PHENOMENOLOGY IN CLINICAL PRACTICE

Phenomenology in Clinical Practice introduces core concepts of Husserlian phenomenology and applies them to the understanding and treatment of affective and personality disorders in clinical settings.

Dr. Susi Ferrarello illuminates the source of emotional cycles and instability and offers mental health practitioners guided approaches to addressing affective disorders, alleviating disturbances, and promoting integration. Designed for mental health professionals and students in psychology, psychiatry, and medical humanities, this book bridges theory and practice through case-based applications and accessible explanations of philosophical concepts. It offers a non-reductionist, lived-experience approach to mental health and aims to expand both academic and therapeutic perspectives on conditions such as CPTSD, alexithymia, BPD, narcissism, and schizophrenia. Asserting that philosophical investigation can deepen an understanding of mental illness and care, the author invites readers to develop transformative approaches to address mental suffering with greater compassion and holistic awareness.

This book is an indispensable tool for those working in mental health care, especially for those looking for new lived experience-based solutions for clinical and psychopathological problems. It is also an invaluable resource for graduate students and researchers, as well as people who are not philosophers but seek support in reflecting on the ethical, psychological, and social challenges that are present in clinical practice.

Susi Ferrarello, Ph.D., is Associate Professor at CSU East Bay and author of *The Phenomenology of Pregnancy and Early Motherhood*, *The Ethics of Love*, and *Human Emotions and the Origin of Bioethics*. She is also a philosophical counselor and writes for Psychology Today.

PHENOMENOLOGY IN CLINICAL PRACTICE

Working with Affective and Personality Disorders in Therapeutic Contexts

Susi Ferrarello

Routledge
Taylor & Francis Group
NEW YORK AND LONDON

Designed cover image: Getty Images

First published 2026
by Routledge
605 Third Avenue, New York, NY 10158

and by Routledge
4 Park Square, Milton Park, Abingdon, Oxon, OX14 4RN

Routledge is an imprint of the Taylor & Francis Group, an informa business

For Product Safety Concerns and Information please contact our EU representative GPSR@taylorandfrancis.com. Taylor & Francis Verlag GmbH, Kaufingerstraße 24, 80331 München, Germany.

ISBN: 9781041125884 (hbk)
ISBN: 9781041125877 (pbk)
ISBN: 9781003665557 (ebk)

DOI: 10.4324/9781003665557

Typeset in Times New Roman
by codeMantra

To Susanna, Valentina, Dalila

CONTENTS

INTRODUCTION

The fruitful intersection of phenomenology and clinical practice—both in mental health and in broader care contexts—continues to yield valuable insights that merit attention for their contribution to individual well-being.

In this book, I offer a chronological overview of Edmund Husserl's life and philosophical development, interwoven with applied chapters focused on specific affective disorders. The aim is twofold: to introduce foundational theoretical concepts in phenomenology as they relate to clinical practice and to demonstrate their practical relevance through concrete applications.

The first chapter introduces the concepts of psychologism and logicism, which I later explore in the context of complex post-traumatic stress disorder (PTSD). Chapter 2 presents Husserl's notions of *epoché* and phenomenological reduction, setting the stage for an analysis of practical intentionality and the volitional body—topics central to the chapter on schizophrenia and the chapter on trauma and CPTSD.

The second half of this book turns more directly to affective disorders. Chapter 6 addresses the crisis of the sciences and the parallel crisis of meaning in contemporary medical practice. Chapter 7 serves as a bridge, offering a phenomenological framework for understanding affective disorders, including alexithymia, borderline personality disorder (BPD), and narcissistic traits. These are examined through key phenomenological lenses: empathy, axiological activity, and representational acts, respectively.

Although the chapters are structured thematically and conceptually, readers are welcome to engage with them in any order that suits their interest or needs. While Husserl's phenomenology is the central reference point throughout this book, the analysis also draws on thinkers influenced by his legacy. Due to space constraints, extended discussions of this intellectual lineage are included in the footnotes.

Below is the final structure of this book:

Part	Theoretical Chapter	Bridging Chapter	Praxis Chapter
Part I	1. Husserl the Philosopher 2. Epoche and Reduction		3. A Phenomenological Account of CPTSD 4. Psychologism and Logicism in Complex PTSD 5. Husserl's Ethics and Schizophrenia
Part II	6. The Crisis of Medical Sciences as a Crisis of Meaning	7. Affects' Disorders	8. Alexithymia and Empathy
			9. Borderline Personality Disorder: Affects and Value Disruptions 10. Affects and Narcissistic Traits

The Book

The first chapter explores the intellectual and biographical foundations of Edmund Husserl's phenomenology and its enduring relevance to psychology, psychiatry, and bioethics. It traces Husserl's transition from mathematics and empirical psychology to a rigorous critique of scientific reductionism, culminating in his development of phenomenological *epoché* and *reduction* as tools to investigate the structures of consciousness and sense. The chapter situates Husserl's thought in historical and existential context, including his Jewish background, his academic influences, and the cultural trauma of early 20th-century Europe. Against logical psychologism and psychological logicism, Husserl defends a non-reductive view of meaning (Sinn) that respects the complexity of lived experience. This framework is applied to mental health, particularly schizophrenia and CPTSD, where phenomenological analysis reveals a breakdown in temporality, embodiment, and intersubjectivity often overlooked by mainstream psychiatry. Drawing on thinkers such as Sass, Minkowski, Foucault, and Merleau-Ponty, the chapter advocates for a phenomenological and ethical approach to abnormality, emphasizing empathy, interaffective resonance, and the relational nature of meaning. Husserl's legacy is ultimately shown to be a call to attend to experience in its fullness, offering a philosophical foundation for more humane clinical and ethical practices.

The second chapter explores the practical and theoretical relevance of Husserl's concepts of *epoché* and *reduction*, particularly in the context of clinical practice and psychopathology. Contrary to the widespread belief that transcendental phenomenology is too abstract for application, the chapter argues that Husserl's reflective method enables a deeper understanding of human experience by revealing the structures that shape how phenomena appear. Beginning with Husserl's shift from a realist to a transcendental standpoint, the chapter illustrates how *epoché* and *reduction* allow clinicians to bracket preconceived models and engage with patients' lived worlds. Drawing on Husserl's mereology, the work highlights how phenomenology resists reductionist models—especially in diagnostic psychiatry—by emphasizing the relational and structured unity of symptoms and experience. The discussion is enriched by historical reflections on Descartes, the transcendental subject, and embodied temporality, showing how Husserl reinterprets the cogito in non-dualistic, embodied terms. Further sections explore the role of intersubjectivity, empathy, and the constitution of normality and abnormality within interaffective communities. By connecting foundational phenomenological insights with clinical examples, the chapter demonstrates the enduring power of *epoché* and *reduction* as transformative tools for understanding and addressing mental suffering in a more compassionate and holistic way.

The third chapter applies some of the concepts explored in these first two chapters. It uses, in fact, the epoché as a healing tool for CPTSD. This chapter offers a phenomenological analysis of CPTSD, reframing trauma as a disruption of the affective, temporal, bodily, and narrative structures that constitute subjectivity. Drawing on Husserl's concepts of passive synthesis, time-consciousness, and affectivity, trauma is shown to persist not as a past event, but as a latent and recurring presence that fragments the self. Complementary insights from Heidegger and Lévinas highlight trauma as an ontological rupture and ethical accusation that resists assimilation into narrative meaning. CPTSD is explored across five axes—time, affect, body, imagination, and identity—revealing how trauma distorts memory, disrupts bodily orientation, colonizes symbolic thinking, and fractures the ego's coherence. First-person testimonies are used to illustrate these effects. The chapter concludes by proposing a healing approach grounded in phenomenological epoché and interaffective exercises, emphasizing the reconstitution of presence rather than a return to pre-trauma normalcy. This model centers embodied awareness, emotional regulation, and relational attunement as the basis for recovery. Trauma is thus recast not merely as a clinical condition, but as a fundamental existential disturbance that requires philosophical, therapeutic, and ethical attention.

The fourth chapter continues the exploration of the philosophical implications of CPTSD through a phenomenological lens, focusing on the lived experience of the author's mother. Drawing on Edmund Husserl's critique of psychologism and logicism, the chapter shows how these reductionist frameworks distort the complexity of trauma by conflating psychological functioning with logical coherence. Using excerpts from the mother's journal, the author illustrates how societal norms, shaped by reductive attitudes, deny individuals with CPTSD the intersubjective and affective space necessary for sense-making. Three phenomenological approaches—evidence, representation, and axiological reason—are developed to distinguish between symbol, expression, and sense and to resist the epistemic silencing often experienced by trauma survivors. The chapter argues that CPTSD involves not just psychological distress but a breakdown in the validation of lived experience within one's community. Through this personal and philosophical narrative, the chapter advocates for a phenomenology of care that preserves the complexity of sense, validates the intentional essence of trauma narratives, and sustains the moral and epistemic responsibility to recognize each person's unique mode of making sense. Only by resisting reductive diagnoses can we affirm the meaningfulness of lives marked by complex trauma.

The fifth chapter is a revised version of a chapter published in Englander's edited book (2018). It explores the relevance of Edmund Husserl's ethical phenomenology for psychotherapy and psychiatry, particularly in the treatment of schizophrenia. Drawing on the concept of epoché and reduction, the volitional body, and Husserl's notions of practical intentionality and time-consciousness, the chapter proposes an alternative to reductionist models in mental health. It builds on the work of Carl Rogers and Eugene Gendlin, who emphasized empathetic, client-centered approaches that prioritize the individual's lived experience over diagnostic labels. The first part of the chapter surveys key contributions from phenomenological psychopathology—particularly by Fuchs, Minkowski, Sass, and Parnas—highlighting schizophrenia as a disorder of temporal and embodied selfhood. The second part applies Husserl's ethical framework to therapy, arguing that the therapist must engage both emotionally and cognitively with the client's worldview. Concepts such as Daseinswert, practical intentionality, and the volitional body offer a deeper understanding of how ethical agency and self-recognition can emerge through therapeutic care. Ultimately, this chapter reframes schizophrenia not as a deviation from normality, but as an existential condition that invites a broader ethical understanding. It proposes that Husserlian ethics can support a more humane and integrative approach to mental health care—one that respects the complexity and dignity of lived experience.

Chapter 6 explores the growing disconnection between science and human experience, particularly within clinical practice, through the lens of Edmund Husserl's later phenomenology. Drawing on concepts such as the lifeworld (*Lebenswelt*), intersubjectivity, and empathy, the chapter critiques the reductionism inherent in modern scientific paradigms that prioritize utility and objectivity over meaning. Using historical examples—from the legacy of Galileo to contemporary medical practices—the chapter illustrates how science's detachment from lived experience can lead to alienation, dehumanization, and a crisis in ethical care. Husserl's notion of *methexis* (participation in truth) and his call to return to the "things themselves" are presented as vital philosophical correctives. Special attention is given to how these ideas inform patient care, particularly in psychiatry, nursing, and bioethics, where the subjective dimension of illness is often overlooked. The chapter also considers practical implications for the clinician-patient relationship, arguing for a re-integration of the subjective and objective dimensions of care. By foregrounding the patient's lived experience and ethical agency, this chapter advocates for a phenomenologically grounded practice that bridges the gap between scientific advancement and human well-being.

Chapter 7 is a bridging chapter that encompasses the theoretical point of Chapter 5 and moves toward the application of some of these concepts on three types of affects disorders. This, too, is a revised version of an article published in *Human Studies* (2024) and explores the phenomenology of affectivity as foundational to the constitution of selfhood, intersubjectivity, and ethical agency. Drawing on Husserl's later works, the chapter presents a layered model of affective intentionality—comprising interest, value activity, and representational acts—as key to understanding how human beings engage meaningfully with the lifeworld (*Lebenswelt*). The discussion then maps dysfunctions in these affective processes onto three clinical phenomena: alexithymia, BPD, and narcissistic personality traits. Each condition is interpreted as a breakdown at a specific level of feeling intentionality, offering a new phenomenological framework for understanding emotional disorders. The chapter proposes integrative approaches combining bodily awareness, narrative reconstruction, and intersubjective engagement to restore access to meaning and ethical life.

Chapter 8 moves to the analysis of the first triad of problems presented in Chapter 6. It explores the lived experience of alexithymia through both phenomenological analysis and clinical reflection, using José Saramago's *Blindness* as a metaphor for emotional opacity. Alexithymia, which affects up to 10% of the population, is characterized by difficulty in identifying and expressing emotions, often resulting in impaired empathy and interpersonal disconnection. Drawing on Husserl's theory of affectivity, intentionality, and empathy, the chapter examines how alexithymic individuals perceive their emotions cognitively rather than bodily, using abstract reasoning like a "cane" to navigate a world of feelings they cannot access directly. Through clinical examples, forum testimonies, and phenomenological descriptions, the chapter highlights how basic bodily empathy—the perceptive, pre-reflective awareness of another's emotional state—is disrupted in alexithymia, while cognitive empathy often remains intact. This disruption stems from impaired bodily interest, which prevents the coupling of affect with perceptual awareness. The chapter proposes therapeutic strategies grounded in movement, musical rhythm, metaphor, and emotion-labeling exercises to foster embodied emotional awareness. Ultimately, it argues that alexithymia is not merely a deficit in emotional expression but a disorder of affective enaction, one that requires a holistic, embodied, and phenomenologically informed approach to therapeutic care.

Chapter 9, which is an expanded version of a previous article (2021), explores the phenomenological structure of emotional dysregulation in individuals with BPD, focusing on how affective valuing disrupts the intentional coherence of meaning-making. Drawing on Husserl's theory of intentionality and mereological foundation, it analyzes how axiological acts overpower ontological concreteness, leading to fragmented intersubjective experiences. The chapter examines how these disruptions result in erratic emotional resonance and unstable identity, contributing to the clinical features of BPD. Integrating lived-experience narratives, phenomenological psychopathology, and first-person testimony, it highlights how emotional excess distorts affective and cognitive representation, creating existential dissonance in relationships and self-perception. The chapter proposes that emotional instability in BPD is less about emotional intensity per se and more about the structural inability to integrate affective values with stable self-world meaning. It further argues that clinical treatment must address this axiological distortion by reinforcing continuity in the affective lifeworld. Therapeutic suggestions include phenomenological interventions that restore embodied intersubjectivity, clarify intentional content, and reduce existential opacity. By highlighting the co-foundational role of value in experience, this chapter aims to offer a new diagnostic and therapeutic framework that links affective instability to disruptions in the very act of making sense of one's world and place within it.

The last chapter offers a phenomenological exploration of narcissistic personality traits, focusing on the affective disconnection at the heart of narcissism. Moving beyond reductive cultural narratives, it draws on Husserl's theory of intentionality to reveal how narcissistic individuals experience a blockage in practical and affective intentionality—specifically, a disruption between passive emotional experiences and active meaning-making. This disconnection prevents Narcissistic Personality Disorder individuals from forming authentic emotional bonds, leaving them reliant on external validation and vulnerable to existential instability. Through an interpretation of Ovid's myth of Narcissus, the chapter illustrates how a distorted self-image emerges from emotional neglect and a lack of interaffective resonance. Theoretical analysis is complemented by clinical insights, suggesting that narcissistic traits are rooted in a failure to integrate bodily affectivity into a coherent sense of self. The chapter concludes by proposing a therapeutic framework grounded in phenomenology that emphasizes embodied awareness, ethical neutrality, and the cultivation of affective resonance. These interventions aim to help narcissistic individuals reconnect with their volitional body and reconstitute their emotional world through meaningful, lived experience. Ultimately, the chapter argues that healing narcissism involves reactivating the flow between emotion, meaning, and ethical connection with others.

Conclusion

This book has aimed to demonstrate the enduring value of Husserlian phenomenology in clinical practice, particularly in addressing affective and psychiatric disorders. By grounding theoretical insights in lived experience—from the epoché and reduction to the volitional body and affective intentionality—I have sought to show how phenomenology provides clinicians and scholars with a powerful framework for understanding the complexities of mental life. The chapters engage with a range of conditions—schizophrenia, CPTSD, alexithymia, BPD, and narcissistic traits—not as isolated pathologies but as disruptions in the structures of sense, embodiment, and intersubjective meaning. Throughout, phenomenology is not treated as an abstract theory but as a practical, ethical orientation—one that resists reductionist tendencies and honors the irreducible dignity of subjective life. My hope is that this book will invite clinicians, researchers, and students alike to cultivate a renewed attention to the textures of experience, and to consider how philosophical reflection can enrich both our understanding of mental illness and our care for those who suffer.

References

Ferrarello, S. (2018). Husserl's ethics and psychiatry. In M. Englander (Ed.), *Phenomenology and the social context of psychiatry*. London/New York: Bloomsbury.

Ferrarello, S. (2021). Meaning-making activity in the emotional experience of borderline personalities. *Psychopathology*, *54*(5), 221–231. https://doi.org/10.1159/000517932

Ferrarello, S. (2024). Affect disorders: A Husserlian interpretation of alexithymia, BPD, and narcissistic traits. *Human Studies*, *47*, 535–551.

1

HUSSERL AND PHENOMENOLOGY

The Risk of Reductionism in Clinical Practice

Husserl's Influences in His Life and Work

This chapter introduces the reader to the life and central concepts of Husserl's phenomenology, as well as to phenomenology more broadly, in order to lay the groundwork for its practical application in clinical practice. The following chapters will delve into specific concepts and explore how they manifest in clinical settings. The guiding thread of this introduction is Husserl's struggle against reductionism, which led him to develop a form of phenomenology that reveals a new sense of intentionality, ultimately feeding into a transcendental perspective. This perspective gives rise to key notions—such as empathy, the lifeworld, intersubjectivity, interaffectivity, epoché, and reduction—that are essential for understanding the human being and for informing clinical approaches to enhance well-being.

Edmund Husserl (1859–1938) is known as the founder of phenomenology, a philosophical contemporary movement that contributed to the humanistic and existential approach in philosophy and psychology (Giorgi, 1970; Hoffman, 2006; Watson & Bohart, 2015). While Hegel's *Phenomenology of Spirit* (1807/2018) and Peirce's phenomenology as an early formulation of pragmatist semiotics (1878/1992) each made significant contributions to philosophy, it was Husserl's phenomenology that had a direct and lasting influence on the development of phenomenological psychology and our understanding of human existence as situated in the *Lebenswelt*—the lived, pre-reflective world of everyday experience. His philosophy notably influenced key figures in French, German, English, Italian, and American psychiatry and in humanistic psychology, including Rogers (1951), Gendlin (1973), Perls (1969), Laing (1960), and

DOI: 10.4324/9781003665557-1

Frankl (1963). He encouraged us to set aside our assumptions and describe the immediate experience of the phenomena as they appear to us. "Back to things themselves" (Husserl, 2000, 168) is, in fact, the motto that animates Husserl's phenomenology.

Even though his appearance points to the typical male German philosopher of our Western (and maybe dated) textbooks, he lived as a minority. Being born Jewish in a small town, Prossnitz (today belonging to the Czech Republic) marked his life and his approach to philosophy in a peculiar way. In order to assimilate, in 1886, Husserl and his wife converted to Protestantism as many other Jewish academicians did in Germany and Austria at that time.[1] Yet, as we well know, the turn of events that will lead up to the Holocaust will make any attempt at assimilation vain. On May 4, 1933, he writes to his longtime friend Dieter Mahnke:

> Finally, in my old age I had to experience something that I didn't deem possible: the erection of a spiritual Ghetto into which my children and I (…) are to be driven. We have no longer the right to call ourselves German; Our spiritual work is no longer to be included in German Cultural history.
>
> *(Husserl, 1994, 481–482)*

Husserl is among those philosophers who will be forced into early retirement and will be forbidden to give public talks. Father Van Breda will save his manuscripts from destruction in a small house that is still today the center of Husserl's Archives in Leuven. The death of his son in World War I and the sudden racial limitations are probably among the factors that contributed to keeping his philosophy open to a deep understanding of human fragilities and far from the temptations of nationalistic idealism. For this reason, it is not a surprise that his philosophy will influence important contemporary interpretations of the human, such as in Levinas' notion of transcendence (Levinas, 1969), Jaspers' (1955) and Binswanger's (1992) existential psychiatry, Heidegger's hermeneutics (Overgaard, 2010), and Merleau-Ponty's psychology of perception (2002). He attracted some of the most brilliant minds across several generations of European philosophy students. Among those who studied directly with him were Heidegger, Gadamer, Arendt, Marcuse, and Levinas. Others—such as Sartre, Merleau-Ponty, Ricoeur, Derrida, Habermas, and Adorno—did not study with him personally but engaged deeply and creatively with his thought.

Husserl's Philosophical Background

Husserl's academic journey began at the University of Halle, where, as a young mathematician, psychologist, and philosopher, he defended his postdoctoral dissertation, *On the Concept of Number*, on June 28, 1887. His examining board included two prominent innovators in their fields—Georg Cantor in mathematics and Carl Stumpf in experimental psychology (Schuhmann, 1977, 17). Husserl had previously served as an assistant to Carl Weierstrass, another major figure in the "foundational crisis" that gave rise to set theory, formal mathematics, and modern symbolic logic. In Vienna, under the mentorship of Franz Brentano, Husserl was introduced to empirical psychology, which shaped his development of the concept of intentionality, a key tool for his later phenomenological theory of consciousness. It is important to reflect on this unique intersection of mathematics and psychology, as it sheds light on Husserl's effort to map life through a structured framework capable of generating meaning and deepening our understanding of human experience.

In Stumpf's laboratory, where they worked together, Husserl contributed to early "experimental phenomenology" (Albertazzi, 2013), conducting pioneering studies on perception. He continued this work while preparing *Philosophy of Arithmetic* (Husserl, 1891/2003) and, later, *Logical Investigations* (Husserl, 2000, 2008). As can be seen from the intersection of these two disciplinary domains, Husserl's thought emerged at the crossroads of two scientific revolutions: one in the realm of ideal objects and a priori reasoning, and the other in empirical experience and a posteriori knowledge. Preserving the distinct status of these two elements—the abstract and the concrete—without conflating them forms the core of phenomenology, giving rise in Husserl's work to a novel understanding of both realms and the profound connection between them (Husserl, 1931/1977, 7–18). As I will demonstrate later in this chapter and throughout this book, conflating these two layers—the ideal and the concrete, the logical and the psychological, and the abstract and the factual—would leave no room for investigating the psychological realm, as it would be reduced to mere empirical facts. Conversely, symbolic forms such as numbers or geometrical figures would become meaningless constructs—arbitrary tokens mistakenly treated as representations of a reality independent of our experience. Husserl's phenomenology emerges precisely from the tension between these layers and from the profound insights that arise when we explore their correlation with rigor and care.

Logical Psychologism and Psychological Logicism

What I believe animated Husserl's philosophical research was his commitment against reductionism in science. In general, reductionism refers to the attitude that reduces the complexity of human life to simplistic answers.[2] Examples of reductionism that Husserl more often cites are psychological logicism and logical psychologism (Husserl, 2000; Kusch, 1995, 2020).

In his *Prolegomena to Pure Logic* (1900/2000), Husserl criticizes psychological logicism—as found in thinkers like J.S. Mill—for reducing logic to empirical psychology. He argues that this reductionism treats logical laws as merely descriptions of how people happen to think, thereby conflating the normativity of logic with contingent mental processes. Such a view risks implying that individuals who cannot perform certain cognitive or expressive acts—for example, due to impairments—are incapable of logical thought, thus excluding them from the community of rational minds. Against this, Husserl defends logic as an ideal, objective discipline grounded in meanings and validity, not in psychological functioning.

On the other hand, logical psychologism—exemplified in part by thinkers like Herbart—claims that psychology can be reduced to formal propositions or laws, treating mental life as a system of causally determined contents expressible in symbolic form (Husserl, 2000, 30). From this standpoint, understanding the psyche becomes a matter of analyzing symbolic representations governed by syntactic rules. Both this and Mill's psychological logicism represent forms of reductionism that oversimplify the complex task of making sense of human experience. They reduce the richness of meaning either to cognitive capacities or to formal-symbolic structures.

Reductionism in Healthcare Professions and Bioethics

The risk of reductionism is particularly relevant in psychology, care ethics, bioethics, and clinical contexts. One form of this reductionism—*psychological logicism*—suggests that cognitive processes alone determine the capacity to make sense of the world. From this view, individuals with cognitive impairments might be wrongly perceived as lacking the ability to access meaning. For instance, Mill's (1843/1973, 1974) empiricist approach, grounded in principles of utility, tends to frame psychological functioning in terms of measurable outcomes. While not explicitly pathologizing, this perspective risks equating diminished utility or responsiveness with a deficit in personhood.

Equally concerning is the view associated with *logical psychologism*, which reduces mental life to the correct manipulation of symbols and rules. Under such assumptions, those who cannot use conventional grammar or symbolic structures fluently may be seen as incapable of meaningful thought. Herbart's psychology and pedagogy, for example, emphasized knowledge as the assimilation and association of ideas within consciousness—a model that privileges formal coherence over lived experience (Baker, 1969). These reductionist frameworks overlook the rich, embodied, and affective dimensions of human understanding that phenomenology seeks to preserve.

Mill and Herbart are two of the targets of Husserl's criticism. In fact, freeing knowledge from these reductionist simplifications will be his lifelong project. The road ahead is not easy and the young Husserl himself will learn the lesson from Frege who in 1894 will publish a negative review of his early book,

Philosophy of Arithmetic, accusing him of logical psychologism[3]; particularly according to Wundt's interpretations of his early logical writings.[4]

A powerful illustration of the dangers of reductionism in understanding the human psyche is evident in the medicalization of schizophrenia. Chapter 5 will explore the problem of schizophrenia through this Husserlian phenomenological lens, while also drawing on insights from Sass (1992), Gozé (2024), and Minkowski (1927/1970). These tendencies remain active in contemporary approaches to mental illness, particularly in psychiatry's treatment of disorders such as schizophrenia. As Sass (1992) argues, dominant models frequently reduce schizophrenic experience to malfunctioning psychological mechanisms or biochemical irregularities, overlooking the nuanced disruptions in meaning, embodiment, temporality, and selfhood that patients themselves live through. From a phenomenological perspective—as explored by thinkers like Sass (1992) and Minkowski (1927/1970)—experiences associated with schizophrenia cannot be fully understood through symbolic logic, grammatical accuracy, or purely cognitive and neurological models. Instead, they reflect significant alterations in the structures through which individuals relate to time, space, self, and others. These experiences reveal shifts in the patterns of sense-making and embodied presence, often rich in meaning and deeply embedded in the person's lived world. However, clinical discourse too often interprets them solely through diagnostic frameworks, overlooking the existential dimensions they express.

From a phenomenological standpoint, Minkowski (1927/1970) emphasizes the "loss of vital contact with reality" in schizophrenia—not as a mere cognitive error but as a fundamental existential disruption. Similarly, Maurice Merleau-Ponty (2002) stressed that our sense of self and world is rooted in *embodied intentionality*, which cannot be reduced to symbolic functions or grammatical forms. In schizophrenia, this intentionality may be fractured, but it still demands interpretation on the level of lived experience, not just neural representation. In this sense, Michel Foucault (1961/1988) warned against the societal control embedded within medical discourse. When interpretation is absent and diagnostic categories are applied rigidly, what is labeled as "madness" risks becoming a political tool of control rather than a framework for care. Reductionist approaches have historically shaped the evolution of mental health as a mechanism of social regulation, producing classifications that often silence the voices of those deemed "insane." Foucault argued that the clinical gaze tends to objectify the patient, reducing complex and meaningful expressions of suffering to pathological signs that must be diagnosed, treated, and brought into conformity.

These examples illustrate how both cognitive-psychological and biomedical reductionisms oversimplify the complex human quest for meaning—either by reducing meaning to behaviors considered statistically normal or socially acceptable or by framing deviations from the norm as biomedical problems to be corrected through pharmacological solutions. It is precisely these reductionist tendencies that phenomenological psychiatry and existential approaches seek to resist by re-centering the lived experience of the person. The key to avoiding these forms of reductionism is to be loyal to the complexity of sense. Today phenomenological bioethics (Ferrarello, 2026; Svenaeus, 2001, 2017; Toombs, 1987) and phenomenological psychiatry (Brencio, 2024; Fuchs et al., 2019; Jaspers, 1955) emphasize the need to avoid reductionism, especially in the interpretation of the mind-body problem, and the importance of the relational and embodied quality of making sense within the intersubjective and interaffective community (Fuchs & De Jaegher, 2019; Fuchs & Koch, 2014).

Symbol, Reference, and Sense

The question that arises from Husserl's critique of reductionism in logic and psychology is—What is sense (*Sinn*)? Does sense belong to the expressions that we use? Or does it lie in universal symbols that we all acknowledge as true, like the numbers? Does sense cease to exist if one does not make sense? To address these questions, Husserl borrows key concepts from Frege and Bolzano. From Bolzano (Husserl, 2008, 229), in fact, he gathers the idea that a symbol does not need a sentence to denote something. Contrary to what logical psychologism believes, a symbol can be evocative of a manifold of meanings without the need to be organized in sound sentences or coordinated within a set of symbols. It is the reference, in fact, that functions as a connecting bridge between the symbol that makes sense and the sense of the symbol itself.

The importance of the role played by reference in approaching sense has been emphasized by Frege's work.[5] Symbols, expression, and sense are three separate elements. Symbols are a form of technology that we use to translate the complexity of sense. The expression is that combination of norms (grammar, logic, etc.) that, if correctly applied, allows something or someone to make sense. The sense itself is something different and more essential at its core. While human beings can express themselves through symbols (numbers, words, or any expressive token), sense itself is something that exists independently of us being able to express it. Sense is possessed by a name whether it has a reference or not. As Frege reminds us (1892), the morning star and the evening star are the same object providing different senses according to different references we use to point to that object. Reference is a truth value that I attribute to that object, while sense is the thoughts that it expresses (1892/1997, 25–50). If we apply this concept in mental health, the sense of truth that guides the actions of a person in existential crisis is there independently of their ability to express it to others or not. Moreover, its sense would seem different according to the references this person would use to point to that sense. Being able to at least see this three-layered sense would prevent us from reductionism; for example, from accusing people of not making sense because they do not make *the sense* that we expect. Being open toward the unexpected moments of sense that life, in all its forms can disclose for us, is the direction to which Husserl's early phenomenology points us.

Sense and Intentionality

In Husserl's vocabulary, evidence and sense go hand in hand. Sense is a living evidence, an incognitum perceivable through our body. As he puts it: "the original evidence or necessity is discovered/felt by the organic body (*Koerper*) which feels its organ, lived body (*Leib*), as the title of such evidence." (2014, 452). This means that the best chance we have to get closer to sense is by investigating this embodied necessity that we discover through feelings of clarity in our biological body (*Koerper*) and lived body (*Leib*).

The body, interpreted by Husserl both as a center of orientation aware of its movements (*Leib*) and as an organic body (*Koerper*), expresses sense (*Sinn*) in an infinite number of correlations according to a "how" and a "what"; this correlation of how and what Husserl called intentional essence. The intentional essence points to how the phenomenon becomes visible to us (Husserl, 2000, 212, 122) even before we can see it. In this sense, Husserl's phenomenology cautions us, especially in its psychological and psychiatric applications (with Merleau-Ponty, Jaspers, Fanon, and Binswanger, for example), to not overestimate the sole use of spoken language to bring sense to visibility and expression (Husserl, 1973).

In Prolegomena Section 16, Husserl presents sense as a necessity (*Notwendigkeit*) that we can explain as a theoretical core (an ought/*Sollen*) that dictates to us the rules of how things should be for them to be as they are. For example, for a triangle to appear to us as a triangle, it must have three angles. If I see a three-angled geometrical shape, I feel with evidence that this must be a triangle. Sense appears to us at its most basic level as a necessary legality that regulates how the phenomena must be there for us to be seen (Husserl, 2000, section 38, 183). The vast concrete matter of life becomes a visible phenomenon for us when it appears to us according to a legality that expresses itself in the correlation of how and what to which we are used (that is, the layers of pre-predicative experience that we build throughout our life). The correlation of how and what is the main layer of the intentional essence through which objects are made present to us; for this reason, the intentional essence is said to be expressed in an objectifying act. The instrument Husserl employs to investigate the intentional essence at its very origin is transcendental phenomenology.

Transcendental Turn

After Logical Investigations, Husserl's quest takes on a transcendental quality that was still silent in his early logical work. As a consequence, some of his students will leave, considering Husserl's transcendental turn a betrayal of the realistic approach of his early philosophy.[6] Notably, redacting the entry Phenomenology for the *Encyclopedia Britannica* (1929) and the publication of Sein und Zeit (1927/1962) will show Husserl the gap between Heidegger's and his approach to phenomenology. Heidegger, at the time his assistant, could no longer be his successor. To secure the tradition of transcendental phenomenology, Husserl starts lecturing across Europe. In particular, the Paris Lectures (later on published as Cartesian Meditations—1964, 1931/1977) will be used to introduce new minds to his transcendental phenomenology. Although the room of the Sorbonne will not be as crowded as Husserl would hope, this small group of students (among whom are Levinas, Merleau-Ponty, Cavailles, Hearing, Koyre, and Aron)[7] will change the history of French, but not only, philosophy.

At the time of Logical Investigations, it was not yet clear how phenomenology helped to come back to the things themselves, as Husserl's motto stated. The intentional essence was an important direction but it was still unclear how we could look at the intentional essence without conflating that essence with our personal point of view. The central question remained: how can we describe the intentional essence of lived experience without falling into reductionism or succumbing to relativism? Without the transcendental turn, Husserl himself risked reverting to the very forms of reductionism he so vigorously opposed. To address these critical concerns, we must carefully consider the significance of the transcendental turn, beginning with a close observation of the following set of terms:

A house / this is a house/ I see this house / I look at myself glancing at this house.

These sentences point to four different positions that one can take to observe and describe the same house. If returning to the things themselves simply meant reverting to the commonly accepted description of a house, we would once again fall into a form of reductionism. The strength of phenomenology lies in its ability to recognize and reflect on the points of observation through which we perceive the house. The difference in the degree of observation among these positions is determined by two essential devices that phenomenology uses: the epoché and reduction. From Greek, epoché indicates parenthesis, while reduction (from Latin *re-ducere*) points to "a coming back to."

These points describe the following stances. From the natural naive attitude with which I engage with life without thinking about it and I unreflectively perceive a house, I progressively transition to a reflective way of describing this house that culminates in the point where I can see myself looking at the house. This final degree of observation is a phenomenological reflective one, an *ego-cogito-cogitatum* (*lit.* I-think-the thought), that is, I look at myself looking at this content. This transition is possible thanks to the epoché and reduction. Through the epoché, that is, an act of self-determination (*selbst-besinnung*,

Husserl, 1970, 188), I parenthesize myself as a human being living in the world and I commit to witness myself as a neutral observer of this living being. Thanks to the epoché, we discover the world as a content of a reflective subjectivity (in Latin, *ego cogito qua cogitatum*). Depending on how deep I want to go with my analysis, I can choose to apply a philosophical or a scientific reduction with which I parenthesize my philosophical or scientific knowledge when I am looking at a given phenomenon; or I can apply the phenomenological reduction which similarly to the epoché[8] allows me to see the essence (*Wesensshau*) of the phenomenon since I parenthesize any personal existential assumption. Through this reduction, I commit to becoming a phenomenologist, that is, an observer describing the phenomenon as it discloses itself. After the phenomenological reduction, I might even apply a transcendental reduction through which I parenthesize my temporality and witness the being of the phenomenon as an original impression in time (*Urimpression*); that is, a living present from which the horizon of time synthesizes the constitution of our knowledge.

Clinical Applications

As we will explore more at length in Chapters 3—5, the phenomenological concepts of epoché and reduction can illuminate the lived experience of individuals suffering from schizophrenia or complex PTSD in ways that resist the reductionism often found in clinical psychiatry. In these conditions, disruptions in meaning, time, embodiment, and intersubjectivity are not merely symptoms to be diagnosed but profound alterations in how the world is experienced and constituted. Being able to observe the constitutive emergence of meaning as it unfolds from the perspective of the person experiencing it allows us to access the structure of their lifeworld in a truly meaningful way. It enables us to witness the world as it appears to them—not as something imposed by societal norms, medical protocols, or familial expectations but as something that holds sense within their own experiential horizon. By performing the *epoché* and phenomenological reduction—adjusted to the depth of inquiry required—we return to lived experience itself, describing it in its liminal phase, as it begins to disclose its meaning.

Moreover, there are situations in which individuals may enter a state closely resembling the *epoché* without consciously or intentionally applying it. In the case of schizophrenia, Husserl's notion of epoché—the suspension of the natural attitude—can be seen as something imposed rather than chosen. The individual no longer relates to the world as coherent, familiar, or continuous. Sass (1992) argues that in schizophrenia, there is often a pathological form of hyper-reflexivity, where ordinary acts of meaning and perception become over-scrutinized and alienating. The self turns inward in an excessive form of self-awareness, leading to a detachment from embodied, affective engagement with the world. This fragmentation can be understood through a phenomenological lens not simply as a cognitive deficit but as a collapse of the very conditions for meaning-making and intentionality.

Similarly, in complex PTSD, the experience of time, memory, and selfhood is disrupted in ways that echo Husserl's transcendental reduction as applied to temporality and embodiment. As Van der Kolk (2014) explains, trauma is stored in the body and experienced not as narrative memory but as recurring, intrusive presence—what he calls the "living past." Phenomenologists such as Fuchs (2012) and Ratcliffe (2015) have expanded on this by showing how trauma fundamentally alters the temporal structure of experience and the sense of bodily coherence. The reduction, which presents itself in this context as a disruptive unrequested event, helps articulate how traumatic memory distorts the individual's capacity to inhabit time and space as lived dimensions, not merely objective facts.

Rather than viewing these conditions solely through a neurobiological or cognitive framework, phenomenological epoché and reduction reorient attention from pathology to meaning, offering a deeper understanding of what it means for one's world to break down. The epoché and reduction, in fact, help us avoid falling into reductionism by revealing the constitutive origin of meaning—not as a mere alignment with symbols or modes of thought but as the foundational process through which we make sense of the world's original structures. They disclose the transcendental space. This does not provide a clinical solution per se, but it opens up a therapeutic space that listens to experience on its own terms—topics I will explore more in depth in Chapters 3, 4, and 9.

The Origin of Intersubjectivity

In the reflective dimension disclosed by this transcendental turn, it became possible to discover precious notions such as intersubjectivity, empathy, interaffectivity, and lifeworld (to cite some) whose influence is still enduring when observing the peculiarity of the human condition. Cairns (1964), Farber (1940), Gurtwisch (1941), Kaufmann (1940), and Schutz (1962) are among those who contributed to Husserl's influence in the United States and the diffusion of these key concepts.

To see how Husserl arrives at these concepts, it is important to remember that the transcendental ego emerging from the transcendental reduction is coexistent with the naive subject that lives in the lifeworld (*Lebenswelt*).[9] The transcendental ego is a functioning locus of experience from which I can see how every object is an object for a subject in an infinite stream of possible meanings.[10] In this primal flow of living presence, the transcendental ego discovers myself as the original Other looking at me from the origin of being/time. I, myself, appear to this original functioning of being as the primary Other. I discover myself as

I-we[11], that is, as a primordial origin of intersubjectivity.[12] Intersubjectivity can be described as a relationship between me and another. The peculiarity of this relationship lies in the fact that the Other is not alien to me but is "within me," *Leibhaftig* (in person).[13] *The other man is constitutionally the intrinsically first man* (Husserl, 1973b, 124). In fact, when I perceive another person, the other is genetically constituted in the midst of my own flowing experience within the natural attitude; my perception of the other is not posited "before" or "after" my self-presence, but it blossoms as a natural experience alongside my self-presence. In my own simple living and perceiving, the other appears as a natural part of my being-in-the-world: one could almost say, as a companion. This very first experience is called by Husserl "communarization" (*Vergemeinschaftung*) to indicate this originary mode of living in which no *ego* (not even myself) remains absolutely singular. In this monadological intersubjectivity, "the second ego [the other] is not simply there, and strictly given to himself; rather is he constituted as 'alter ego' – the ego indicated as one moment by this expression being I myself in my ownness" (Husserl, 1973b, 94). The other appears via a pairing (*Paarung)*, that is, via its external presence as an animate organism (*Leib*) that is similar to mine. When I perceive this organism as analogous to me, I live an *analogical apprehension* that enables me to recognize myself as a human being partaking in a humanity that is shared with others.

Empathy

Empathy originates exactly in the encounter between the neutral observer and ourselves as the radical other. In this encounter, I can present to myself certain feelings, emotions, and sensations that I experience in my living body. Such presentifications enable me to transform what was given *Leibhaftig* (in person) into a sedimentation that establishes "the unity of world-certainty" and discloses the possibility for any reproductive activity (Husserl, 2000b, 152). In Husserliana XIII (1973a, text 15), Husserl distinguishes between a straightforward and an oblique form of empathy. This latter is an act analogous to recollection. While in the former kind of empathy I have an experience in which I directly presentify the other's experience, in the latter I reflect on the experience of the person with whom I am empathizing and I fulfill the expectation with what I recollect from my past (Husserl, 1973a, 97).[14] The analogy at the basis of my empathizing process is just an indication. If this indication becomes a rigid expectation, the empathizing process becomes projection. Even though my world is first of all solipsistic (my thing, my body, and my mind), empathy is what gives this world windows. The other is given to me as a presence, as another presence tied to the here and now of my body (Husserl, 1973a, 99). In this sense, empathy is a mode of apperception and appresentation (Husserl, 1973a, 229) that is founded on another concrete apperception (the apperception of the living body or the material thing). It is a *Verbildlichung*, that is, an act of analogizing or picture-making. Empathy presupposes the empathized object as a being that is given in the now. Through the empathic act, taken as recollection, we go beyond our own egoic time stream and reach other egos' streams. Empathy constitutes a new form of transcendency (Husserl, 1973b, 8) because, despite the fact that we do not know any of the contents of other persons' streams as first-person experiences, we can interact with them as units constituted in time and recollected in the apprehension.

Abnormality and Interaffective Dissonance

The constitution of empathetic connection and intersubjective validation might carry its limits and interferences. In the text 6 of 1930 manuscript, Husserl raises the problem: How can I be sure that what I perceive from another's state of mind is true for the other as well?

Even if my body stands as a proof that I am a living being like many others and shows by *Paarung* (spontaneous bodily apperception and pairing of myself with others) that my body is similar to that of other human beings, I might trick myself into projecting my meanings onto others. For example, I feel better if I eat when I am hungry. From here, I infer that this is true for all those having a living body similar to mine. Looking at others, I assume that what they feel is the same as I feel. I assume that there are harmonious syntheses taking place on different levels of our lives that bring us together. Yet, the other which holds its own sense of being (*Seinsinn*) is also a *Sosein*, that is, a specific kind of being. Hence, a presupposition might very easily become an assumption that if not confirmed in the intersubjective lived experience turns into prejudice or blindness. I cannot limit the life of the people around me to my assumptions of what normality should be; the Other is a living being as much as I am a living being—so observing its bodily language and keeping this language open and hybrid is essential for mutual respect within the society. It might be safe to assume that if a person smiles, she is happy but I also know that smiling can come from a desire to please or it might come from anxiety. The encounter always occurs within a lifeworld, that is, an embedded context of meaning structured by an intersubjective community within an interaffective network.

The intersubjective expectations often set the limits for what is considered normal and abnormal, e.g., I expect that a smile comes from happiness. This is what I call normal. If someone smiles out of fear, that is somewhat abnormal. Often normality and abnormality represent our "social" allowance to belong to an interaffective community (friends, family, school, etc.) in which we affect and are affected by those parts of the community. Being part of the interaffective community is essential for the well-being of the individual (Fuchs & Koch,

2009). Accordingly, phenomenological psychiatry and psychology emphasize the non-neutrality of the worldviews, especially in the way in which we charge them with axiological expectations (Jaspers, 1955). Wherever strong invalidations of meanings arise which might cause interaffective dissonance (for example, "you think my way of smiling is weird that's why you don't love me"), it might be worthwhile to transform invalidations in a resting moment of suspension (epoché) and attenuate their existential intersubjective tone (which can be expressed in the sentence "you look weird") while insisting on the affective continuity. This approach allows us to access the constitutive structure of the lifeworld as *Leibhaftig*—as directly and bodily given—and to perceive the world as others live it, through their own eyes. It moves us away from reductionist perspectives that elevate average ways of thinking or conventional symbols to the status of normative truths.

Conclusion

This introductory chapter aimed to address the key themes of Husserl's philosophy that are essential for understanding how his ideas can be applied in clinical practice. Husserl's philosophical journey reveals a rich tapestry of influences and intellectual challenges that significantly shaped his approach to phenomenology. His early years in mathematics and psychology, coupled with the mentorship of thinkers like Brentano, Cantor, and Stumpf, provided a foundation that would later lead to his rejection of reductionist approaches in science and psychology. Instead, Husserl championed a rigorous and intentional examination of consciousness and experience, pushing for an understanding of human life that remains loyal to its complexity and depth.

The diversity of Husserl's intellectual background allowed him to address a variety of essential questions that continue to influence contemporary philosophy, psychology, and bioethics. From his critique of logical psychologism and psychological logicism to his development of a phenomenological methodology rooted in sense and intentionality, Husserl strove to avoid simplistic reductions of human experience. His emphasis on the essential structures of consciousness, captured through concepts such as intentional essence and transcendental reduction, redefined the exploration of subjective experience. This approach underpins his profound impact on phenomenological bioethics and psychiatry, fields that emphasize the importance of intersubjective and interaffective relationships within the lived body and its environment.

Through notions of empathy, intersubjectivity, and the transcendental ego, Husserl provided a framework that respects the autonomy of otherness and seeks to build intersubjective understanding. His insights into meditative subjectivity as an origin of intersubjectivity enriched phenomenology with new dimensions of ethical consideration, particularly in understanding abnormality and interaffective dissonance within social frameworks. His legacy continues to inform phenomenological inquiries, fostering an appreciation for the nuanced, embodied experience of self and others.

In sum, Husserl's phenomenology stands as a powerful intellectual legacy that has profoundly influenced fields such as existential psychiatry, hermeneutics, and relational psychology. His call to return "to the things themselves" remains a foundational guiding principle, urging us to recognize and respect the depth, diversity, and interconnectivity of human experience in all its manifestations.

Notes

1 See, for example, Ales Bello (2009) and Ghigi (2002) for a discussion of Husserl's religiosity. According to their reviews, Husserl's conversion was truly animated by a renewed faith.

2 Husserl critiques several forms of reductionism across his writings. In Philosophie also strenge Wissenschaft (1911), he targets both objectivism, which treats scientific knowledge as independent of the knowing subject, and subjectivism, which relativizes knowledge to individual or psychological experience. He argues that both fail to grasp the transcendental conditions of knowledge, which are rooted in intentional consciousness. In The Crisis of European Sciences and Transcendental Phenomenology (1970—1936), he expands this critique to include naturalism, biologism, and historicism (§§7–10), especially as found in Dilthey. Historicism, for Husserl, reduces meaning and rationality to historical development, neglecting the a priori structures of consciousness (§46) that make such development intelligible. His transcendental phenomenology seeks to overcome these positions by grounding science, history, and meaning in the lived experience and constitutive activity of the transcendental subject. For Husserl, such approaches overlook the a priori structures of experience that make historical understanding possible. His transcendental phenomenology sought to overcome these reductionisms by grounding meaning in the structures of intentionality, lived experience, and the lifeworld (Lebenswelt).

3 "I was able to gauge the devastation caused by the influx of psychology into logic" (Frege, 1892/1972, 337). Moreover, "Andrew Osborn visited Husserl in 1935 in the Black Forest to ask him about Frege's influence on the abandonment of the psychological approach of the Philosophie der Arithmetik. Husserl concurred, but also mentioned his chance discovery of Bolzano's work in a second-hand book store." (note by Spiegelberg, quoted in Schuhmann, 1977, 463).

4 In recent literature, doubts have been raised whether Husserl's early position was, in fact, psychologistic. I do not want to discuss this question here. It is important for my point, however, that the years between 1894 and 1900 are characterized by a decisive move in Husserl's philosophy, a move that considerably influenced his relation to Franz Brentano.

5 Although Husserl does not seem to acknowledge his influence in his work. In the Prolegomena he mentions Frege only once in a footnote (cf. Husserl, 2008, 172).

6 See Spiegelberg (1994): among others, Ingarden, Stein, and Hearing became his main assistants, while Heidegger and Pfänder left the group.

7 He introduced De Beauvoir and Sartre to Husserl's phenomenology and would lead Sartre to rush to the nearest bookshop and say, "Give me everything you have on phenomenology, now!" (Bakewell, 2017, 20).

8 In particular, see: *Ideas* I "The Thesis of the Natural Standpoint and its Suspension" (§§27–32).

9 In the first volume of *Ideas,* Husserl had already introduced this concept under the heading of *Umwelt* to mean a surrounding natural world, and it is only after writing the *Cartesian Meditation* and most of all in the *Crisis* that Husserl elaborates a proper "Umweltanalyse" to explicate the idea of an objective world shared within the intersubjective life of a living community (*Husserliana*, vol. IV, p. 222; Husserl, 1989, 234).

10 See Husserl (1970, 105): "in forming and having them. (…) we are subjects for this world, ...experiencing it, contemplating it, valuing it, relating purposefully;... it has an ontic meaning given by our experiencings...; and it has the modes of validity which we as subjects of validity ...bring about or possess from earlier on as habitual acquisitions...which we can reactualize at will (…) There are two attitudes; in one, the perceptive, we are (…) directed straightforwardly toward the object...our gaze passes through the appearances towards what continuously appears through their continuous unification;...In the reflective attitude, (by contrast) ....the sequence of appearances themselves is thematic, rather than what appears in them."

11 Here and similarly in Husserl's manuscripts from 1920s, Husserl often uses the expression "I-Thou-relationship," which closely seems to point to Buber's work I and Thou, published in 1923. Yet, it seems that when in 1920 Husserl used this expression, there was no influence by Buber's writing, because Husserl did not seem to possess in his library any copy of his work as Husserl's collection of books shows at the Husserl Archive in Leuven. In fact, Husserl and Buber met for the first time in 1928, when Buber visited Husserl in Freiburg.

12 Ströker (1993) and Held (2007) defend, in fact, Husserl from the attack of solipsism because the transcendental ego is a meditating stance *functioning for* and not just a *solus ipse*; it is, in fact, the original streaming of time in relation to which being comes to existence and it is the first other through which we can experience this primal empathy (see Husserl, Paris Lectures, section 44 and Husserl VI, 149, 150, 153) that allows us to encounter the radical other.

13 The sources Husserl borrowed to develop his theory of intersubjectivity are especially indebted to Brentano (1973), Stein (1989), and Fink (1981). From Brentano he took the theory of intentionality to explain the subject-object relationship and from Stein the notion of empathy to clarify the manner in which we perceive otherness.

14 As Husserl writes, "The analogy is not in full force and effect (*voll*); it is an indication, not an anticipation (*Vorgriff*) that could become a seizure of the self (*Selbstgriff*)" (Husserl, 1973a, 87).

References

Albertazzi, L. (Ed.). (2013). *Handbook of experimental phenomenology: Visual perception of shape, space and appearance*. London: Wiley-Blackwell.

Ales Bello, A. (2009). The divine in Husserl and other explorations. *Analecta Husserliana, 98*, 12–24.

Baker, H. D. (1969). *Herbart & education*. New York: Random House.

Bakewell, S. (2017). *At the Existentialist Café*. New York: Other Press.

Binswanger, L. (1992). *Traum und Existenz* (Dream and existence). M. Foucault (Trans.). Bern/Berlin: Verlag Gachnang & Springer.

Brencio, F. (2024). *Phenomenology, neuroscience and clinical practice: Transdisciplinary experiences*. Switzerland: Springer.

Brentano, F. (1973). *Psychology from the empirical standpoint,* A. C. Rancurello, D. B. Terrell, & L. McAlister (Eds.). London: Routledge.

Cairns, D. (1964). Translator's introduction. In E. Husserl (Ed.), *Cartesian meditations* (pp. x–xx). New York: Martinus Nijhoff.

Farber, M. (Ed.). (1940). *Philosophical essays in memory of Edmund Husserl*. Cambridge, MA: Harvard University Press.

Ferrarello, S. (2026). *Bloomsbury handbook of phenomenological bioethics*. London: Bloomsbury.

Fink, E. (1981). The problem of the phenomenology of Edmund Husserl. In R. M. Harlan Trans.). W. McKenna, R. M. Harlan, & L. E. Winters (Ed.), *Apriori and world: European contributions to Husserlian phenomenology* (pp. 21–55). The Hague: Martinus Nijhoff. (Original work published 1939).

Foucault, M. (1988). *Madness and civilization: A history of insanity in the age of reason*. R. Howard (Trans.). New York: Vintage Books. (Original work published 1961).

Frankl, V. E. (1963). *Man's search for meaning: An introduction to logotherapy*. New York: Washington Square Press.

Frege, G. (1892). On sense and reference. In M. Black (Ed.), P. Geach (Trans.). *Translations from the philosophical writings of Gottlob Frege* (pp. 209–230). Oxford: Blackwell.

Frege, G. (1892/1997). On sense and reference. In A. P. Martinich (Ed.), M. Black (Trans.). *The philosophy of language* (4th ed., pp. 25–50). Oxford University Press. (Original work published 1892).

Fuchs, T. (2012). *The phenomenology of body memory*. In S. C. Koch, T. Fuchs, M. Summa, & C. Müller (Eds.), *Body memory, metaphor and movement* (pp. 9–22). Amsterdam: John Benjamins.

Fuchs, T., & De Jaegher, H. (2009). Enactive intersubjectivity: Participatory sense-making and mutual incorporation. *Phenomenology and the Cognitive Sciences*, *8*(4), 465–486.

Fuchs, T., & Koch, S. C. (2014). Embodied affectivity: On moving and being moved. *Frontiers in Psychology*, *5*, 1664–1078.

Fuchs, T., Messas, G. P., & Stanghellini, G. (2019). More than just description: Phenomenology and psychotherapy. *Psychopathology*, *52*, 63–66.

Gendlin, E. T. (1973). Experiential phenomenology. In M. Natanson (Ed.), *Phenomenology and the social sciences* (Vol. I, pp. 281–319). Evanston, IL: Northwestern University Press.

Ghigi, N. (2002). La metafisica come ricerca di Dio nella fenomenologia di Husserl. *Dialegesthai. Rivista telematica di filosofia*, *3*, online.

Giorgi, A. (1970). *Psychology as a human science: A phenomenologically based approach*. New York: Harper & Rowe.

Gozé, T. (2024). *Phénoménologie et schizophrénie* (Phenomenology and schizophrenia). Paris: Hermann.

Gurtwisch, A. (1941). A non-egological conception of consciousness. *Philosophy and Phenomenological Research*, *1*, 325–338.

Hegel, G. W. F. (2018). *The phenomenology of spirit*. T. Pinkard (Trans.). Cambridge: Cambridge University Press. (Original work published 1807).

Heidegger, M. (1962). *Being and time*. New York: Harper.

Held, K. (2007). Phenomenology of 'authentic time' in Husserl and Heidegger. *International Journal of Philosophical Studies*, *15*(3), 327–347.

Hoffman, L. (2006). *Humanistic psychotherapy*. Retrieved from https://www.existential-therapy.com/Humanistic Psychotherapy.htm

Husserl, E. (1929). Phenomenology. In *Encyclopædia britannica* (14th ed., Vol. 17, pp. 699–702).

Husserl, E. (1964). *Cartesian meditations: An introduction to phenomenology*. D. Cairns (Trans.). Dordrecht: Kluwer Academic Publishers.

Husserl, E. (1965). Philosophy as rigorous science (Q. Lauer, Trans.). In Q. Lauer (Ed.), *Phenomenology and the crisis of philosophy: Philosophy as rigorous science, and Philosophy and the crisis of European man* (pp. 1–88). New York: Harper & Row.

Husserl, E. (1970). *The crisis of European sciences and transcendental phenomenology*. D. Carr (Trans.). Evanston, IL: Northwestern University Press.

Husserl, E. (1973a). *Zur Phänomenologie der Intersubjektivität. Texte aus dem Nachlass. Erster Teil. 1905–1920* [On the phenomenology of intersubjectivity. Texts from the estate. Part 1. 1905–1920]. I. Kern (Ed.). The Hague: Martinus Nijhoff.

Husserl, E. (1973b). *Zur Phänomenologie der Intersubjektivität. Texte aus dem Nachlass. Zweiter Teil. 1921–28* [On the phenomenology of intersubjectivity. Texts from the estate. Second part. 1921–28]. I. Kern (Ed.). The Hague: Martinus Nijhoff.

Husserl, E. (1977). *Cartesian meditations: An introduction to phenomenology*. D. Cairns (Trans.). Martinus Nijhoff. (Original work published 1931).

Husserl, E. (1994). *Briefwechsel* [Correspondence] (Vol. III). The Hague: Kluwer Academic Publishers.

Husserl, E. (2000). *Logical investigations*. J. N. Findlay (Trans.). London: Routledge.

Husserl, E. (1891/2003). *Philosophy of arithmetic: Psychological and logical investigations with supplementary texts from 1887–1901*. D. Willard (Trans.). Dordrecht: Kluwer Academic Publishers. (Original work published 1891).

Husserl, E. (1989). *Ideas pertaining to a pure phenomenology and to a phenomenological philosophy: Second book: Studies in the phenomenology of constitution*. R. Rojcewicz & A. Schuwer (Trans.). New York: Kluwer Academic Publishers. (Original work published 1952).

Husserl, E. (2008). *Logical investigations*. D. Moran (Ed.) (Vol. 1). Milton Park: Routledge.

Husserl, E. (2014). *Grenzprobleme der Phänomenologie. Analysen des Unbewusstseins und der Instinkte. Metaphysik. Späte Ethik* (Texte aus dem Nachlass 1908–1937) [The limit problems of phenomenology. Analyses of unconsciousness and instinct, metaphysics, late ethics. (Texts from the estate 1908–1937)]. R. Sowa, & T. Vongehr (Eds.). New York: Springer.

Jaspers, K. (1955). *Reason and existence*. New York: Noonday Press.

Kaufmann, F. (1940). Art and phenomenology. In M. Farber (Ed.), *Philosophical essays in memory of Edmund Husserl* (pp. 187–202). Cambridge, MA: Harvard University Press.

Kusch, M. (1995). *Psychologism: A case study in the sociology of philosophical knowledge*. New York: Psychology Press.

Kusch, M. (2020). Psychologism. In *The Stanford encyclopedia of philosophy* (Spring 2020 Edition). Retrieved from https://plato.stanford.edu/archives/spr2020/entries/psychologism/

Laing, R. D. (1960). *The divided self: An existential study in sanity and madness*. Harmondsworth: Penguin.

Levinas, E. (1969). *Totality and infinity: An essay on exteriority*. A. Lingis (Trans.). Pittsburgh: Duquesne University Press.

Levinas, E. (1987). *Collected philosophical papers*. Dordrecht: Martinus Nijhoff Publishers.

Merleau-Ponty, M. (2002). *Phenomenology of perception*. New York: Routledge.

Mill, J. S. (1843/1973, 1974). *A system of logic ratiocinative and inductive: Being a connected view of the principles of evidence and the methods of scientific investigation*, cited from *The collected works of John Stuart Mill* (Vol. 7) (Books I–III), 8 (Books IV– VI). J. M. Robson (Ed.). London and Toronto: Routledge and University of Toronto Press.

Minkowski, E. (1970). *Lived time: Phenomenological and psychopathological studies*. N. Metzel (Trans.). Illinois: Northwestern University Press. (Original work published 1927).

Overgaard, S. (2010). *Husserl and Heidegger on being in the world*. Dordrecht: Kluwer Academic Publishers.

Peirce, C. S. (1992). How to make our ideas clear. In N. Houser, & C. Kloesel (Eds.), *The essential Peirce: Selected philosophical writings, Volume 1 (1867–1893)* (pp. 124–141). Indiana: Indiana University Press.

Perls, F. (1969). *Gestalt therapy verbatim*. Lafayette, CA: Real People Press.

Ratcliffe, M. (2015). *Experiences of depression: A study in phenomenology*. Oxford: Oxford University Press.

Rogers, C. R. (1951). *Client-centered therapy: Its current practice, implications and theory*. London: Constable and CompanySchutz, A. (1962–1966). *Collected papers I: The problem of social reality*. M. A. Natanson, & H. L. van Breda (Eds.). Dordrecht: Martinus Nijhoff Publishers.

Sass, L. A. (1992). *Madness and modernism: Insanity in the light of modern art, literature, and thought*. New York: Basic Books.

Schuhmann, K. (1977). *Husserl-Chronik. Denk- und Lebensweg Edmund Husserls*. Dordrecht, Boston, MA and London: Kluwer.

Schutz, A. (1962). *Collected papers I: The problem of social reality* (M. Natanson, Ed.). New York: Martinus Nijhoff.

Spiegelberg, H. (1994). *The phenomenological movement*. Holland: Springer.

Stein, E. (1989). *On the problem of empathy*. W. Stein (Trans.). Washington, DC: ICS Publications.

Ströker, E. (1993). *Husserl's transcendental phenomenology*. Stanford, CA: Stanford University Press.

Svenaeus, F. (2001). *The hermeneutics of medicine and the phenomenology of health: Steps towards a philosophy of medical practice*. New York: Springer.

Svenaeus, F. (2017). *Phenomenological bioethics*. London: Routledge.

Toombs, S. K. (1987). The meaning of illness: A phenomenological approach to the patient-physician relationship. *The Journal of Medicine and Philosophy, 12*(3), 219–240.

Van der Kolk, B. (2014). *The body keeps the score: Brain, mind, and body in the healing of trauma*. New York: Viking.

Watson, J., & Bohart, A. (2015). Humanistic/existential/phenomenological psychotherapy. In *The encyclopedia of clinical psychology* (pp. 30–42). New York: John Wiley & Sons.

2

EPOCHE AND REDUCTIONS

Dualism, Normality, and Abnormality in the Lifeworld

Introduction

The notion of the transcendental in phenomenology and philosophy might initially seem irrelevant for understanding everyday psychological experiences, let alone for deepening our comprehension of psychopathological conditions. When Husserl shifted from his realistic approach to transcendental phenomenology, he lost many followers who believed this turn rendered his philosophy less applicable to life, especially compared to his work in Logical Investigations. However, this chapter seeks to challenge this misunderstanding of Husserl's transcendental phenomenology.

By approaching the transcendental, Husserl's philosophy actually delves even deeper into the origins of lived experiences. Staying true to the phenomenological motto of "Back to the things themselves," transcendental phenomenology scrutinizes the conditions that allow a certain aspect of life to appear in one way rather than another. Much like examining a hair under a microscope reveals a far more detailed and complex structure, transcendental phenomenology reveals new depths in any phenomenon.

In what follows, I will provide a basic understanding of Husserl's notion of epoche, reduction, and transcendental and I will show its applications to common ideas of normality and abnormality.

Why Transcendental Phenomenology in Nursing and Clinical Work?

Husserl considered himself a student of Socrates, always a "beginner" in philosophy. He repeatedly emphasized the danger of a sophistic attitude that "deprives

DOI: 10.4324/9781003665557-2

life of any rational sense" and separates the lived experience from truth and value. This concern drove his philosophical inquiries and his commitment to an "examined life" (Husserl, 1956/1969, 11). Following the Socratic footsteps, he saw himself as a "functionary of humanity," taking on a caring, almost medical, attitude toward the obstacles that hinder personal growth, inner freedom, moral responsibility, and cognitive flexibility (Husserl, 1981, 15). He managed to pursue this goal even in the most abstract and theoretical investigations.

For example, if we consider Husserl's account of mereology—the theory that examines how parts and wholes relate—which I will draw upon in Chapter 9 to discuss borderline personality disorder, we can see how phenomenology rejects sensory atomism, the view that the phenomenal world lacks inherent structure. Contrary to Kant's notion of a formless "manifold of intuition," Husserl argued that every phenomenal object has an inherent form or structure as it is given to the senses. Central to Husserl's mereology is the notion of unity of containment (or "unitary foundation"—*Einheitliche Fundierung*), which refers to the interdependent variations of a content's parts. For example, in a melody, you cannot change a note without affecting the entire structure of the melody. Each part is not an independent or separable bit, but a dependent or inseparable moment within the whole (Husserl, 1983, 235–236).

For how abstract this concept might look, it has direct applications in psychopathology. The current Diagnostic and Statistical Manual of Mental Disorders does not account for how the various symptoms of each disorder coherently manifest in an individual case. Much like a melody composed of individual notes, each symptom occupies a specific place within the structure of a disease. Altering the sequence in which symptoms appear or the context of their manifestation can significantly reshape our understanding of the structure of a given phenomenon. Hence, simply identifying the presence of a minimal number of symptoms does not adequately capture the "invariant style" (Binswanger, 1947) or the "living plot" of the individual's symptoms (Minkowski, 1933).

Psychopathology influenced by phenomenology holds into account the idea that the phenomenal world has a structure whose composition of parts and whole is interdependent and our understanding of its givenness cannot be altered without altering the phenomenon itself. For this reason, the classics of phenomenological psychopathology aimed not only to identify the varieties of mental disease but also to understand the varieties of persons experiencing mental suffering. These case studies serve as paradigms to explore the bounds of normality and create gestalten—ideal-typical cases that simultaneously retain personal individuality, consistent with the "inseparability of matter of fact and essence" (Husserl, 1983, 12).

Yet, we cannot intend these models to be pre-existing and ever-changing. In that sense, especially in nursing and clinical work, Husserl's notion of the transcendental is pivotal for enhancing the depth and quality of patient care by moving beyond the limitations of pre-existing models and theories. The models and paradigms produced by phenomenological research are types that originate from a phenomenological observation of the lived experience. At the heart of Husserl's phenomenology is the concept of epoché, which involves a deliberate suspension of preconceived judgments and the bracketing of the natural attitude, enabling clinicians to set aside, at each time they approach a case, their ingrained assumptions and heuristics (Husserl, 1931/1960, 20, 1936/1970, 168). This is what makes the observation of reality phenomenological. This process is crucial in the clinical setting, where reliance on ready-made models can inadvertently overshadow the rich, nuanced experiences of patients. Being able to listen to the patient and observe their medical history without biases is vital for improving their well-being. While heuristics serve as valuable tools for pattern recognition and diagnostic accuracy, they can become insidious when they dominate the clinical encounter, reducing patients to mere subjects of predefined categories. Husserl's epoché and transcendental reduction (more on this in the following sections), therefore, becomes a means by which clinicians can return to "the things themselves," allowing them to engage more authentically with the patient's lived experience, free from the distortions of preconceived notions (Husserl, 1913/1983, 111).

This phenomenological approach encourages clinicians to truly listen to their patients, fostering a more empathetic and holistic understanding of the patient's embodied world. By doing so, it not only enriches the clinician-patient dialogue but also challenges the tendency to oversimplify complex emotional, physical, and social phenomena, ultimately leading to more compassionate and effective patient care.[1] In essence, Husserl's transcendental phenomenology provides a rigorous foundation for nursing and clinical practice, urging practitioners to engage deeply with the unique, personal realities of their patients, beyond the constraints of traditional medical models.

Paris Lectures

The Paris Lectures (February 23 and 25, 1929) serve as a valuable introduction to Husserl's phenomenology, particularly in tracing its evolution since the Logical Investigations. After the publication of Heidegger's *Being and Time* (1962) and difficulties with the Encyclopedia Britannica entry on phenomenology (Husserl et al., 1997), Husserl, sensing a divergence from Heidegger's approach, embarked on a rigorous lecturing tour across Europe. His aim was to defend his transcendental phenomenology. During this period, he was supported by scholars like Ingarden, Stein, and Hering, while Heidegger and Pfänder, who were critical of Husserl's transcendental shift, distanced themselves. Offering these seminars at La Sorbonne aligned perfectly with his aim to introduce more scholars to transcendental phenomenology and to preserve his vision of phenomenological philosophy.

Husserl's Inspiration from Descartes

In these lectures, the discussion begins with a tribute to Descartes and then moves to compare Husserl's phenomenology with Descartes' philosophy. Both thinkers focus on exploring the rational foundations of science and use a meditative, introspective approach in their inquiries. For each, the pursuit of rational foundations is a deeply personal endeavor that precedes its scientific implications. Both Descartes and Husserl possessed a profound understanding of mathematics and shared a growing dissatisfaction with the foundations of scientific knowledge. Each sought a personal starting point for exploring the nature of truth—one that could withstand even the most pervasive doubts.[2] For this reason, both chose a meditative approach, viewing their quest as, above all, a deeply personal search for a solid foundation of truth. But how can such personal meditation be of public value? Husserl explores this question in his essay *The Origin of Geometry* (1936/1970), where he seeks to address it through the concept of evidence.

For both philosophers, evidence is the end point of their investigations, yet each interprets this key concept in subtly different ways. Similar to Husserl, *clara et distincta perceptio*, using Descartes' term, serves as the starting point for acquiring true knowledge. For Descartes, evidence is tied to clarity and distinctness—qualities that ensure the certainty of knowledge. In *Meditations on First Philosophy*, Descartes emphasizes that clear and distinct perceptions are the "criteria of truth" (Descartes, 1641/1996, AT VII:35). His approach focuses on identifying an indubitable foundation for knowledge, culminating in the *cogito* ("I think, therefore I am") as the ultimate example of self-evident truth.

Husserl, while influenced by Descartes, redefines evidence within the context of his phenomenological project. In *Ideas I*, Husserl describes evidence as the "consciousness of fulfillment" experienced when an intentional act coincides with the presence of its intended object (Husserl, 1913/1983, §136). Unlike Descartes, Husserl sees evidence as a dynamic and ongoing process rooted in the lived experience of phenomena, which includes temporal and embodied dimensions.

Secondary sources highlight the divergence between the two philosophers. Moran (2000) explains that while Descartes focused on methodological certainty, Husserl sought to ground all knowledge in the experiential structures of consciousness. Zahavi (2003) elaborates that Husserl's concept of evidence extends beyond Cartesian intellectual intuition by addressing the relational and intersubjective aspects of how phenomena are given to consciousness. Evidence, in fact, is for Husserl the most concrete expression of our understanding of the world. Although both philosophers' inquiries lead to an understanding of the world as *cogitatio* (thought), what this *cogitatio* reveals differs for each thinker. It is crucial to avoid the outdated and mistaken interpretation of Husserl's phenomenology as mere intellectualism, which reduces *cogitatio* to a purely cognitive starting and end point (Dreyfus, 1991). Instead, attention should be directed toward Husserl's effort to bridge the mind-body gap introduced by Descartes' concept of *cogitatio* and the dualism it entails. For Husserl, *cogitatio* is embodied evidence as I will explain below and in the following section.

Both Descartes and Husserl believed that confronting the possibility of relativism required embracing radical doubt. They viewed the *epoché* (or *Einklammerung*, parenthesizing) as a crucial method for suspending all knowledge and presuppositions, enabling us to seriously consider the possibility that an evil genius could be deceiving us about everything we believe to be true. Even if this evil genius were real and succeeded in undermining the very foundation of our being, one truth remains undeniable—the doubt itself. Indeed, there is one thing I cannot doubt: the fact that I am doubting. *Cogito sum* ("I think/ I am," ideally without the *ergo* to capture the immediacy of this realization) stands as the self-evident truth revealed to both Husserl and Descartes through their radical application of doubt. Even when I question the ground beneath my feet or the air I breathe, I cannot question the fact that I am questioning. In this act of questioning, the truth *I am* emerges—a unity where "I" signifies the mind and "am" represents the body, both so profoundly interconnected that one cannot fully make sense without the other. This unity becomes the first, indubitable truth.

Thus, while both philosophers identify the *ego cogito* ("I think") as the first evidence in their pursuit of an ultimate truth that can withstand doubts about the foundations of scientific knowledge, their interpretations of it differ significantly. Descartes' notion of evidence, expressed by the *ego cogito*, emphasizes intellectual clarity and distinctness as guarantees of certainty, while Husserl broadens the concept to include the fulfillment of intentional acts, reflecting his phenomenological focus on embodied experience and its structures. This shift illustrates the progression from Cartesian foundationalism to Husserl's more comprehensive account of truth as rooted in lived experience. For Husserl, the *cogito*, as we will better see in the next two sections, is a living body.

Cogito Existo *and Its Body*

The dualism expressed in Descartes' "*cogito, existo*" is quite complex to define. According to Hart (1996, 265–267), Descartes introduced a form of substance dualism which is not to be confused with the property and predicate dualism that are its consequences. Property dualism asserts that the properties of the mind and those of the matter are substantially different; for this reason, consciousness cannot be reduced to neurobiology. This dualistic way of categorizing matter/mind properties generates a predicate dualism according to which while there is only one ontological category of substances and properties of substances (usually physical), the predicates that we use to describe mental events remain mental representations. Descartes' substance dualism separates the substance of mind and body as irreducible to each other. The thinking ego becomes the object of its body as the thought experienced by this machine. Similarly, to the scientific world of nature, the human world is a thought (*cogitatum*) with the difference that the lifeworld (the world in which we live) is the thought (*cogitatum*) of the mind while nature is the thought (*cogitatum*) of the body. Descartes' interpretation of the *cogito* reduces the human psyche to a mechanistic entity, functioning like a detached operator controlling the body, much like a machine or, as Dennett describes, a "Cartesian theater" where the mind observes and directs the body's actions from a central command (Dennett, 1991). This dualistic framework reinforces a sharp division between mind and body, portraying the psyche as an immaterial agent separate from the physical world.

The pineal gland, situated within the larger machinery of the human body, is tasked with mediating the interaction between the thinking substance (*res cogitans*) and the extended substance (*res extensa*). This reinforces a dualistic view of health and medical care that strongly separates the body from the mind.

Husserl's main criticism of Descartes goes toward his apodictic acceptance of the truthfulness of the *ego cogito* and its contents. This stance reinforces the dualism between mind and body.

> He does not see that, by being convinced of the possibility of the goal and of this means, he has already left this radicalism behind. (...) The ego is not a residuum of the world but is that which is absolutely apodictically posited.
>
> *(Husserl, 1936/1970, 80)*

The *ego cogito* ("I think") that Husserl critically examines is, for Descartes, the unshakable self-evident truth grounded in the certainty of an omniscient God. This divine perfection,[3] implanted the self-evident idea of the *ego cogito* within the machine-like body, which explains why humans experience sensory knowledge in a coherent and reliable manner.[4]

Having a Body vs Being a Body

While Husserl distances himself from Descartes by rejecting the notion that the *ego cogito* is tied to a divine, self-evident idea and by refuting the intellectualism and dualism inherent in this view, he remains deeply interested in the implications of substance dualism, particularly regarding the temporal structural differences between *res cogitans* (thinking substance) and *res extensa* (extended substance). The temporal experience of *having* a body (*res cogitans* and in Husserl's terms *Leib*) is quite different from the temporal experience of *being* a body (*res extensa* and in Husserl's terms *Koerper*). Acknowledging the complexity of this problem, he wrote, "The same Body which serves me as means for all my perception obstructs me in the perception of itself and is a remarkably imperfectly construed thing" (Husserl, 1913/1983, 167). To have a body is to be aware of our physical limits (*Grenzen*) within the space we occupy as one object among others. In contrast, to be the body is to experience these same limits through a lived, unreflective awareness.

The main difference between these two modalities of being is temporal because it is in time that things (our own body included) appear to us. A temporal extended object will never appear to us if it exists only in the here and now, as a living presence. For something to be,[5] a temporal horizon or field should be present. As mentioned above, the celebre example that Husserl gave is that of the melody: we would not be able to retain the melody if the tones in which it is expressed were not retained, anticipated in a "constantly gradated coming" (Husserl, 1991). This ability does not belong to our being a thing among other things because in that sense we are a living presence without any skill to anticipate or retain what has just been; that ability belongs to our mind. Having a body, being a *res cogitans*, means being able to figure in time the appearance of the lifeworld; as Zahavi remarks (2003), the two are not distinguished only in an object-relation way but in a temporal way. On the one hand, the temporal experience which characterizes the being a body opposes the pre-reflective and thematizing temporal presupposition of having a body. Having a body is the phenomenological presupposition for the body to be perceived and described in scientific terms.[6] This I *am*, that emerges from radical doubt and points to Husserl the radical difficulty of having a body and being a body in time discloses the door of phenomenology as a method and a discipline of knowledge. As will be demonstrated in the next section, *I am* serves as the foundational core of our intersubjective world.

To *be* a body, in Husserl's terms, refers to the lived experience of the body (*Leib*), where the body is not separate from the self but is the very medium through which we perceive, act, and experience the world. This is the pre-reflective, immediate mode of being, where the body is not an object of awareness but the center of all intentional activities. For instance, when walking or gesturing, the body seamlessly integrates into our actions, enabling us to inhabit time as a flow of continuous experiences. Wehrle (2019a, 2019b) emphasizes that this lived embodiment situates us temporally, as our bodily movements and sensations are always experienced within the dynamic flow of past, present, and future.

On the other hand, to *have* a body points to a reflective and objectifying stance, where the body is perceived as a physical entity (*Körper*) distinct from the self. This perspective emerges when we analyze or observe our body, such as when we notice fatigue or view our reflection. In this mode, the body is situated in objective, measurable time rather than the lived, subjective temporality of *Leib*. According to Wehrle, this objectification of the body introduces a temporal distance, as the body becomes something we possess and evaluate from an external standpoint, disrupting the immediacy of lived time.

The interplay between these two modes of embodiment is deeply temporal. The lived body (*Leib*) anchors us in the present, allowing us to move through time fluidly, whereas the physical body (*Körper*) situates us within a framework of chronological time, subject to decay and the finite nature of existence. As Wehrle points out, this distinction becomes particularly significant in contexts of disruption—when illness, pain, or fatigue draw attention to the body as an object, we are reminded of its material limits and its temporal finitude. This intuition proves to be particularly useful when discussing psychopathological disturbances connected to time experiences (Fuchs, 2010) of people suffering with schizophrenia, for example (Stanghellini et al., 2016). The integrity of time both from the perspective of having a body and the perspective of being a body is essential to build a coherent sense of identity in the world as an embodied being.

I *Am*

As demonstrated above, what lies behind the concept of "I/am" differs between Husserl and Descartes. In Descartes' philosophy, the statement "*Cogito, ergo sum*" ("I think, therefore I am") serves as a foundational truth, asserting the certainty of one's existence as a thinking being. Descartes posits that this self-evident idea is placed in the human mind by a divine essence, providing an indubitable basis for knowledge. In contrast, Husserl interprets the *ego cogito* not as an end in itself but as the starting point for a rigorous investigation into the contents of consciousness. Husserl's phenomenological approach seeks to explore the structures and experiences of the "I am," aiming to uncover the essence of phenomena as they present themselves to consciousness.

While Descartes' focus was on providing a method for Galileo's science and justifying the separation between religion and science (Schmaltz, 2015), Husserl was influenced by Dilthey's ideas. Dilthey understood the world in terms of motivation rather than the physical concept of causality (1910/2002) which implied a participatory view of the human being as an agent in the world which changes with and through the world. He also viewed empathy as the apperception of another's body (1910/2002). This means that, unlike Descartes, for Husserl, the *ego cogito* is not the center of a representational content where we find the idea of God; it is not an intellectual representation merely connected to the living body. Instead, for Husserl, the *ego cogito* is a renewed, embodied attitude with which the living being engages with the world through the temporal flow of time. The lifeworld is exactly the expression that Husserl uses to explain the kind of reality that emerges from the repeated interaction between the human beings and the reality they are interacting with. From a psychopathological perspective, this offers a privileged view on the meaning-making process of the individual whose life might be misaligned with their interaffective environment.

Accordingly, the subject is never an isolated monad detached from its own environment but it is an agent shaping its environment while being recursively shaped by it. The *ego cogito* is an *ego cogito cogitatum*—an "I" that engages with the world reflectively, distinct from the "I" that interacts with the world in a natural, unreflective way (again, the contrast between being a body while having a body). This reflective "I" serves as a constitutive pole of meaning, coexisting and co-functioning with the natural "I" that participates in the world without self-reflection. One "I" is living a story, while the other assigns meaning to it. Between these two poles exists a witness that discovers itself as the original "other" in relation to the life that naturally flows in the natural attitude. This witnessing is the original source of the transcendental attitude. Strengthening this inner witness enables individuals with various psychopathological issues to gain control over their problems while staying connected to their core identity. In fact, this witness has a body in time, which forms the foundational condition for any possible ways their body may manifest in practical life. Deciding to observe and describe this foundational condition marks the very beginning of the phenomenological attitude (Fuchs, 2007; Wehrle, 2019b).

In this sense, Husserl's idealism and transcendental turn cannot be compared to traditional German idealism because there is no recourse to a primal being. The primal being is, in this case, one of the positions that the *ego cogito* can take in the flow of time. These egos are co-existent and co-functioning positions; there is no reification of ideas because the meaning constituted by the transcendental ego is incarnated within the coexisting life of the living body. Moreover, there is no rigid method, as the phenomenological approach is presuppositionless, tailored to lived experience, and grounded in a never-ending beginning. Training individuals to become aware of these ego stations can help them to get to know their blind spot and correct them when they bring harm or disrupt regular life (Bürgy, 2010).

Ego Cogito Cogitatum

The *ego cogito cogitatum* is that initial step in which we discover the world as a content of its reflective being. The *ego cogito* (I think) becomes an *ego cogito cogitatum* (I think thoughts) through an act of *selbst-besinnung* (self-determination) (Husserl, 1931/1960, 1936/1970a, 188) by which we choose to adopt a phenomenological attitude to look at the contents of the first emerging truth that resists the radical doubt. It is through this act of self-determination that we come to understand the generation of time and its contents. The epoché is the phenomenological tool that can initiate this specific act of self-determination. It is, in fact, through the attitude of self-doubt that an individual chooses to adopt in response to the free flow of events in their life that we encounter the phenomenon as it reveals itself to us. This change of attitude allows the subject to shift from the naive ego that lives in the world to the ego who looks at this world with a questioning attitude—the ego cogito. The phenomenologist finds in this *ego cogito* a *cogitatum* that explains the generative flow of time and being. The epoché represents a return to the things themselves, but through observation rather than analysis.

If I choose to examine the cogito from a different observational standpoint, I begin to perceive the structure of the world as it is experienced through that perspective. Initially, a phenomenon may appear to me in a naïve way—as an object external to my being (for instance, a house). However, when I adopt a phenomenological reflective attitude, that same house reveals itself not merely as an external object, but as something I am intentionally directed toward. It becomes an object of interest, something that engages my attention. At this point, the house takes on the form of a noematic correlate of my perception—an intentional object I can now describe and analyze through phenomenological reflection. Within this experience, objectivity reveals itself as a function of my role as an observer—both psychologically and logically. It emerges as a correlation between the noesis—the bodily and intentional activity (*Leistung*) through which I touch or see—and the noema, the meaning constituted in being touched or seen by the subject. Thus, the *cogito cogitatum* is the reason/world/comprehensive being (á la Jaspers)[7] that structures my understanding of being according to the specific functioning in which reality appears to me and I determine this reality through the body. My categories of meaning are not static boxes in which I organize knowledge; they are operative categories that live within me and evolve with me. They have a body and are a body which operates in and through time. Each perception opens up a horizon of meanings, and each perception represents an index of possible meanings that this object can embody. The world is a dispositional property that functions for us and within us.

Reductions

In Husserl's Formal Transcendental Logic, the epoché becomes an essential step for perceiving the essence of a phenomenon (*Wesensschau*). To grasp the essence of a specific portion of the world I engage with, I must understand the conditions that make its appearance possible to me.[8] For example, for a triangle to appear to me as a triangle, it must have three angles—this is its essence. It is more complex, however, to discern the essence of certain feelings or interpersonal phenomena.

Since the scope of my experience is boundless, a methodological approach to organizing my knowledge is necessary. For this reason, in his Ideas, Husserl organized being into ontological regions (Ideas I–III), meaning that each region corresponds to specific areas of being with which human experience typically engages. Formal ontology relates to how we express the concrete essence of a specific being through intelligible forms, primarily logic and mathematics (*Ideas I: "Fact and Essence,"* §§1–17).[9] Material ontologies represent concreteness according to three broad categories: Nature, Spirit (*Geist*), and Consciousness. Nature corresponds to any science that studies objects in space-time, Spirit concerns the study of persons and their interactions within personal and institutional contexts, and Consciousness focuses on the intentional acts of consciousness itself. As explained above, Husserl does not adopt Descartes' dualism but instead views formal and material ontologies as the relationship between facts and essences necessary for reality to appear to us. For instance, a dog is both an object in space that interacts with me and a concept I can refer to using the formal token "dog." There is no before and after between its matter and form, nor is there a dualism between concrete matter and its formal expression. To delve into the concreteness of a phenomenon and the form through which it expresses itself, I must apply the epoché and a reduction. Through the *epoché*, I set aside my personal assumptions and biases, committing myself to observe the phenomenon as it presents itself to me. Through the *reduction*, I direct my attention back (*re-ducere*, from Latin) to a specific ontological domain of the phenomenon under observation. This approach brings me as close as possible to the ontology—the essence of the phenomenon before me—while bracketing the human characteristic of the naïve ego that usually engages with that aspect of reality. Depending on the depth of my analysis, I can choose to apply either a philosophical or scientific reduction. These forms of reduction bracket my philosophical or scientific knowledge when examining the formal and regional aspects of a phenomenon. Alternatively, I can apply the phenomenological reduction, which, similar to the epoché,[10] allows me to perceive the essence (*Wesensschau*) by bracketing any personal existential assumptions. Through this reduction, I commit to becoming a phenomenologist, fully focused on observing and describing the phenomenon that appears before me in an absolute[11] moment in time. After the phenomenological reduction, I might even apply a transcendental reduction, through which I bracket my temporality and witness the being of the phenomenon as an original impression in time (*Urimpression*)—a living present from which the horizon of time synthesizes the constitution of our knowledge.

Seven Epochai

Embree, in his article *Seven Epochēs* (1992), expands the traditional understanding of the *epoché* by identifying seven distinct types, each tailored to a specific domain of phenomenological inquiry. His analysis enriches the methodological landscape of phenomenology by showing how the *epoché* can be adapted to explore various dimensions of human experience.

The *transcendental epoché* forms the cornerstone of classical phenomenology, where all presuppositions about the existence of the external world are suspended to focus solely on the structures of consciousness. This approach aligns closely with Husserl's original project of grounding knowledge in the immediacy of experience. The *eidetic epoché* shifts attention to the essence of phenomena by bracketing empirical variations. Through this method, phenomenologists aim to uncover the invariant structures that define a phenomenon, moving beyond its contingent manifestations. Embree also highlights the *ontological epoché*, which sets aside assumptions about the being of entities to investigate their modes of appearance. This method resonates with phenomenological efforts to describe how entities present themselves within specific contexts of experience. Beyond these foundational forms, Embree introduces specialized *epochai* for exploring specific fields. The *phenomenological psychological epoché* suspends theoretical frameworks in psychology to analyze lived experiences as they are given, free from interpretive overlays. Similarly, the *phenomenological sociological epoché* brackets sociological constructs, enabling a first-person exploration of social phenomena. The *phenomenological anthropological epoché* invites the suspension of cultural assumptions, facilitating a phenomenological investigation of human experience across diverse cultural contexts. Finally, the *phenomenological historical epoché* involves bracketing historical interpretations to access historical events as they were lived and experienced. Embree's classification is particularly useful in light of the ongoing debate over whether the *epoché* should be understood as a practical methodological tool or as a purely theoretical construct within phenomenology.[12] Since we are bringing phenomenology in clinical practice, I believe this article demonstrates the adaptability of the *epoché* to different domains, providing phenomenologists with a refined set of tools for uncovering the structures of experience. Phenomenology is not a static methodology but a dynamic approach that evolves to meet the needs of various fields of inquiry.

The Transcendental Subject and the Origin of Intersubjectivity

After applying the transcendental epoché and reduction, we discover transcendental subjectivity as the original ground of all being, truth, and value. In *The Crisis*, Husserl explains that by "transcendental," he broadly refers to:

> the motif of inquiring back into the ultimate source of all formations of knowledge; the motif of the knower's reflecting on himself and his knowing life, in which all the scientific structures that are valid for him occur, purposefully stored up as acquisitions, and have become and continue to become freely available.
>
> *(1936/1970a, 97–98)*

Accordingly, the transcendental ego is a meditating subject that functions as the "performer of all validities," which "continuously carries out a retaining function," preventing what has been explicated from sinking into nothingness as perception progresses. It "crosses out what is illusory" and "attends to decisions about uncertainties and doubt" (1936/1970a, 171). The transcendental ego that emerges from the transcendental reduction still coexists with the naïve subject that lives in the world but operates as a functioning locus of experience. This ego is the residue of consciousness, observing and producing meanings as *cogitatum* coexistent with the empirical ego. It is the pure stream of living presence through which being appears in different phenomena. Within this stream, I can see how every object is an object for a subject and an infinite point of possible meanings.[13] In clinical practice, a relevant example of the transcendental ego's functioning can be seen in mindfulness-based cognitive therapy for individuals with depression. In this therapeutic approach, patients are guided to become more aware of their thoughts, emotions, and bodily sensations without immediately reacting to them nor identifying with them (Segal et al., 2002). This process aligns with the idea of the transcendental ego as the "performer of all validities," which continuously observes and retains experiences, ensuring they do not simply fade into oblivion as new perceptions arise.

During mindfulness exercises, patients are encouraged to recognize their thoughts as transient mental events rather than objective realities. This practice helps them "cross out what is illusory"—such as negative automatic thoughts—and focuses on making decisions in moments of doubt or uncertainty. The transcendental ego, in this context, acts as the observer of these mental events, allowing the individual to maintain a sense of self that is separate from the immediate experience of distress. It functions alongside the naïve, everyday self, enabling the patient to perceive their thoughts and emotions as objects within a broader stream of consciousness, thus allowing for a more detached and reflective approach to their experiences (Kabat-Zinn, 1990).

This dual perspective—where the empirical ego lives in the world while the transcendental ego observes and interprets—enables patients to see their depression not as an all-encompassing identity, but as one of many possible interpretations within their lived experience. This realization can be empowering, providing patients with a greater sense of agency and helping them navigate their symptoms with a renewed sense of clarity and purpose.

Intersubjectivity and Empathy

In this primal flow of living presence, the transcendental ego discovers myself as the original Other, observing me from the origin of being and time. I appear to this original functioning of being as the primary Other. In this sense, through the transcendental reduction, I discover myself as an "I-we"—what Zahavi calls a neutral metaphysics—resulting in a radical and primal constitution of intersubjectivity. Similarly, Ströker (1993) and Held (2003) successfully defend Husserl against accusations of solipsism, arguing that the transcendental ego functions *for* something, not merely as a *solus ipse*. It is the original stream of time in relation to which being comes into existence, and it is the first Other through which we experience this primal empathy (Husserl, 1929/1964, section 44 of Paris Lectures; Husserl, 1931/1960; 1936/1970, 149, 150, 153), enabling us to encounter the radical Other. Empathy originates precisely in this encounter with ourselves as the radical Other, and it can be understood through three interconnected steps: associative pairing, reflexive revelation, and co-experiencing.

First, I can bring into my awareness certain feelings, emotions, and sensations that I experience in my living body. These presentifications enable the subject to transform what was given *Leibhaftig* (in person) into a sedimentation that establishes "the unity of world-certainty" and reveals the possibility for any reproductive activity (Husserl, 2000b, 152). Husserl's earliest unpublished work on the problem of empathy and the constitution of the living body dates back to 1908 (Husserl, 1973/Hua 13). In *Husserliana 13* (text 15, 97), Husserl distinguishes between a straightforward and an oblique form of empathy. The latter is an act analogous to recollection while the former points to a kind of empathy in which I presentify the other's experience in a spontaneous perceptive way. Oblique empathy instead holds a more cognitive component where I reflect on the experience of the object and fulfill the expectation with what I recollect from my past (Husserl, 1973/Hua 13, 97). My world is initially solipsistic (my thing, my body, my mind), and empathy opens windows in this otherwise blind structure. The other is given to me as a presence, as another presence tied to the here and now of my body (Husserl, 1973/Hua 13, 99).

Thanks to the transcendental reduction, the other appears primordially as a "now" with its field of protentions and retentions. In this "now," I encounter a mode of being, posited as self-given, where experiences that are not my own are directly present to me. In this sense, following a text from 1910 to 1911 (Beilage XXVIII in Husserl, 1973, 229), empathy is a mode of apperception and appresentation, founded on another concrete apperception (the apperception of the living body or the material thing). It is a *Verbildlichung*, an act of analogizing or picture-making. Empathy presupposes the empathized object as a being that is given in the now. The now is not continuously self-intuited; in the empathic act, you do not feel this continuity, as it is pre-temporal and already constituted in the point of now. In the empathic act, understood as recollection, the now is mirrored or given by another ego in the constitution of a harmonious spatio-temporal nature. Through the empathic act, taken as recollection, we move beyond our own egoic stream and reach into the streams of other egos. Empathy thus constitutes a new form of transcendence (Husserl, 1973b, 8) because, even though we do not know the contents of other persons' streams as first-person experiences, we can interact with them as units constituted in time and recollected in apprehension.

Accordingly, in this first step, empathy begins as a form of perception involving apperception and appresentation (Husserl, 1973; Stein, 1989). It is an act of analogizing or picture-making, where we recognize each other as human beings facing similar challenges. This initial empathetic connection allows the subject to perceive the essence and stylistic nuances of the other's expressions.

The second step, reflexive revelation, involves learning about ourselves through perceiving the other. For example, the direct intention to carry a pregnancy to term teaches the mother about her own changes, vulnerabilities, and responsibilities. This reflexive revelation strengthens the bond between, for example, a mother and her baby, regardless of the pregnancy's outcome or the mother's future decisions regarding the child. When the baby begins to kick, those small movements reflexively reveal the presence of a human being in the womb—one that is, in every essential way, similar to her own being. In perceiving the other, we experience both our similarities and differences—a process Husserl calls pairing association (Husserl, 2000; Ricoeur, 2004). This resonance creates a passive synthesis of meaning that connects individuals. Pairing aspects of each other's lives involves a reflexive revelation of both the subject and the other, highlighting the meaningful expressions of the other's life.

The final step of empathetic unfolding, co-experiencing, may or may not occur in the presence of the other. This step involves expanding one's interaffective world into the world of the other, creating new shared realities. At this step, we might develop interaffective interactions. Interaffectivity, the intertwining of embodied affectivity, means that partners' emotional states and bodily resonances continuously influence each other (Fuchs & Koch, 2014).

Abnormality and Interaffective Dissonance

The constitution of empathetic connection and intersubjective validation has its limits and interferences. In the 1930 manuscript, text 6 (1973b), Husserl raises the question: How can we trust the veracity of the mental and psychological life we perceive in others? How can I be sure that what I perceive about another's state of mind is true for them as well?

Even though my body tells me that I am a living being among other living beings, and it tells me through *Paarung* (the apperception and pairing of myself with others) that my body is similar to that of other humans, I realize in apperception and appresentation that my bodily sensuousness might be fulfilled by a meaning similar to that of another human being. I observe others and assume that what they feel is akin to what I feel. I assume that there are harmonious syntheses taking place on different levels of our lives that bring us together. The Other, which holds its own sense of being (*Seinsinn*), is also a *Sosein*—a specific kind of being. The Other has its own unique body, but the similarity between our bodies serves as a presupposition for empathy and for the constitution of the Other and its world (Husserl, 1952/1989, *Idee II*, text 16, Hua 4).

Of course, a presupposition can easily become an assumption, which, if not confirmed in intersubjective lived experience, turns into prejudice or blindness. The problem is that I cannot confine the lives of those around me to my assumptions; the Other is a living being just as much as I am—so observing their bodily language is as important as understanding the meaning that this embodied expression assumes. It might be reasonable to assume that if someone turns off the radio, they simply don't like music or that particular song. However, it could also mean that the person feels overwhelmed by sensory input and is trying to return to a more regulated or calm state.

The encounter always occurs within a lifeworld where an intersubjective community constitutes meanings that structure life within an interaffective context. It is intersubjective perception that defines what is considered normal or abnormal; often, these categories reflect our social permission and intersubjective validation to belong within an interaffective community—such as friends, family, or school. "Interaffectivity is regarded as an intertwinement of two cycles of embodied affectivity, continuously modifying each partner's affective affordances and bodily resonance" (Fuchs & Koch, 2014, 61).

> Interaffectivity includes body feedback (i.e., the impression function within self and other), which is necessary for interbodily resonance. Components of interbodily resonance are: mirroring or complementing movements, body awareness (via proprioceptive body feedback), and kinaesthetic empathy; these are psychotherapeutically important in phenomena such as somatic countertransference.
>
> *(Fuchs & Koch, 2014, 62)*

Normality and abnormality are the two possible extremes of my eidetic variation within my intersubjective perception. What is normal and what is abnormal are two limit points on the same continuum of expectations that I can tolerate and accept from the Other within myself. Unfortunately, the gray area that is neither normal nor abnormal risks being overlooked entirely because it may not even fall within the scope of our expectations, and we may be completely blind to it.

The Assumption of Normality

"Man is a normative animal," as Husserl has it (Husserl, 1988, 59), and a pretty reluctant one.

Husserl's detailed analysis of embodied normality has a profound influence on the field of psychopathology, leading to two key conceptual developments. First, it contributes to the typology of (deviant) norms and forms of being-in-the-world, as explored by Binswanger (1963), Straus (1966), and von Gebsattel (1954). Binswanger illustrates the connection between these two concepts by referencing a passage from Husserl's Formal and Transcendental Logic: "The real world is only under a presumption, constantly renewed, that experience ought to always unfold in the same constitutive style" (Binswanger, 1963, 24).

These typologies correspond more to significant alterations in the entire personality than to standard nosographic categories (Minkowski, 1933). Second, it helps identify the fundamental and pervasive nature of pathological deviations from normality, described by Blankenburg (1971) as a "loss of natural evidence." Husserl's "constitutive" analyses reveal that the ordinary "constitutive style" of reality is dependent on at least four interrelated variables: the structures of lived space, lived time, intersubjectivity, and basic self-constitution. A significant deviation from the norm can occur along any of these axes, resulting in a different "constitutive style" of lived experience and giving rise to the phenomenology of psychiatric alienation, as described by phenomenological psychopathologists.

"Negative" symptoms, such as affective flattening, speech impoverishment, anhedonia, and attentional impairment, can underpin major positive symptoms of schizophrenia like hallucinations and delusions. However, these negative symptoms can also persist independently, manifesting as chronic difficulties in a person's relationship with reality and others. Husserl's constitutive analysis provides a powerful framework for understanding these difficulties. Husserl's phenomenology invites us to see the "presumption" regarding the usual style of evidence as a tentative way to understanding our intersubjective and interaffective lifeworld. The disruption it creates is akin to the phenomenological epoché, where a person's tacit assumptions of common sense are suspended, leading to the disintegration of the foundational aspects of normal interaction and linguistic communication. These foundational aspects, referred to by Wittgenstein (1953) as the "background" of tacit rules and by Schneider (1950) as the "underground" of such rules, ensure the "continuous consistency [Kontinuierliche Einstimmigkeit]" of ordinary experience (Husserl, 1973b, 206). Wolfgang Blankenburg famously termed this condition "a loss of natural evidence" (Blankenburg, 1971), resulting in a world where nothing can be taken for granted and the habitual fluidity of action disintegrates, leading to the collapse of "common sense." Feeling detached from what is generally deemed acceptable fosters an inner sense of insecurity, rendering even the simplest actions emotionally exhausting and difficult to articulate.

Normality and Intersubjectivity

According to phenomenology, normality is a social construction constituted through empathy, time, and intersubjectivity. "Normal" is what we expect to live according to an already constituted "style," and "abnormal" is what disrupts or breaks these pre-delineated expectations. While normality indicates "concordance" (*Einstimmigkeit*) with regard to certain objects (Husserl, 1973a, §21), or practical familiarity with expected experiences (Husserl, 1952/1989, §59), abnormality signifies a lack of certain faculties and capacities to relate to the world in the expected or outlined way (Husserl, 1931/1960, §55).[14]

As seen above, the intersubjective experience is what I first encounter in the discovery of my "I." My "I" emerges as distinct from the intersubjective matter, leading me to realize that I am intimately interwoven with others and responsible for my own actions.

This empathetic and intersubjective understanding of my nature occurs through time; our interpretation and constitution of what we are is shaped by and takes place within time. As Merleau-Ponty remarks:

> To analyze time is not to follow out the consequences of a pre-established conception of subjectivity; it is to gain access, through time, to its concrete structure. If we succeed in understanding the subject, it will not be in its pure form, but by seeking it at the intersection of its dimensions. We need, therefore, to consider time itself, and it is by following through its internal dialectic that we shall be led to revise our idea of the subject.
>
> *(Merleau-Ponty, 2012, 410–411/469–470)*

I gain access to what I am through time, and it is within time that the intersection of the different dimensions of me in time and space becomes apparent. Unfortunately, most of the time, our minds and eyes are not yet attuned to perceive what this intersection means. It is time, understood as a synthetic concept, that generates what we are. It is this time that defines the normality of a person and labels their identity.[15]

Common Sense, Social Interaction, and Cognition

Husserl's work, alongside that of his collaborators, highlights that both self-constitution and the creation of a shared, intersubjective world rely on primary intersubjectivity. Understanding intersubjectivity allows clinicians to form meaningful therapeutic relationships, where the clinician's "patient consciousness" can act as a mirror, helping patients reconstruct or repair a fragmented sense of self (Calvi, 1996, 2013).

The discovery of mirror neurons has provided neurobiological support for the concept of primary intersubjectivity (Rizzolatti & Sinigaglia, 2006), reaffirming phenomenological insights into pre-reflective attunement and social interaction. This has revived interest in empathy research and its significance in clinical practice, particularly as a counter to models like theory of mind and simulation theory (Zahavi, 2011). Empathy, based on primary intersubjectivity, is essential for understanding patients' experiences, especially in psychopathology and conditions such as autism, where social interaction may be impaired (Ballerini et al., 2016).

Husserl's ideas about self-constitution and primary intersubjectivity offer a valuable framework for clinical practice, psychopathology, and nursing studies. By focusing on patients' lived experiences and the intersubjective aspects of care, these concepts help clinicians grasp the complexities of selfhood, agency, and empathy in therapeutic settings. This phenomenological approach strengthens the relationship between healthcare providers and patients, promoting more personalized and compassionate care.

Conclusion

In this chapter, I have reflected on the role of transcendental phenomenology in clinical practice to enhance the mental health and well-being of individuals. As demonstrated, the reflective attitude inherent in phenomenological practice helps to move beyond heuristics and predefined models, prioritizing an understanding of the lived experience of each individual.

Through the epoche and reduction—where we bracket our personal assumptions and explore various ways of uncovering the essence of phenomena—we can focus our observation and description on a specific moment in time and space, examining how this presence interacts with the world around it. This process also brings us into contact with the origins of intersubjectivity and empathy, as the discovery of the initial "I am" introduces us to the first experience of otherness within the naïve flow of life. In adopting a reflective attitude, I discover myself as the primary other who lives and operates in the world, producing specific meanings.

The concepts of normality and abnormality are shaped by the common consensus on the meanings generated by the "I-we." Therefore, rather than focusing strictly on normality and abnormality, it would be more beneficial to rely on an intersubjective understanding of shared meanings and to consider how we can train ourselves to expand the inclusiveness of our meaning-making processes.

Notes

1 In this context, Sass (2021) engages deeply with transcendental phenomenology in his exploration of psychopathology, especially in severe mental disorders like schizophrenia. Sass argues that transcendental phenomenology is essential for understanding the subjective experiences of individuals with mental disorders, offering insights into consciousness and subjectivity that conventional psychological methods often overlook. He emphasizes the importance of phenomenological epoché and reduction to avoid errors such as the distortion of reflection and the neglect of ontological difference to achieve a more accurate understanding of the human mind.

2 "It is apparent that, as a consequence of the fact that I am striving after the presumptive goal of true science, I cannot as a beginner in philosophy make any judgment or accept one which I have not drawn from evidence, from 'experiences' in which the respective things and states of affairs are present to me as 'they themselves'" (Husserl, 1960, 9).

3 In a dialogue from his Gelassenheit, Heidegger writes "If thinking is what distinguishes man's nature, then surely the essence of this nature, namely the nature of thinking, can be seen only by looking away from thinking." (From Discourse on Thinking: A Translation of Gelassenheit by Anderson and Freund, Harper & Row, 1966). By "thinking" Heidegger refers to representational thinking in that sense distinct from contemplative or profoundly awareness.

4 "Now we consider all the above as things or qualities or modes of things. When, however, we recognize that it cannot happen that something is made from nothing, then the proposition 'nothing is made from nothing' is considered, not as if it were something that exists or even as a mode of a thing, but as some kind of eternal truth that is present in our mind, and it is called a common notion or an axiom" (Descartes, 1639, retrieved online https://www.marxists.org/reference/archive/descartes/1639/meditations.htm).

5 I do not imply here any Meinongian or Heideggerian difference between being and existing. More simply, I use this term to express the concreteness of the phenomenon.

6 According to Waller (2014), Descartes' dualism can be expressed in temporal terms. In Principles II. 23, for example, Descartes used time as a means to describe bodies as individuals since he claimed that "any variation in matter or diversity in its many forms depends on motion." For Waller, Descartes used two temporal attributes: (1) successive duration and (2) an innate idea of time (2004, 8). The former characterizes the *res cogitans* in the way in which it organizes the knowledge pertaining to its *res extensa* and the world it comes in contact with; the latter indicates the temporal quality in which the *res extensa* is. Differently from the sense of time in Plato's philosophy which Julia Annas described as a "mysterious cosmic entity or container" (Laws, 818c), both in Descartes and Husserl time is a constitutive quality that allows to distinguish the dual nature of our being as a thing among other things (being a body or res extensa) and as a reflecting subject (having a body or *res cogitans*). The substantial difference is not determined by a point of discontinuity between the two but by the nature of the time that constitutes every single fiber of both. Descartes and his followers did not conceive the mind-body dualism as a disconnection between the two. Their interaction and its laws, in fact, were conceived according to regular relations that inform the domain of natural philosophy and physics. Regis, one of his followers, named these regular interactions between brain states and resulting sensory experiences as laws of mind-body relations (see Hatfield, 2000).

7 The concept of the *cogito-cogitatum* aligns with Karl Jaspers' notion of the "Encompassing" (*das Umgreifende*), which refers to the all-encompassing reality that structures our understanding of being. Jaspers elaborates on this in his work *Philosophy of Existence*, where he discusses how the Encompassing shapes our perception of reality. He states, "The Encompassing is that which we ourselves are and that which we are not, that in which we live and that which we are" (Jaspers, 1938/1971, 27). This perspective suggests that our understanding of being is structured by the specific functioning through which reality appears to us, resonating with the idea of the *cogito-cogitatum*.

8 In the opening section of *Ideas* I, Husserl writes, "The world is the totality of objects of possible experience and experiential knowledge" (§1).

9 Fact covers what experience posits as "the real [as] *individual,* … as spatio-temporal existent *[Daseiendes],* as something which is at *this* time-place" (§2). Essence covers

"what" (Was) an individual is, but an essence is ideal and can be shared by other individuals (§3). Indeed, *"The essence (eidos) is a new type of object [Gegenstand],"* an ideal object that can be experienced or known in essential intuition *(Wesensanschauung)* (Husserl, *Ideas* I, §3).

10 See, Husserl, *Ideas* I in the chapter "The Thesis of the Natural Standpoint and its Suspension" (§§27–32).

11 By absolute here it is meant ab-solutus, that is, untied from any other moments in time. It is not the linear form of time always connected to a before and after but the phenomenological sense of time as this here-now.

12 The debate over the *epoché* centers on whether it should be seen primarily as a lived, practical act of bracketing assumptions in the process of reflective experience (as emphasized by practitioners like Amedeo Giorgi [2009] and other phenomenological psychologists), or as a theoretical ideal that structures the transcendental standpoint without requiring its actual psychological enactment (as argued by critics who follow a more Husserlian-transcendental or formalist line). Some, like Zahavi (2003), stress its function in opening access to transcendental subjectivity, while others, such as Merleau-Ponty (1945/2012), reinterpret it as a gesture embedded in embodied reflection rather than a discrete suspension. Embree's typology (1992, 1997) attempts to clarify these diverse interpretations by distinguishing various modes and uses of the *epoché* across phenomenological traditions.

13 Husserl (1970, 105): in forming and having them. "…we are subjects for this world, …experiencing it, contemplating it, valuing it, relating purposefully;… it has an ontic meaning given by our experiencings…; and it has the modes of validity which we as subjects of validity …bring about or possess from earlier on as habitual acquisitions…which we can reactualize at will…." There are two attitudes; in one, the perceptive, we are "…directed straightforwardly toward the object…our gaze passes through the appearances towards what continuously appears through their continuous unification;…In the reflective attitude (by contrast) ….the sequence of appearances themselves is thematic, rather than what appears in them."

14 Regarding empathy, Zahavi (2012) engages with Habermas's (1994) disparaging comment that phenomenology cannot escape its preoccupation with subjectivity. Zahavi successfully demonstrates that the constitutive ground of phenomenology is, first and foremost, intersubjective. He illustrates this by discussing the different positions taken by phenomenologists like Stein, Scheler, Merleau-Ponty, and Schutz on empathy and intersubjectivity. For example, against the theory that equates empathy with analogy, Scheler argued that to gain access to other people's minds, we need to consider the other as a lived body with its *Ausdrückenheit* (1954, 261). The body is a psychophysical unit that communicates something of itself to us. As Merleau-Ponty stated, we find the other when we find ourselves in the world. Or, as Levinas suggested, the other is manifest to us in his elusiveness and inaccessibility (2010, 94). According to Scheler, we can be empathetically capable of experiencing other minds (1954, 9, 220).

15 Adjacent to phenomenology, other voices have also critiqued the fluidity of time, meant as a form of sedimented historicity in which we constitute the meaning of what we define normal. The most famous is Foucault, who stated, "The history of psychiatry in the 19th and 20th centuries is a history of the continuous attempt and failure to isolate functional areas of the psyche that would give conceptual unity and clarity to the differential clinic of psychopathological disorders" (*The Birth of the Clinic*, 1973, passim). Additionally, Szasz, a psychiatrist who likened psychiatry to witchcraft and slavery, devoted a book (if not his entire career) to defining the myth of mental illness. He questioned the legitimacy of labeling psychological experiences as diseases. He argued that such classifications often reflect societal control mechanisms rather

than genuine medical conditions. Similarly, R. D. Laing sought to challenge and expand the traditional understanding of normality, particularly in the context of mental health. In his seminal work *The Divided Self* (1960), Laing argued that the concept of normality is often shaped by societal expectations and cultural norms, which may pathologize behaviors and experiences that fall outside conventional boundaries. He believed that so-called abnormal experiences, such as those of individuals diagnosed with schizophrenia, could often be understood as meaningful responses to untenable life situations or as attempts to preserve a sense of self in a fragmented world. Laing's exploration of normality also emphasized the relational and existential dimensions of human experience. He suggested that what is considered "normal" or "abnormal" often reflects broader societal dynamics, including alienation and the breakdown of authentic interpersonal connections. By reframing these experiences, Laing sought to humanize mental illness and highlight the importance of understanding individuals within their unique personal and social contexts. His work continues to influence debates on normality, mental health, and the role of society in shaping these concepts. In a less radical manner, Guggenbühl-Craig, in his work *Eros on Crutches*, examines the tendency within clinical psychology to dichotomize psychopathy and morality. He highlights how this division often leads to the assumption that an abnormal psyche equates to a morally bad person, perpetuating a simplistic and stigmatizing narrative. Fromm even coined the term "pathology of normalcy" as a bias into which practitioners can easily fall: "The 'pathology of normalcy' rarely deteriorates to graver forms of mental illness because society produces the antidote against such deterioration. When pathological processes become socially patterned, they lose their individual character. On the contrary, the sick individual finds himself at home with all other similarly sick individuals. The whole culture is geared to this kind of pathology and arranges the means to give satisfactions that fit the pathology. The result is that the average individual does not experience the separateness and isolation the fully schizophrenic person feels. He feels at ease among those who suffer from the same deformation; in fact, it is the fully sane person who feels isolated in the insane society—and he may suffer so much from the incapacity to communicate that it is he who may become psychotic" (Fromm, *The Anatomy of Human Destructiveness*, 1973, 356). Normality is a synthetic concept that generates isolated and stigmatized individuals through and in time; it is often incapable of addressing the problem that leads to the diagnosis and may contribute to creating an insane society. As Verhaeghe (1994, 35) wrote, "Every clinician has experienced in his life a certain amount of anxiety, depression, relationship problems, problems in growing up, etc. As long as what he encounters in his client is situated within the limits of his own experience, he will consider this more than likely as 'normal.' However, if what he encounters in his client is situated outside his quantitative field of experiences, he will suddenly diagnose it as pathological, and if it is situated outside his qualitative field of experiences, the diagnosis will become psychosis."

References

Ballerini, M. (2016). Autism in schizophrenia: A phenomenological study. In G. Stanghellini & M. Aragona (Eds.), *An experiential approach to psychopathology: What is it like to suffer from mental disorders?* (pp. 281–300). New York: Springer International Publishing/Springer Nature.

Binswanger, L. (1947). Über Phänomenologie [On phenomenology]. In L. Binswanger, *Ausgewählte Vorträge und Aufsätze* [Selected lectures and essays] (Vol. 1, pp. 13–49). Bern: Francke. (Original work published 1923).

Binswanger, L. (1963). *Being-in-the-world: Selected papers of Ludwig Binswanger*. New York: Basic Books.

Binswanger, L. (1992–1994). *Ausgewählte Werke* [Selected works] (Vols. 1–4). Heidelberg: Roland Asanger.

Blankenburg, W. (1971). *Der Verlust der natürlichen Selbstverständlichkeit: Ein Beitrag zur Psychopathologie symptomarmer Schizophrenien*. Stuttgart: Enke.

Bürgy, M. (2010). Zur Psychopathologie der Ich-Störungen: Geschichte und Phänomenologie [The psychopathology of ego disturbances: History and phenomenology]. *Der Nervenarzt, 81*(9), 1097–1107.

Calvi, L. (1996). Il corpo come linguaggio: Percorsi di psicopatologia fenomenologica. Milano: FrancoAngeli.

Calvi, L. (2013). Fenomenologia della cura. Milano: FrancoAngeli.

Dennett, D. C. (1991). *Consciousness explained*. Boston, MA: Little, Brown and Company.

Descartes, R. (1996). *Meditations on first philosophy*. J. Cottingham (Trans.). Cambridge: Cambridge University Press. (Original work published 1641).

Dilthey, W. (2002). *The formation of the historical world in the human sciences*. R. A. Makkreel, & F. Rodi (Eds. & Trans.). Princeto: Princeton University Press; Der Aufbau der geschichtlichen Welt in den Geisteswissenschaften. In B. Groethuysen (Ed.), *Gesammelte Schriften* (Vol. 7). Leipzig: Teubner, 1910.

Dreyfus, H. L. (1991). *Being-in-the-world: A commentary on Heidegger's being and time, division I*. Cambridge: MIT Press.

Embree, L. (1992). Seven epochēs. *Research in Phenomenology, 22*(1), 3–14.

Embree, L. (1997). What is phenomenology? In L. Embree (Ed.), *Encyclopedia of phenomenology* (pp. 1–10). Dordrecht: Kluwer Academic Publishers.

Foucault, M. (1973). *The birth of the clinic: An archaeology of medical perception* (A. M. Sheridan, Trans.). Tavistock Publications. (Original work published 1963). Cambridge: Cambridge University Press & Assessment.

Fromm, E. (1973). The anatomy of human destructiveness. New York: Holt, Rinehart and Winston.

Fuchs, T. (2007). Fragmented selves: Temporality and identity in borderline personality disorder. *Psychopathology, 40*(6), 379–387.

Fuchs, T. (2010). Temporality and psychopathology. *Phenomenology and the Cognitive Sciences, 9*(4), 567–594. https://doi.org/10.1007/s11097-010-9189-4

Fuchs, T., & Koch, S. C. (2014). Embodied affectivity: On moving and being moved. *Frontiers in Psychology, 5*, 1664–1078.

Giorgi, A. (2009). *The descriptive phenomenological method in psychology: A modified Husserlian approach*. Pittsburgh, PA: Duquesne University Press.

Habermas, J. (1994). Three normative models of democracy. *Constellations, 1*, 1–10. https://doi.org/10.1111/j.1467-8675.1994.tb00001.x

Hart, W. D. (1996). *The engines of the soul*. Cambridge: Cambridge University Press.

Heidegger, M. (1962). *Being and time*. New York: Harper.

Heidegger, M. (1966). Discourse on thinking (J. M. Anderson & E. H. Freund, Trans.). New York City: Harper & Row. (Original work published 1959 as Gelassenheit).

Held, K. (2003). Husserl's phenomenological method. In D. Welton (Ed.), *The new Husserl: A critical reader* (pp. 3–31). Bloomington: Indiana University Press.

Husserl, E. (1929). Phenomenology. In *Encyclopædia britannica* (14th ed., Vol. 17, pp. 699–702). New York: Kluwer Academic Publisher.

Husserl, E. (1960). *Cartesian meditations: An introduction to phenomenology*. D. Cairns (Trans.). The Hague: Martinus Nijhoff. (Original work published 1931) (Hua I).

Husserl, E. (1964). *The Paris lectures*. P. Koestenbaum (Trans.). Leiden: Martinus Nijhoff. (Original lectures delivered 1929).

Husserl, E. (1969). *Formal and transcendental logic*. D. Cairns (Trans.). Leiden: Martinus Nijhoff. (Original work published 1956) [Hua XVII].

Husserl, E. (1970a). *The crisis of European sciences and transcendental phenomenology: An introduction to phenomenological philosophy*. D. Carr (Trans.). Evanston, IL: Northwestern University Press. (Original work published 1936) [Hua VI].

Husserl, E. (1973a). *Zur Phänomenologie der Intersubjektivität. Texte aus dem Nachlass. Erster Teil: 1905–1920*. I. Kern (Ed.). The Hague: Martinus Nijhoff. [Hua XIII].

Husserl, E. (1973b). *Zur Phänomenologie der Intersubjektivität. Texte aus dem Nachlass. Zweiter Teil: 1921–1928* (I. Kern, Ed.). The Hague: Martinus Nijhoff. [Hua XIV].

Husserl, E. (1981). Renewal: Its problem and its method. In P. McCormick, & F. A. Elliston (Eds.), J. M. Allen (Trans.). *Husserl: Shorter works* (pp. 326–331). Notre Dame: University of Notre Dame Press. [Hua XXVII].

Husserl, E. (1983). *Ideas pertaining to a pure phenomenology and to a phenomenological philosophy: First book*. F. Kersten (Trans.). Dordrecht: Kluwer Academic Publishers. (Original work published 1913) [Hua III).

Husserl, E. (1988). Formale Typen von Kultur in Menschheitsentwicklung (1923). In E. Husserl (Ed.), *Aufsätze und Vorträge. 1922–1937* (pp. 59–94). Dordrecht: Kluwer Academic Publishers. [Hua XXVII].

Husserl, E. (1989). *Ideas pertaining to a pure phenomenology and to a phenomenological philosophy: Second book*. R. Rojcewicz, & A. Schuwer (Trans.). Dordrecht: Kluwer Academic Publishers. (Original work published 1952) [Hua IV].

Husserl, E. (1991). *On the phenomenology of the consciousness of internal time (1893–1917)*. J. B. Brough (Trans.). Dordrecht: Kluwer Academic Publishers.

Husserl, E. (2000a). *Logical investigations*. J. N. Findlay (Trans.). London: Routledge. (Hua XIX/1; XIX/2).

Husserl, E. (2000b). *Aktive Synthesen: Aus der Vorlesung "Transzendentale Logik" 1920/21. Ergänzungsband zu "Analysen zur passiven Synthesis"* . R. Breeur (Ed.). Dordrecht: Kluwer Academic Publishers. [Hua XXIV].

Husserl, E., Sheehan, T., & Palmer, R. E. (1997). *Psychological and transcendental phenomenology and the confrontation with Heidegger (1927–1931) : The Encyclopaedia Britannica article, the Amsterdam lectures "Phenomenology and anthropology," and Husserl's marginal notes in Being and time, and Kant and the problem of metaphysics*. New York: Kluwer Academic Publishers.

Jaspers, K. (1971). *Philosophy of existence*. R. F. Grabau (Trans.). Philadelphia: University of Pennsylvania Press. (Original work published 1938).

Kabat-Zinn, J. (1990). *Full catastrophe living: Using the wisdom of your body and mind to face stress, pain, and illness*. New York: Delacorte Press.

Laing, R. D. (1960). *The divided self: An existential study in sanity and madness*. London: Tavistock Publications.

Merleau-Ponty, M. (2010). *Institution and passivity: Course notes from the Collège de France (1954–1955)* (L. Lawlor & H. Massey, Trans.; C. Lefort, Foreword). Evanston, Illinois: Northwestern University Press.

Merleau-Ponty, M. (2012). *Phenomenology of perception*. D. A. Landes (Trans.). London: Routledge. (Original work published 1945).

Minkowski, E. (1933). *Le temps vécu: Études phénoménologiques et psychopathologiques*. Paris: Collection de l'évolution psychiatrique.
Moran, D. (2000). *Introduction to phenomenology*. London: Routledge.
Ricoeur, P. (2004). *Memory, history, forgetting*. Chicago: University of Chicago Press.
Rizzolatti, G., & Sinigaglia, C. (2006). *Mirrors in the brain: How our minds share actions and emotions*. Oxford: Oxford University Press.
Sass, L. A. (2021). Everywhere and nowhere: Reflections on phenomenology as impossible and indispensable (in psychology and psychiatry). *Critical Inquiry, 47*(3), 544–564.
Schmaltz, T. M. (2015). Galileo and Descartes on copernicanism and the cause of the tides. *Studies in History and Philosophy of Science Part A, 51*, 29–35.
Schneider, K. (1950). *Klinische Psychopathologie* (Clinical psychopathology) (7th ed.). Stuttgart: Georg Thieme.
Segal, Z. V., Williams, J. M. G., & Teasdale, J. D. (2002). *Mindfulness-based cognitive therapy for depression: A new approach to preventing relapse*. New York: Guilford Press.
Stanghellini, G., Ballerini, M., Presenza, S., Mancini, M., Raballo, A., Blasi, S., & Cutting, J. (2016). Psychopathology of lived time: Abnormal time experience in persons with schizophrenia. *Schizophrenia Bulletin, 42*(1), 45–55.
Stein, E. (1989). *On the problem of empathy, trans*. Washington D.C.: Waltraut Stein, ICS Publications.
Straus, E. W. (1966). *Phenomenological psychology: The selected papers of Erwin W. Straus*. E. Eng (Trans.). New York: Basic Books.
Ströker, E. (1993). *Husserl's transcendental phenomenology*. Stanford, CA: Stanford University Press.
Verhaeghe, P. (1994). *On being normal and other disorders: A manual for clinical psychodiagnostics*. (S. Jottkandt, Trans.). New York: Other Press.
von Gebsattel, V. E. (1954). *Prolegomena einer medizinischen Anthropologie*. Berlin: Springer.
Wehrle, M. (2019a). *The normative body: The role of embodiment in phenomenology and bioethics*. Dordrecht: Springer.
Wehrle, M. (2019b). Being a body and having a body: The twofold temporality of embodied intentionality. *Phenomenology and the Cognitive Sciences, 18*(3), 517–540.
Wittgenstein, L. (1953). *Philosophical investigations*. G. E. M. Anscombe (Trans.). London: Blackwell. (Original work published 1953).
Zahavi, D. (2003). *Husserl's phenomenology*. Stanford, CA: Stanford University Press.
Zahavi, D. (2011). Empathy and direct social perception: A phenomenological proposal. *Review of Philosophy and Psychology, 2*(3), 541–558.
Zahavi, D. (2012). *The Oxford handbook of contemporary phenomenology*. Oxford: Oxford University Press.

3

A PHENOMENOLOGICAL ACCOUNT OF CPTSD

Introduction

In this chapter and the next, I will apply several concepts introduced in the two theoretical chapters to the phenomenon known as complex post-traumatic stress disorder (PTSD). I begin by posing the following question.

Why was the word *trauma* chosen to describe the emotional pain an individual might experience in life? Its etymological root traces back to the Greek *τραῦμα* (*traûma*), which originally referred to a strictly physical injury caused by accidents or acts of violence. Initially, its use was strictly medical, referring to physical injuries caused by external forces—such as cuts, blows, or fractures (Luckhurst, 2008). This definition remained dominant through the classical period and well into the early development of Western medicine.

In the 18th and 19th centuries, the term continued to be used in medical and surgical contexts. However, by the late 19th century, a new understanding began to emerge: traumatic injury could be emotional as well as physical. The absence of visible wounds did not necessarily indicate the absence of harm. This insight became increasingly evident with the rise of industrial accidents. The phenomenon known as "railway spine"—a term used to describe persistent symptoms following railway crashes despite the lack of observable bodily injury—led physicians to theorize that intense emotional shock could give rise to genuine and enduring symptoms (Scull, 2009).

Something can break you from within even if it is not visible and can leave lasting effects on you as much as a physical wound could.

This shift in meaning laid the groundwork for a psychological interpretation of trauma. Sigmund Freud and Josef Breuer played a crucial role in this

DOI: 10.4324/9781003665557-3

transition with their *Studies on Hysteria* (1895/2000). They proposed that emotionally painful experiences could become repressed, later manifesting as physical or emotional disturbances—a foundational concept for psychoanalysis (Freud & Breuer, 1895/2000).

- Nevertheless, it was in the 20th century that scholarly work started focusing on the problems that traumas could generate in one's life. Trauma took on a broader and more prominent psychological meaning, particularly in the context of war. Soldiers returning from World War I with what was then called "shell shock," and later from World War II with "combat fatigue" exhibited symptoms that would today be recognized as psychological trauma (Young, 1995). These experiences directly influenced the emergence of what we now call PTSD, which was formally included in the third edition of the *Diagnostic and Statistical Manual of Mental Disorders* (DSM-III) in 1980 (American Psychiatric Association, 1980). While the modern clinical diagnosis of PTSD only emerged in the late 20th century, descriptions of trauma-like symptoms can be found in ancient Greek literature, especially in accounts of warfare. In Homer's *Iliad*, the character of Achilles, following the death of Patroclus, displays behaviors that resemble contemporary understandings of PTSD: uncontrollable rage, emotional detachment, and a withdrawal from the social and moral order of the Greek camp (Homer, trans. Fagles, 1990). Similarly, Sophocles' tragedy *Ajax* portrays the title character descending into confusion, shame, and suicidal despair after suffering a loss of honor in battle—what might today be described as a dissociative or depressive episode linked to psychological trauma (Sophocles, trans. Lloyd-Jones, 1994).

Contemporary scholars such as Jonathan Shay (1994) have drawn direct parallels between these ancient texts and the experiences of modern combat veterans, arguing that the psychological wounds depicted in Homeric epics closely resemble the clinical symptoms of PTSD. Shay's comparative work suggests that, although ancient Greeks lacked a medicalized vocabulary for trauma, they possessed a sophisticated literary and cultural understanding of the psychological aftermath of violence and moral injury.

In the 20th century, the concept of trauma has expanded significantly to include not only single catastrophic events but also chronic, developmental, and intergenerational forms of suffering. Like the Greek heroes of ancient epic, the battles we fight are not always visible; they can be quietly and systematically waged within one's family during childhood or repeatedly endured in the context of an abusive marriage. Contemporary trauma theory—shaped by thinkers such as Judith Herman (1992), Bessel van der Kolk (2014), and Cathy Caruth (1996)—emphasizes how trauma can disrupt memory, identity, and relational life and how healing requires attention to the embodied and narrative dimensions of experience.

Returning to the earlier question—why did we choose the word *trauma* to describe an emotional wound?—we might say that *trauma* serves as a reminder that the wounds endured by the soul, though invisible, are no less painful or devastating than physical injuries. Unfortunately, their invisibility often makes their impact harder to recognize and their suffering more difficult to validate, especially for the person experiencing them. This is particularly true in cases of complex trauma, where the effects are prolonged, layered, and deeply embedded in one's sense of self. Today, trauma is understood not only as a physical or emotional wound, but also as a multidimensional disruption of human life that calls for integrated psychological, social, and ethical responses.

In this chapter, I will explore how Husserl's phenomenology can deepen our understanding of the multilayered dimensions of complex PTSD (CPTSD) and offer philosophical resources for mitigating its effects. I begin by examining the altered relationship between the subject and the trauma, treating trauma as if it acquires agency and begins to structure the subject's life from within. I then provide an overview of how phenomenology, particularly in the Husserlian tradition, conceptualizes CPTSD and its experiential structure. This will lead to a closer analysis of the lived experience of this disorder. The final section focuses on how key Husserlian concepts—especially his theories of affectivity, epoché, and egology—can be mobilized as tools to support therapeutic reflection and existential reorientation in the face of complex trauma.

My Self and My Trauma

Children don't get traumatised because they are hurt. They get traumatised because they're alone with the hurt (The Wisdom of Trauma, 2021).

Trauma, fundamentally, is not reducible to the hurt itself but to the existential aloneness in experiencing it. One might ask: would trauma still be trauma if we were not left alone in its aftermath? The answer may be yes—but the presence of another allows for that formation of meaning which creates a crucial bridge across the rupture, offering coherence to a self that would otherwise fracture. In this sense, meaning-making within an interaffective context becomes crucial for a therapeutic and structurally reparative intervention later on. Yet, phenomenology emphasizes how the meaning-making process is obstructed after traumatic events.

Phenomenologically, trauma often arises from emotionally charged events that rupture the individual's self-concept, giving rise to experiences of dysmorphia, intense shame, anxiety, and explosive affect. What remains in the wake of such events is frequently a shattered core self, fragmented in both its temporal continuity and affective coherence. As I will argue later in this chapter, healing may require a dual movement: first, a reflective suspension (*epoché*) of past affective imprints, allowing the subject to bracket habitual patterns of reactive self-understanding; and second, the enactment of interaffective connection exercises, which aim to reintegrate the fractured elements of subjectivity into the evolving continuity of the lived "I." This reintegration is not a return to a pre-traumatic self, but the cultivation of a renewed coherence capable of holding the trauma within a broader narrative of embodied meaning.

Husserlian Account of Trauma

Edmund Husserl's exploration of *passive synthesis* offers a foundational framework for understanding the latent and affectively charged structures that underlie traumatic experience (2001). His analyses of sedimentation, diffusion (*Fortpflanzung*), and affective resonance describe how experiences are passively retained, repeated, and echoed in consciousness without active intentional direction. These mechanisms—especially sedimentation—suggest that past experiences do not vanish but are silently inscribed into the subject's experiential horizon, where they continue to influence perception, mood, and reaction in opaque, pre-reflective ways (Husserl, 2001). In the context of trauma, this means that traumatic events may persist not through conscious recollection, but through latent affective traces that shape the subject's temporal, embodied, and emotional life.

Husserl's *Bernau Manuscripts on Time-Consciousness: 1917–18* (2008) are particularly revealing in this regard. There, he explores the intricacies of retention, protention, and the continuous flow of inner time—concepts that are essential for understanding the temporality of trauma. Each unit of time can be phenomenologically described as a living present now that retains what has just been lived and anticipates what is about to come. From this perspective, trauma can be explained as a disruption in the fabric of this flow, where retentional layers become overly charged, frozen, or disconnected from the present. These moments of *disruptive stasis* or *temporal rupture* may correspond to what trauma theorists today describe as flashbacks, intrusive memories, or the collapse of narrative continuity (Durt, 2014; Husserl, 2008).

Furthermore, Husserl's reflections on affective acts—particularly in the *C-Manuscripts* and in *Ideas II* (1989)—address how emotions are not merely add-ons to cognition but are structurally integrated into the dynamics of attention and perception. Affective acts can sustain or disrupt the unity of experience, shaping how events are synthesized or fragmented. As we will explore further in Chapter 7, affects awaken our subjectivity to each moment in life and reveal how reality is inscribed upon the body. Traumatic affect, in this sense, may hyper-sediment or desynchronize the affective field, leading to attentional anomalies such as *hypervigilance*, *emotional blunting*, or *compulsive rumination* (Husserl, 1989; Wilde, 2022).

In *Ideas I* (1982) and *Analyses* (2001) Husserl also investigates attentional mutations—shifts in the focus and structure of intentional acts—and the conditions under which memory is deactivated or reactivated. These analyses provide conceptual tools for understanding how traumatic memories may be rendered inaccessible, not through forgetting, but through a form of attentional withdrawal or affective inhibition. Such mechanisms mirror contemporary accounts of trauma-related dissociation, where memories remain latent but emotionally charged and prone to involuntary reemergence under certain conditions (Depraz, 2021; Ferrarello & Baglieri, 2025; Zahavi, 2003).

Husserl's insights reveal that trauma is not simply a cognitive failure or pathological memory but a disturbance in the passive-affective architecture of subjectivity. We will explore this point more in depth in Section "The Lived-Experience of CPTSD." Trauma affects the very modalities through which consciousness holds onto time, meaning, and selfhood. His detailed descriptions of the pre-reflective layers of experience, and the affective dynamics of passive synthesis, open a vital path for grounding a phenomenological understanding of trauma as a temporally diffuse, emotionally saturated, and structurally disintegrative phenomenon.[1]

Heidegger and Lévinas on Trauma

Heidegger, too, offers important conceptual resources for understanding the existential dimensions of trauma, even if he does not address trauma in clinical terms. Central to his thought is the idea that *Dasein*—the human being as the being for whom Being is a question—is fundamentally constituted through its sense of belongingness or *Being-in-the-world* (1962). Trauma, from a Heideggerian perspective, can be interpreted as an abrupt rupture in this ontological structure of embeddedness, a sudden and disorienting interruption of the meaningful relations that anchor Dasein to its world (Polt, 2019). Such an interruption is not merely psychological but ontological—it fractures the coherence of existence itself.

Heidegger's theory of *Stimmungen* (moods or affective attunements) provides a powerful lens for this interpretation. His distinction between fear (*Furcht*) and anxiety (*Angst*) is particularly significant. Fear is directed toward specific, identifiable threats, while anxiety reveals the nothingness that underlies existence—the uncanniness (*Unheimlichkeit*) of being itself. In the experience of anxiety that follows a traumatic experience, the world loses its familiar contours, and Dasein is exposed to the abyssal groundlessness of its own being. Trauma, understood in this light, can be seen as a *radical disattunement*—a collapse of the affective and existential framework that allows the world to appear as meaningful, navigable, and secure.

Polt (2019) develops what he terms a "traumatic ontology"—a Heideggerian reading of existence that foregrounds experiences of crisis, emergency, and rupture as central to the human condition. Rather than treating trauma as an anomaly or dysfunction, Polt positions it as a revealing moment of ontological truth, in which the fragility and contingency of Dasein's world-relation is laid bare. Trauma becomes, in this sense, not just a disruption, but a radical disclosure of the groundlessness of existence.

Building on Heidegger's insights, Stolorow (2011) offers a phenomenologically informed psychoanalytic perspective that re-centers affectivity as the core of psychic life. In contrast to classical models that emphasize intrapsychic structures or drive-based conflict, Stolorow proposes that trauma is best understood as the experience of unbearable affect, arising not merely from the intensity of the injurious event but from its failure to be metabolized within a responsive relational context. As he puts it:

> Trauma is the experience of unbearable affect. Such a state cannot be explained solely, or even primarily, on the basis of the quantity or intensity of the painful feelings evoked by an injurious event. Traumatic affect states can be grasped only in terms of the relational systems in which they are felt.
>
> *(Stolorow, 2011, 387)*

In this framework, trauma emerges from a breakdown in intersubjective attunement—a failure of the relational world to provide the resonance and containment needed for emotional integration. This view is deeply consonant with Heidegger's notion of *Mitsein* (Being-with) as a structural condition of Dasein (1962). When the relational matrix collapses, the subject is not only overwhelmed emotionally but existentially deworlded—cast into a mode of being that lacks coherence, grounding, and orientation.

To return to the question raised at the beginning of this section: a trauma remains a trauma even if we are not alone. However, the collapse of the relational network makes it impossible for any new sense of self to emerge—one that could illuminate the affective disruption and restore our sense of belonging in the world.

Lévinas takes this further: for him, *traumatisme* is a radical alterity, irreducible and irrecoverable (*irrécupérable*), a condition of persecution that transcends representation. Trauma here is not only an affliction but also a metaphysical *accusation* that arrests subjectivity itself. Lévinas takes the phenomenological discourse on trauma into radically ethical and metaphysical terrain. For Lévinas, *traumatisme* is not simply an event that wounds the psyche or body, but a radical alterity—an encounter with something wholly other that breaks into the self from beyond comprehension or anticipation. This otherness is *irreducible* and *irrecoverable* (*irrécupérable*), meaning it cannot be integrated into the structures of representation, memory, or narrative continuity that typically enable healing or reconciliation. In this sense, trauma resists all hermeneutic appropriation—it cannot be "made sense of" in the usual phenomenological terms.

At the heart of this experience is what Lévinas calls a "passivity more passive than all patience" (*passivité plus passive que toute patience*) (1974/1988, 20) that makes any attempt at making-meaning process extremely challenging. Experiencing trauma places the subject in a condition where they are no longer an autonomous agent, but rather held hostage by an event that overwhelms their capacity for self-determination. This passivity is not to be confused with inertia; rather, it is a profound vulnerability in which the subject is exposed, accused, and persecuted by the trauma itself, hence the sense of shame, self-exclusion, and loop rumination. As Lévinas writes in *Otherwise than Being*, this trauma is not just an event suffered—it is a metaphysical accusation, a kind of ethical calling or disturbance that precedes the self's ability to respond or defend itself. The subject becomes a *sub-jectus*—thrown beneath the trauma's weight, exposed in a condition of ethical captivation (Levinas, 1974/1998).

In this view, trauma does not merely interrupt the continuity of experience; it arrests subjectivity at its root, suspending its capacity to intend, to signify, or to recuperate meaning. It is, in Lévinasian terms, a pre-original rupture, a moment of suffering that destabilizes the foundational intentionality of consciousness. What follows is not healing through recollection or symbolization, but a kind of ongoing exposure—a wound that signifies not what was lost, but the infinite and unresolvable obligation toward what has inflicted it.

Thus, for Lévinas, trauma opens not to narrative closure but to ethical infinity. It is a demand that cannot be discharged, a suffering that resists both autonomy and therapeutic mastery. It challenges the very conditions of phenomenological presence, situating trauma not in what can be experienced, but in what exceeds experience.

Drawing from the analyses of trauma[2] offered by Husserl, Heidegger, and Lévinas, we can describe trauma as a disruption of the affective and existential attunement—a moment when the world no longer coheres, and the subject experiences not only pain but also a profound loss of existential intelligibility and agency. Trauma constitutes a metaphysical accusation that holds the subject hostage, distancing them from any access to ethical agency. In the following section, I will focus on the relationship between phenomenology and CPTSD, while in the third section, I will examine the lived experience of CPTSD and how the themes discussed here intersect with that experience.

CPTSD and Phenomenology

Contemporary philosophers have increasingly sought to bridge the gap between trauma theory and the intentional and egological structures articulated in Husserlian phenomenology, particularly in relation to PTSD and its psychoanalytic elaborations through Freud and Lacan. This intersection recognizes that trauma not only disrupts memory and emotion but also destabilizes the very structures of consciousness, such as temporality, affectivity, and selfhood, which Husserl positioned at the heart of intentional experience.

Psychology

One significant contribution to this dialogue is found in Simon Critchley's *Ethics-Politics-Subjectivity* (1999), where he phenomenologically confronts the subject with what resists assimilation—alterity, suffering, and ethical demand. In this framework, trauma is not merely a pathological disturbance but a limit-experience that reveals the fragility and exposure inherent in subjectivity. By attending to the ethical dimensions of suffering, Critchley frames trauma as an event that calls the subject into question, disrupting the coherence of its intentional structures and exposing a form of selfhood that is constituted through vulnerability rather than autonomy.

Guy-Félix Duportail, in his work *Intentionnalité et trauma: Levinas et Lacan* (2005), offers a more focused treatment of this convergence, explicitly linking Levinas's account of trauma as radical alterity with Lacanian psychoanalysis and the phenomenological model of intentionality. Duportail argues that trauma cannot be adequately grasped within traditional egological frameworks that presuppose the self's transparency and control over its experiences. Instead, trauma points to a crack in intentional life—an encounter with something unassimilable that both overwhelms and reconfigures the field of experience. Drawing from Lévinas, he understands trauma as a *de-structuring irruption* of Otherness, while from Lacan he borrows the idea of trauma as a real—an encounter that eludes symbolization and leaves a trace (*trace traumatique*) that continually disrupts psychic integration.

These contemporary approaches reveal that trauma cannot be accounted for solely through empirical or clinical models. Rather, it must be understood as a phenomenological rupture—a breakdown in the basic structures that allow the self to intend, relate, and narrate its world. Trauma interrupts not only memory or cognition but the very constitutive flow of intentional time, the horizon of meaning, and the self's affective orientation toward the world. Through the contributions of Critchley, Duportail, and others, a new post-Husserlian phenomenology of trauma is emerging—one that remains faithful to Husserl's foundational insights while also acknowledging the psychic fractures that resist integration and demand ethical and philosophical rethinking.

Psychiatry

Several psychiatrists and clinical researchers working with complex PTSD have emphasized the value of phenomenology as a methodological lens for capturing the lived complexity of trauma. Unlike diagnostic frameworks that rely primarily on symptom clusters or behavioral metrics, a phenomenological psychopathology seeks to describe trauma from the first-person perspective, attending to the temporal, bodily, emotional, and imaginative structures that are uniquely disrupted in traumatic experience.

Claude Barrois, in *Les névroses traumatiques* (1988), was among the early clinicians to advocate for a shift away from reductive, psychometric models toward a more nuanced understanding of trauma as a crisis of subjectivity. Drawing from existential-phenomenological traditions, Barrois explored how psychic shock engenders a profound disturbance in the subject's lived world, undermining the coherence of memory, identity, and temporal continuity. He described trauma as an existential rupture, one that radically reconfigures how individuals experience their own bodies, relationships, and future horizons. For Barrois, therapy must begin with a phenomenological attentiveness to the person's felt disorientation and, as in Husserlian terms, passive affects, rather than simply attempting to normalize or extinguish symptoms.

Similarly, Ehlers et al. (2004) have argued for a phenomenologically informed approach to intrusive reexperiencing in PTSD—arguably one of its most defining symptoms. In their influential article, they highlight that reexperiencing is not merely a "memory" in the conventional sense, but rather an involuntary, embodied reliving of the traumatic event that disrupts the linear flow of time and the integrity of the self. The traumatic event acquires its own agency, beginning to organize the layers of affect that regulate an individual's habits and behaviors. These experiences, often characterized by fragmentation, timelessness, and vivid perceptual immersion, suggest that trauma is fundamentally a disorder of temporality and narrative integration—a view consonant with phenomenological accounts of time-consciousness and retention. Their work demonstrates that phenomenology can provide critical insight into both the mechanisms of trauma and the design of therapeutic interventions, particularly those that aim to restore narrative coherence and bodily grounding.

Louis Crocq, in *Seize leçons sur le trauma* (2007), also points to the importance of phenomenological reflection in clinical contexts. Drawing on both psychiatric case studies and philosophical analysis, Crocq portrays trauma as an event that suspends the subject's ordinary relationship with meaning—a condition he likens to existential exile. For Crocq, the clinician's task is not merely to diagnose but to reestablish meaningful world-relations, often through therapeutic dialogue that allows patients to rearticulate their experience in phenomenologically faithful terms. This work contributes to a growing recognition that trauma does not simply cause dysfunction—it constitutes a transformation of the subject's existential horizon, one that cannot be captured without attending to the subtleties of lived time, embodied memory, and emotional atmosphere.

Together, these contributions point to an emerging consensus that Husserlian phenomenology provides essential tools for understanding CPTSD as a disorder not only of behavior or cognition, but also of affective being-in-the-world. Whether through the disruption of temporal synthesis, the breakdown of bodily integrity, or the collapse of intersubjective meaning, trauma reconfigures the very structures that make experience possible. As such, phenomenologically informed psychiatry holds promise for a more ethically attuned and experientially accurate clinical practice—one that views healing not just as symptom reduction, but as the reconstitution of existential coherence.

The central hypothesis of this evolving field is that trauma alters the fundamental architecture of subjectivity. Trauma is not only an object or a clinical label—it is a *lived experience* that resists objectification. Its rupture is particular, individualized, and nontransferable.

A Preliminary Cartography of Trauma

Based on this philosophical, psychological, and clinical foundation, we can sketch a preliminary cartography of trauma's structural dynamics which alters the individual's selfhood map according to these coordinates: time, affect, body, imagination, and identity. As we will explore in greater depth in the next section—but outline preliminarily in Table 3.1—trauma manifests across multiple dimensions. Temporally, it disrupts linear continuity, replacing it with latency, where passive sedimentations of meaning are repeatedly reactivated. Affectively, it amplifies emotional resonance into ruminative loops that fail to reach catharsis. Bodily, it fragments the body schema, producing zones of dysmorphia or dissociation. Imaginally, it induces symbolic breakdown and intrusive imagery. As a result, on the level of identity, trauma disintegrates coherence and arrests the formation of a continuous narrative self.

TABLE 3.1 A Preliminary Cartography of Trauma

Trauma Characteristic	*Phenomenological Disturbance*	*Husserlian Reference*
Temporal	Replaces linear flow with latency; reactivates sedimented meanings	Bernau Manuscripts
Affective	Locks resonance in ruminative loops; no catharsis	Analyses Concerning Passive Synthesis
Bodily	Fractures body schema; induces dysmorphia, dissociation	Ideas II
Imaginal	Produces symbolic breakdown and intrusive imagery	Experience and Judgment
Identity	Disintegrates narrative self and halts coherent self-formation	Cartesian Meditations, Bernau Manuscripts

This dynamic results in what Depraz calls a loosening of the aftermath: chronic repetitions, partial memories, associative cascades, and compulsive reexperiencing without a clear beginning or end (2018). The subject is caught in a loop of passive reactivation, unable to "move on," held hostage by a *present that does not pass*.

The Lived Experience of CPTSD

In the United States, studies indicate that nearly 90% of adults report exposure to at least one potentially traumatic event during their lifetime (Kilpatrick et al., 2013). Among those exposed, approximately 5%–6% of men and 10%–12% of women develop PTSD, making it one of the most frequently encountered psychiatric conditions in clinical practice (Olff et al., 2005). While around 8% of trauma-exposed individuals develop PTSD, the majority show natural recovery following the initial exposure.

Trauma exposure is widespread across geographic contexts. Notably, urban and rural populations in the United States, for example, show comparable overall rates of trauma exposure, though the types of traumatic experiences differ: wartime trauma is more prevalent in rural areas, while urban populations report higher exposure to substance abuse-related events (McCall-Hosenfeld et al., 2014).

The risk of developing CPTSD appears to follow a bimodal distribution, with heightened vulnerability during childhood, adolescence, and again after age 65 (Brewin et al., 2000). Furthermore, current evidence suggests that the type of trauma plays a decisive role in predicting trauma-related pathology. Recurrent physical violence, particularly in the context of combat, and all forms of sexual violence carry the highest risk, with some studies indicating (C)PTSD development rates between 13% and 14% (Kessler et al., 1995). In contrast, the unexpected death of a loved one and direct exposure to death or grave injury confer moderate risk, with PTSD rates ranging from 5% to 8%—nonetheless significant due to their high prevalence in the general population (Kessler et al., 2005).

Applying the interpretive grid developed in the previous section to testimonies of individuals suffering from CPTSD, we can describe the lived experience of CPTSD as follows.

Temporal Latency

In the lived experience of Complex PTSD, trauma is not simply something that happened—it is something that continually happens, something that endures through affective traces and latent anticipation. The structure of time is no longer linear but fragmented, haunted by affectively charged remnants that return unbidden. As one survivor expresses it, "*Calm doesn't feel calm. It feels dangerous.*

Because when your whole life was built around chaos, stillness is unfamiliar. And unfamiliar feels unsafe."[3] Stillness becomes a temporal dimension that often generates anxiety rather than calm. The horizon opened by moments of quiet can, in fact, reactivate unwelcome and unresolved feelings. "*And then the same image of myself resurfaces—covered in scars that only I can see, and day by day they become redder, more swollen, a bit more concerning.*" In Husserlian terms (2001), the passively synthesized temporal layers sedimented in experience are reactivated through affectivity, not through deliberate memory but through bodily readiness, pre-reflective expectation, and a sense that danger is imminent even in moments of apparent peace. The scars are invisible to everyone else—barely even noticeable to the person who carries them, except when they flare-up. While the sedimented past is usually stored and organized in a substrate layer of meanings, in CPTSD, the past is still a living present that can intrude in the affective horizon of the individual. As we will see in the next section, it even becomes the agent, progressively taking over and replacing the individual's own sense of will and agency. In his writings on internal time-consciousness (Husserl, 1990), Husserl conceptualizes time not as a linear sequence but as a dynamic synthesis of protentions (anticipations) and retentions (immediate memories). Each "now" moment is embedded within a temporal horizon shaped by these anticipatory and retentive structures. Memory, especially in the form of recollection, allows us to grasp the present as multidimensional, structured by what has just occurred and what is about to unfold. For instance, perceiving a melody requires retaining the previous tones and anticipating the next—an act through which the "I" composes a coherent temporal experience. For individuals suffering from this disorder, the melody does not flow smoothly but is continuously disrupted—like a radio struggling to find the right frequency. In CPTSD, the past does not remain in the past but is an embodied present that can intrude in different layers of existence. In this sense, it replaces linear flow with latency and spontaneous affections with reactivation of sedimented meanings.

Affective Resonance

Affections are the means by which individuals come into contact with the perceptual flow of their own life. They represent a pre-intentional dynamic—the silent, non-volitional pull of certain experiences that force the subject into attention. In his *Analyses Concerning Active and Passive Synthesis*, section 58, Husserl adds the concept of "substrate" to explain how an object comes to our attention as a whole. The term substrate refers to what exercises a unitary affection upon the ego, emerging in our attentive perception. "A substrate can stem from passivity or from activity" (Hua XL, 42; En. tr. 312). The active substrate involves the ego's constitution of itself and its objects, explicitly identifying what has already been constituted. The passive substrate, by contrast, is pre-given as a foundation for the whole, objectivated by the active ego's receptivity. In CPTSD, it seems that the active substratum emerging from the attentive perception of the subject exercises unitary affection on the ego while being affectively charged by the event. The traumatic impressions remain affectively charged and continually press forward from the background of consciousness. These affective "awakenings" do not bring clarity but rather overwhelm the individual and amplify the loss of agency. One narrative captures this poignantly: "*You have 100 tabs open in your brain... and you haven't felt your face or fingers for 45 minutes.*" The past is not behind the individual; it is inside the present, affectively coursing through every moment as tension, hypervigilance, or numbness.

Hence, the emotional field is marked not by catharsis but by ruminative intensification. "*Mine is shame. Sadness. Self-deprecation. It's a quiet kind of devastation. A collapse inward. A spiral that feels like losing my sense of identity—like I've stopped existing as a whole person.*" The reactivity of the substratum simultaneously leads to a loss of agency in the individual while imposing ethical demands that corner them into positions of impossible choice. This leaves the individual unable to defend themselves or respond to the traumatic event. As a result, rumination becomes a habitual response to these triggers, often lacking any constructive outlet. This dynamic may generate an excess of empathy—making it easier to empathize with the source of the trauma or with triggers that reactivate it, rather than with oneself. This occurs because the traumatic substratum exerts more agency within the individual's life than the individual feels permitted to exercise themselves.

As one person describes it:

> And instead of getting angry at them, I try to understand them. I give them grace. I search for reasons why they did what they did—because it must've been me. It has to be me, right? That's how it feels. Before I can even process the possibility that someone else was wrong I have to convince myself I was.

As very precisely this person puts it, CPTSD often leads individuals to hide behind acts of empathy and enter ruminative loops in which they affectively connect with those who have harmed them. This counterintuitive process draws them closer to themselves—toward the very substratum that awakens them to the core of their existence. The problem, however, is that this core is the traumatic event itself, that is, the emotionally charged substratum that acts as an agentic force in their life. Instead of distancing themselves from those who harm them, they intensify their empathic connection—drawing closer to what feels familiar: the trauma itself, as it resides in the depths of their affective core.

Affective life in CPTSD becomes a recursive structure, where feelings no longer orient the subject toward meaningful fulfillment but instead arrest attention in circuits of self-erasure. As one CPTSD survivor puts it:

> CPTSD doesn't always look like what people expect. But that doesn't make it less real. It just makes it easier to miss. And easier to judge. But I'm done judging myself for it. And I hope one day, the world catches up.

Affects organize themselves into this substratum that functions as an ever-present field, making trauma not merely an event of the past but an ongoing agent eroding the space typically available for the self to thrive.

Husserl's writings on emotional fluctuation and affective attention reveal how moods and feelings fundamentally shape the ego's structure and orientation. In Hua XVI, Husserl notes that "the sensuousness – which comprises feelings and drives – has its own unity" (205), forming the affective ground of intentional life. Even the perception of physical objects presupposes a sensuous basis: "The experience of the physical thing proper provides the mere 'This', an empty X which becomes the bearer of (...) determinations." This "empty X" serves as a kind of practical index, or what we might call an inner *telos* or vocation, which calls for further affective and perceptual organization to create a unified field of sense.

This process is central to Husserl's account of intentionality: objects are not merely given, but constituted through a "unity of construing (...) grounded in the essence of those construings" (Hua XVI, §41; Eng. trans. p. 88). Even affective states like pleasure require intentional grounding. As he puts it, "feeling considered in itself involves nothing intentional, that is, it does not point beyond itself to a felt object" (Hua XIX, 388; Eng. trans. p. 107). Yet in practice, feelings are rarely self-contained; rather, "only in union with a representation gives [feeling] a certain relation to an object" (Hua XIX, 388; Eng. trans. p. 107). Thus, feelings owe their intentional structure to the underlying presentations they are bound up with (more on this in Chapter 4, V.1).

In the case of CPTSD, however, this dynamic is disrupted. The representational substratum remains subordinated to the trauma, which occupies disproportionate space in the affective field. Instead of orienting the subject toward coherence or ethical agency, feelings lose their intentional trajectory—disconnected from the lifeworld and openness to future meaning—and collapse inward, obstructing the formation of viable representations of their life and new unities of self. The trauma continues to call affective and cognitive resources back into its orbit, silencing the emergence of alternative possibilities for integration or healing.

Disembodied Feelings

In states of prolonged trauma, the body ceases to function as a reliable ground of orientation. The usual bodily schemas are fractured by the trauma and they build habituations around a disembodied self. Individuals may continue to perform socially expected behaviors—"*You smile. You talk. You nod. But inside, you're gone.*"—yet inhabit a dissociative state so normalized it becomes invisible even to themselves. As this person continues: "*And the scariest part? You've done it so often, it feels normal.*"

As described in Chapters 1 and 2, the bodily schema refers to the pre-reflective, dynamic organization of bodily movements and postures that enables a person to interact fluently with the world. It is not a conscious image of the body, but a lived, embodied orientation that structures perception, action, and spatial awareness without the need for deliberate control. A common example of bodily schema is how you reach for a cup of coffee on your desk without consciously calculating the position of your arm or hand. Your body "knows" the movement automatically because it is oriented toward the world through a pre-reflective sense of space, proportion, and action. In the narrative cited above, this habitual dissociation of smiling even if you are not there signals a breakdown of embodied intentionality and accordingly bodily schema, which Husserl's phenomenology can help us to understand, particularly through his theory of kinaesthetic passivity and the body as the *zero-point* of orientation.

At the most basic stratum, the human being appears as a physical body (*Körper*), described by Husserl as "a thing among other things" (Hua-Mat IV, 182). This *Körper* is not immediately available to perception as a lived subject, but manifests as a hyletic whole—an ensemble of sensations and passive syntheses—upon which the ego's still-unformed traits are grounded (1989, §§36, 44). As long as the body remains merely physical, we do not perceive it in the usual sense. Rather, we *are* it. The *Körper* is our sensory medium—our instrument for apprehending both the external world and our own inner sense of being. In complex PTSD, the body becomes the primary repository of trauma—holding the memory of the event even as the individual struggles not to relive it repeatedly.

Husserl emphasizes this in *Cartesian Meditations*, where he describes the physical body as the "*there-ness-for-me*" (Hua I, 124). The body, as perceptually given, unfolds within an open, infinite horizon of undisclosed internal possibilities. It is not just an object but a primordial *transcendence*—the very platform from which perception, action, and subjectivity emerge. In complex PTSD, the individual is often unable or unwilling to fully grasp the "thereness" of their body, as doing so may reawaken painful memories or sensations.

In trauma, this zero-point of embodied experience becomes destabilized. The body no longer grounds the subject's perceptual or affective field. Instead, it is hollowed out—no longer experienced as a cohesive locus of sensation or agency, but as a site of evacuation. The dissociative self may still move through the world, but the body is no longer lived; it becomes merely *animated*, a container for a self that has withdrawn.

Imaginal Intrusiveness

This disintegration also affects the individual's imaginative resources: the ability to dream of a better future, to think positively about the present, or to envision the best possible outcome given the circumstances becomes profoundly diminished. Not only are symbolic systems disrupted, but they are also colonized by the logic of trauma. CPTSD is not merely a psychological injury; it produces a breakdown in the symbolic structure through which a person understands themselves and the world. As mentioned earlier in the section on Affective Resonance, this disruption fractures the intentional arc of feelings, dissociating affect from its representational foundation. This breakdown extends deeply into the realm of imagination, transforming it from a space of possibility into one dominated by compulsive and accusatory narratives. "*I become the one who disappears. I become the one who dehumanizes myself... Instead of getting angry at them, I try to understand them. It must've been me, right?*" Through these words, we see how trauma colonizes symbolic logic: the self is no longer the locus of agency but the target of internalized blame, while the other is shielded by rationalizations. The symbolic world—normally a source of self-articulation and ethical orientation—is turned against the subject.

This inversion echoes Levinas' metaphysics of accusation, where the self becomes incapable of defending themselves from the offense and Husserl's notion of affective deformation of horizonality, where future meanings no longer appear as open possibilities but are saturated by the compulsive return of traumatic affect. Horizonality, which ordinarily allows the ego to project itself into future meanings and make sense of experience, is obstructed; symbolic interpretation becomes entangled in self-negation.

This symbolic collapse is mirrored in the body's role as a ground of perception and selfhood. As seen before, Husserl's phenomenology distinguishes between the physical body (*Körper*) and the lived body (*Leib*). The *Körper* is experienced as a thing among things (Hua-Mat IV, 182), while the *Leib*—the animated body—is what constitutes the zero point of orientation and opens up the world of self-recognition. "As perceptively active, I experience (or can experience) all of Nature, including my own animate organism... I 'can' perceive one hand 'by means of the other'... the functioning organ must become an Object and the Object a functioning organ" (Hua I, 128). In trauma, this reflexive perception collapses. The self, instead of perceiving itself as a lived unity, experiences a disjointed and alienated body.

Moreover, Husserl emphasizes that it is through the *Leib* that we realize our sphere of ownness—a phenomenological sense of self anchored in the contrast between lived embodiment and physical structure.

> Nature brings to light my Leib, 'my animated organism, reduced to what is included in my ownness (…) I as this man (…). If I reduce myself as a man, I get 'my animate organism' and 'my psyche', or myself as psychophysical unity — in the latter, my personal Ego, who operates in this animate organism and, by means of it'.
>
> *(Hua I, 128)*

This Ego or "I" (Ich) is not passive. As Husserl notes in his later writings (2012), the "awakened I" (wache Ich) responds to life's ruptures by making ethically meaningful decisions (jetzigen Wahl), even in the face of disruption. These decisions are shaped by the subject's embodied affectivity, past habits, and motivational horizon (Hua-Mat IX, 120, 128–133). The trauma, however, interferes with this process of ethical agency. It impairs the ability to retain salient affective impressions, distorts motivation, and interrupts the intentional arc of "acting according to one's best knowledge and conscience" (nach bestem Wissen und Gewissen) (Husserl, 2012, 133).

Fragmentation of Identity

This culminates in the fragmentation of identity. As one survivor puts it, "*It feels like losing my sense of identity—like I've stopped existing as a whole person.*" In Husserlian terms, trauma does not annihilate the ego; rather, as seen before, it disjoins the temporal, affective, imaginative, and bodily syntheses through which the ego is constituted. The self becomes a patchwork of adaptive gestures, protective reflexes, and suspended coherence. It is not absence, but dispersion—an erosion of continuity and unity within the structure of the self.

And yet, within these fractured narratives, a quiet resistance persists: a plea not to be seen as broken, but as still becoming—someone surviving, adapting, and protecting. "*You're not broken. You adapted. Your body protected you the best way it could. And now, little by little, it's learning that it's safe to come home.*" Even in the most painful affective awakenings, phenomenology reveals a horizon of possible reconstitution where it is safe to come home. As Husserl maintained, the ego is not a fixed point, but an evolving formation structured through layered syntheses. "In receptivity, although the ego is indeed actively turned toward what affects it, it does not make its knowledge, and the individual steps of cognition (…) an object of will" (Husserl, 1973a, 198). The ego is moved, shaped, and attuned through affective and cognitive encounters—its coherence not lost, but suspended, waiting for the conditions of return.

This receptivity creates a horizon of apprehensive attention—a tension between the fragmented "not yet I" and the pull toward integration. As Husserl writes, "In general, attention is a tending of the ego toward an intentional object, toward a unity which appears continually in the change of the modes of its givens (...); it is a tending toward realization" (Husserl, 1973a, p. 80). When this tension is accepted, it can evolve into interest (*dabei sein*), enabling the ego to participate once again in its world. The will begins to operate through objectification—not as control, but as a reaching toward renewed meaning, toward the reconstruction of a predicative and practical identity. As mentioned before, trauma does not simply cause dysfunction—it constitutes a transformation of the subject's existential horizon.

Healing, then, is not a return to an original or coherent self, but the slow and courageous reweaving of affective continuity. It is the act of staying—of participating again in one's embodied experience and gradually rebuilding a life in which it feels safe to exist, to remember, and to act.

A Phenomenological Healing Approach

While therapies such as CBT, EMDR, NLP, and art therapy offer vital relief, I believe that a rigorous, first-person inquiry into the subjective texture of trauma is necessary to help recovering from the recurring traumatic experience. By suspending presuppositions and following the contours of lived experience, a phenomenological lived-experience-based approach can offer new descriptions of traumatic temporality, affectivity, embodiment, and identity that can meaningfully contribute to both theory and applicative care. In doing so, it would also be possible to respond to a deeper philosophical imperative: to let the traumatized subject speak, not merely as an object of diagnosis, but as a source of insight into what it means to survive and remember.

Exercising Epoché

Hence, to address the shattered core self—whose unity is continually disrupted by the reemergence of a present past—we must acknowledge how trauma reawakens affective traces and distorts the sense of time. The logic of trauma begins to populate the imagery of the individual's consciousness, leading to a growing disconnection from the body. To counter this, I propose the use of *epoché*, allowing emotionally charged events from the past to be observed fully and ultimately relocated in their proper temporal place.[4] Epoché entails an act of emotional acceptance—of both the past and ourselves as agents within it—paired with a suspension of judgment, analysis, and reflection. It is a gesture of pure, unconditional observation and acceptance. The substratum from which the affective emergence activates intruding thoughts or triggers ruminative loops would then progressively become less reactive. This substratum would start being passively populated with less charged affections that actually belong to the individual's bodily schema rather than to the bodily impact of the traumatic event(s). Suspending judgment about how individuals *should* feel—and how emotionally charged their responses ought to be—can help reduce reactivity in the present. This, in turn, may lessen the lingering effects that past events imprint on the layers of habituation the subject forms in relation to their emerging embodied self, including experiences such as dysmorphia, intense shame, anxiety, or explosive emotions.

Interaffective Exercises

Consecutively, in order to begin restoring embodied unity to a fragmented sense of self, interaffective exercises may prove beneficial. These exercises should initially focus on engaging with the various parts of the self, allowing them to be acknowledged as they are—free from shame, anxiety, or judgment. For this reason, they are ideally practiced after earlier stages of self-awareness and stabilization through epoché. The exercises might involve dialogical journaling with different affective parts of the self (e.g., the fearful child, the angry protector, the silenced adolescent), embodied imagination practices (e.g., visualizing safe or affirming bodily states), and somatic mirroring through guided touch or movement in dyadic settings. These practices aim to reintegrate dissociated bodily experience into present-time awareness by engaging interaffectivity—not merely as an external relational act, but as an internal dialogue between fragmented affective states.

In a more private setting, one might begin by choosing clothing that feels comfortable and affirming to one's own body, noticing temperature changes while showering, or mindfully tracing the location, intensity, and movement of emotional sensations in the body—without assigning narrative meaning or cognitive interpretation. Another practice involves affective mirroring, where the subject expresses an emotional movement (e.g., through gesture or tone), and a trusted partner echoes it nonverbally, creating resonance and fostering affective validation. Slow, repetitive sensory rituals—such as applying warm compresses or engaging in breathing with touch—can be paired with verbal affirmations of the present time, helping to relocate affective residues in their appropriate historical context.

These embodied interaffective exercises support the grounding and tracking of one's own affective states, while enabling them to be echoed in accordance with the present felt-sense. They also offer a form of temporal anchoring that prevents the past from overpowering the present, allowing the subject to inhabit a more coherent and embodied sense of self in the here and now.

Once a cohesive core sense of self is reestablished, the interaffective work can gradually extend outward, integrating emotionally charged or disruptive aspects of the external world. This phase involves cultivating an intentional suspension of reactive judgments, particularly toward those traits or behaviors in others that tend to provoke CPTSD flare-ups. This includes exercises in affective neutrality, where one practices observing triggering behaviors or traits in others—particularly those that echo past trauma—without assigning immediate meaning or judgment. These stimuli can be gently placed in phenomenological *epoché*, suspending interpretation in order to maintain an authentic connection with the here-and-now of the body. This should allow for an authentic reconnection with the here-and-now of the body. From this grounded presence, interaffective connection—with oneself and others—can unfold. This co-creation of meaning is essential for fostering a renewed sense of imagination and a more serene, fluid participation in one's own life.

Engaging in shared stillness with another—through mutual regulation of breath and posture without the need for words—can help restore nonverbal attunement. Difficult interactions or remembered events can be reapproached through reintegrative role play, where the subject explores alternative responses with new boundaries and pacing, emphasizing emotional self-regulation and embodied choice. Mapping recurring external triggers while tracking their somatic impact, and responding with compassion and soothing gestures, helps shift the meaning of these encounters over time. Eventually, imaginative re-scripting—where past or feared situations are visualized with affirming outcomes—can assist in reclaiming the capacity for agency, flexibility, and emotional range.

From this grounded presence, interaffective connection—with oneself and others—can unfold with more ease and safety. This relational co-creation of meaning is essential not only for reweaving a fragmented sense of self but also for restoring a fluid, creative participation in one's own life. The aim is not to erase trauma, but to re-situate it within a larger, more stable affective horizon—one marked by presence, continuity, and the possibility of becoming otherwise.

Within this condition, recovery is not about returning to a pre-trauma coherence, but about slowly weaving back the threads of attention, embodiment, and relational presence. Interaffective exercises—once the subject regains enough grounding—can help activate this latent openness. They are not quick fixes, but processes that reattune the subject to temporal flow, somatic coherence, symbolic imagination, and ethical engagement. Healing, in this light, is less a restoration than a reorientation: a movement from metaphysical captivation toward phenomenological presence.

Conclusion: From Fragmentation to Reorientation

This chapter has examined how CPTSD undermines the foundational structures of subjectivity, drawing on Husserl's phenomenology to explore its effects across temporal, affective, bodily, imaginal, and narrative domains. We have seen that CPTSD is not merely the persistence of a past event, but an ongoing disruption of the affective and temporal synthesis that grounds selfhood. Trauma unsettles time, not by erasing it, but by reactivating past meanings in the present, interrupting the flow of experience and limiting the subject's capacity to move forward.

Affectively, trauma captures the emotional life of the subject, replacing the natural ebb and flow of resonance with loops of rumination and identification with harm. Bodily experience is no longer a medium of grounded orientation but becomes the site of dysregulation, either through hyperarousal or dissociation. The lived body, once the zero-point of all experience, loses its anchoring function. Symbolic life and imagination become hijacked by intrusive content, foreclosing possibilities for meaningful projection into the future.

And yet, despite these disturbances, Husserl's account of the ego provides a hopeful framework. Even when fractured, the ego retains the capacity for reactivation through attention, affective investment, and shared meaning. From a clinical standpoint, healing must not aim to return the subject to a pre-traumatic wholeness but rather to enable a reorganization of coherence across layers of experience. Phenomenological tools—such as epoché, affective attunement, and embodied presence—offer a way to slow down and reengage with the self as it unfolds in time and relationship.

Therapeutic work thus becomes a process of renewal: holding space for what has fragmented, offering recognition where meaning has collapsed, and cultivating the imaginative and bodily capacities through which life can once again be authored. Crucially, this is not a solitary act. Recovery is intersubjective. Through carefully guided interaffective encounters, the traumatized subject may rediscover the possibility of ethical engagement, where being-with-others becomes not a threat, but a source of grounding and transformation.

In this sense, recovery is not a return to what was, but a phenomenological reorientation—a reawakening of the subject's presence to self, world, and others. Trauma arrests the flow of life; healing begins when that flow is felt again.

Notes

1 Building on Husserl's intuitions, in phenomenology, the internalization of suffering has been powerfully theorized by Michel Henry, whose concept of *self-affection* refers to the immediate, pre-reflective experience of oneself as affected by one's own existence (Henry, 1963/2003). For Henry, suffering is not primarily something the subject *observes*, but something the subject *is*—a mode of affectivity that discloses the radical immanence of life. This account provides a foundational perspective for understanding how trauma imprints itself inwardly, bypassing representational and objectifying modes of experience.

Although not writing explicitly about trauma, Maurice Merleau-Ponty and Jean-Paul Sartre significantly extended the phenomenological project into psychoanalytic terrain. Merleau-Ponty, drawing on Freud and attending to Lacan, emphasized the intertwining of body and psyche, especially in *Phenomenology of Perception* (1945/2012), where he discusses how the lived body can carry meaning that is inaccessible to reflective consciousness—a theme resonant with trauma studies today. Sartre's *existential psychoanalysis* in *Being and Nothingness* (1956/1943) and later texts explores how fundamental affective configurations, including shame and bad faith, are structured by early psychic events and projected through personal history—thus framing a phenomenology of psychic dislocation.

Max Scheler adds a crucial layer to the emotional topology of trauma through his analyses of moral emotions such as *despair*, *guilt*, and *loneliness* (Scheler, 1913/1973). For Scheler, these emotions are not mere psychological states but reveal the axiological structure of the person's being-in-the-world. Despair, in particular, reflects a breakdown in the value-world that sustains the self, offering fertile ground for a phenomenological account of the existential disintegration found in traumatic experience.

2 Among those who directly approached trauma, Henry Maldiney stands out as a pivotal figure. His concept of *effraction*—a term borrowed from psychoanalysis but given a phenomenological twist—describes the violent intrusion of an event that exceeds the subject's capacity for meaning-making, thereby shattering the coherence of one's ontological grounding (Maldiney, 1991). Trauma, in this view, is not only a psychological disturbance but also a rupture of the subject's existential configuration—a breakdown in the fabric of self-world continuity. Close to Depraz's argument (2018), for Maldiney, too, trauma is an effraction that disrupts the natural flow of one's life. Depraz's integrative model, though, which draws from both (micro) phenomenological descriptions and empirical data (neurophysiological, affective, and cognitive), describes trauma as a negative surprise capable of generating a *blank* or *interrupted* lived experience, structured by passive preconscious dynamics.

3 This and the following first-person quotes are taken from the public myptsd/cptsd forum at https://www.myptsd.com/.

4 In some respects, this approach parallels the EMDR method developed by Shapiro in the 1980s; however, the application of the phenomenological *epoché* allows for the integration of additional phenomenological coordinates, thereby enriching the meaning-making process through a grounding in the individual's interaffective lived experience.

References

American Psychiatric Association. (1980). *Diagnostic and statistical manual of mental disorders* (3rd ed.). Washington, DC: Author.

Barrois, C. (1988). *Les névroses traumatiques: Le psychothérapeute face aux détresses des chocs psychiques*. Paris: Dunod.

Brewin, C. R., Andrews, B., & Valentine, J. D. (2000). Meta-analysis of risk factors for PTSD in trauma-exposed adults. *Journal of Consulting and Clinical Psychology, 68*(5), 748–766.

Caruth, C. (1996). *Unclaimed experience: Trauma, narrative, and history*. Baltimore, MD: Johns Hopkins University Press.

Critchley, S. (1999). *Ethics-politics-subjectivity: Essays on Derrida, Levinas and contemporary French thought*. London–New York: Verso.

Crocq, L. (2007). *Seize leçons sur le trauma*. Paris: Odile Jacob.

Depraz, N. (2018). Trauma and phenomenology. *Eidos. A Journal for Philosophy of Culture, 2*(2), 53–74.

Depraz, N. (2021). *Attention and vigilance: A phenomenological investigation.* Springer.

Duportail, G.-F. (2005). *Intentionnalité et trauma: Levinas et Lacan.* Paris: L'Harmattan.

Durt, C. (2014). The temporality of trauma: Husserlian contributions to a phenomenology of post-traumatic experience. *Continental Philosophy Review, 47*(1), 1–18.

Ehlers, A., Hackmann, A., & Michael, T. (2004). Intrusive re-experiencing in post-traumatic stress disorder: Phenomenology, theory, and therapy. *Memory, 12*(4), 403–415.

Ferrarello, S., & Baglieri, D. (2025). Hyperthymesia, the past that does not pass: A phenomenological account. *Human Studies*, 1–21.

Freud, S., & Breuer, J. (2000). *Studies on hysteria.* J. Strachey (Trans.). New York: Basic Books. (Original work published 1895).

Heidegger, M. (1962). *Being and time.* J. Macquarrie & E. Robinson (Trans.). Harper & Row. (Original work published 1927).

Henry, M. (2003). *The essence of manifestation.* G. Etzkorn (Trans.). Springer. (Original work published 1963).

Herman, J. L. (1992). *Trauma and recovery: The aftermath of violence—From domestic abuse to political terror.* New York: Basic Books.

Homer. (1990). *The Iliad.* R. Fagles (Trans.). New York: Penguin Classics. https://en.wikipedia.org/wiki/Homer.

Husserl, E. (1973). *Experience and judgment: Investigations in a genealogy of logic.* J. S. Churchill, & K. Ameriks (Trans.). Routledge & Kegan Paul. [Hua XIX].

Husserl, E. (1982). *Ideas pertaining to a pure phenomenology and to a phenomenological philosophy: First book.* F. Kersten (Trans.). Springer. [Hua III].

Husserl, E. (1989). *Ideas pertaining to a pure phenomenology and to a phenomenological philosophy: Second book.* R. Rojcewicz, & A. Schuwer (Trans.). Kluwer. [Hua IV].

Husserl, E. (1990). *On the phenomenology of the consciousness of internal time (1893–1917).* J. B. Brough (Trans.). Kluwer.

Husserl, E. (2001). *Analyses concerning passive and active syntheses: Lectures on transcendental logic.* A. J. Steinbock (Trans.). Springer. [Hua XXXI].

Husserl, E. (2008). *The Bernau manuscripts on time-consciousness: 1917–18.* R. Böhm & R. Sowa (Eds.). Springer.

Husserl, E. (2012). *Einleitung in die Philosophie. Vorlesungen 1916–1919.* H. Jacobs (Ed.). Springer. [Hua-Mat IX].

Kessler, R. C., et al. (1995). Posttraumatic stress disorder in the National Comorbidity Survey. *Archives of General Psychiatry, 52*(12), 1048–1060.

Kessler, R. C., Berglund, P., Demler, O., Jin, R., Merikangas, K. R., & Walters, E. E. (2005). Lifetime prevalence and age-of-onset distributions of DSM-IV disorders in the National Comorbidity Survey Replication. *Archives of General Psychiatry, 62*(6), 593–602.

Kilpatrick, D. G., Resnick, H. S., Milanak, M. E., Miller, M. W., Keyes, K. M., & Friedman, M. J. (2013). National estimates of exposure to traumatic events and PTSD prevalence using DSM-IV and DSM-5 criteria. *Journal of Traumatic Stress, 26*(5), 537–547.

Levinas, E. (1969). *Totality and infinity.* A. Lingis (Trans.). Duquesne University Press.

Levinas, E. (1988). *Otherwise than being or beyond essence.* A. Lingis (Trans.). Duquesne University Press. (Original work published 1974).

Luckhurst, R. (2008). *The trauma question.* London: Routledge.

Maldiney, H. (1991). *Penser l'homme et la folie.* Éditions Jérôme Millon.

McCall-Hosenfeld, J. S., Mukherjee, S., & Lehman, E. B. (2014). Differences in trauma exposure and mental health among rural and urban veterans. *Journal of Rural Health, 30*(3), 253–261.

Merleau-Ponty, M. (2012). *Phenomenology of perception*. D. A. Landes (Trans.). Routledge. (Original work published 1945).

Olff, M., Langeland, W., Draijer, N., & Gersons, B. P. (2005). Gender differences in posttraumatic stress disorder. *Psychological Bulletin, 131*(2), 133–164.

Polt, R. (2019). *Time and trauma: Thinking through Heidegger in the wake of catastrophe*. Rowman & Littlefield.

Sartre, J.-P. (1956). *Being and nothingness*. H. E. Barnes (Trans.). Washington Square Press. (Original work published 1943).

Scheler, M. (1973). *Formalism in ethics and non-formal ethics of values*. M. S. Frings, & R. L. Funk (Trans.). Northwestern University Press. (Original work published 1913).

Scull, A. (2009). *Madness in civilization: A cultural history of insanity*. Princeton University Press.

Shay, J. (1994). *Achilles in Vietnam: Combat trauma and the undoing of character*. Scribner.

Sophocles. (1994). *Ajax*. H. Lloyd-Jones (Trans.). Harvard University Press.

Stolorow, R. D. (2011). *World, affectivity, trauma: Heidegger and post-Cartesian psychoanalysis*. Routledge/Taylor & Francis Group.

van der Kolk, B. (2014). *The body keeps the score: Brain, mind, and body in the healing of trauma*. Viking.

Wilde, L. (2022). Trauma: Phenomenological causality and implication. *Phenomenology and the Cognitive Sciences, 21*, 689–705.

Young, A. (1995). *The harmony of illusions: Inventing post-traumatic stress disorder*. Princeton University Press.

Zahavi, D. (2003). *Husserl's phenomenology*. Stanford University Press.

4

THE PROBLEM OF PSYCHOLOGISM AND LOGICISM IN CASES OF COMPLEX PTSD[1]

Introduction

"Nothing has really happened until it has been described. So you must write many letters to your family and friends and keep a diary" Virginia Woolf cited in her biography from Nicolson (2001, 2).

My mother's journal spans five pages, chronicling her life from age 7 to 14. A few years after her death, these brief pages were transformed into a theater performance in Rome. Although I could not attend as I was already in California, I thought the director's choice to set the play in a maze captured a crucial aspect of her story. I have only read those pages a handful of times, as it is often emotionally overwhelming. Every time something different catches my attention. Today, the word "silence" stands out, as if each word in the journal became trapped in the maze, deepening the harmful silence with each passing day.

I grew up in a madhouse, deeply in love with the madwoman[2] (Baiasu & Collins, 2026; Schlichter, 2003)—my mother—who managed the house with both care and passion. Our madness was defined by silence, the absence of words, and bursts of intense pain. Every now and then, the end of some inner dialogue—often introduced by the Italian word "dunque" (then, therefore)—would break the silence, offering us a fleeting insight into her reality, and consequently, our own. Her journal, too, starts with the word "dunque":

> Born underweight, thus, I am the youngest of ten daughters.

DOI: 10.4324/9781003665557-4

In several parts of her short journal, she also writes how often she was forced by circumstances to close herself up in her silence:

> I was forced to retreat further and further into my silence.

The silence I want to address as a philosopher—and the silence I most regret as her child—is the one surrounding our intersubjective responsibility as a community to create space for each person's search for meaning and for the noise this search sometimes brings with it. I believe she had the right to speak when the opportunity arose, but she rarely encountered people worth finding words for. We all have the right to find a place where we can grow and expand.

In this chapter, I will focus on the intersubjective experience of care drawing on Husserl's critique of psychologism. Using parts of my mother's journal, I will focus on Husserl's Prolegomena (Husserl, 2001) to show how both logical psychologism and psychological logicism are forms of reductionism that taint our ability to open up in our relationships of care. In particular, these forms of reductionism tend to simplify the difficult quest for sense, reducing the complexity of sense either to psychological skills or to logical symbols. If we oversimplify our ability to make sense, too many people in our world would cease to make sense. Accordingly, either we would apply the category of "otherness" (Bhugra et al., 2023; Davidson & Moss, 2008) on too many individuals until none is left to be intersubjectively part of our world; or we would reduce to nonsense what everyone has to say. In the next section, I will focus on complex post-traumatic stress disorder (CPTSD) and the adjacent lived experience of becoming "mad," while the following sections will be dedicated to the phenomenological analysis of sense considered against a reductionistic background.[3] Specifically, I will take three approaches—evidence, representation, and axiology—to illustrate how to avoid reductionist perspectives and the harm they cause in cases of CPTSD. Each approach emphasizes a distinct aspect—sense, symbol, or expression—that must remain separate to avoid reductionist conflation. Phenomenology, moral psychology, and epistemological logic are closely interconnected, yet each plays a unique role in understanding the legality, normativity, and factuality of a phenomenon. Table 4.1 summarizes this framework, which will be further explored in the following sections.

The Lived Experience of Becoming Mad

Although we never received a formal diagnosis—and I am not writing this chapter to diagnose my mother—I can say, as her daughter, that her life was emotionally exhausting. She was exposed to trauma from a very young age through her

TABLE 4.1 Interrelations of Phenomenology, Moral Psychology, and Epistemological Logic in the Analysis of Legality, Normativity, and Factuality

Criteria to Access Meaning	*Key Aspect of Expression*	*What They Express*	*Discipline*
Evidence	Sense	Legality	Phenomenology
Representation	Symbol	Ought	Epistemological logic
Axiology	Reference/ expression	Is	Moral psychology

twenties. This prolonged exposure may have made her vulnerable to complex PTSD. As described in Chapter 3, CPTSD is a severe mental health condition marked by chronic difficulties in emotion regulation, identity, and interpersonal relationships. It is typically associated with prolonged or repeated trauma, such as childhood abuse or ongoing domestic and community violence (Maercker et al., 2022).

At birth, my mother lacked the intersubjective network that any human being needs to feel safe in the world and at peace with themselves:

> I was born underweight (1 kg), the last of ten daughters. The oldest is 20 years older than me. When I was born, my mother became very ill during childbirth. I was told that when I was just born, they placed me in a shoebox with some cotton. And so, life went on. The second oldest sister moved to Rome and asked my mother to send one of the younger sisters to Rome. So, it fell to me.

Once at her sister's home, she recounted how, at just seven years old, she was asked to care for her sister's children, even though her husband was unemployed and at home. Gradually, she revealed how her sister's husband began to regularly abuse her—I will spare, for decency, the details of that. She tearfully begged her sister to let her return to their mother. Over time, her sister grew tired of her tears and eventually sent her back to their hometown in Sicily. "I was returned to my mother covered in lice; I was nine years old"—she writes. However, her time in Sicily did not last long. They did not have enough food, and she never felt at ease. Moreover, she writes that her family seemed ashamed of her. A year later, she was sent back to Rome to live again with her sister. As she grew older, her brother-in-law became more cruel, she writes, but she also became more astute in finding ways to avoid him. She worked as a house cleaner, but he would take all the money she earned. He would even show up at her workplace to ensure he could harass her on the way back. She tried to explain this to the homeowners she worked for, but they called her sister, and things got worse and more cruel. Eventually, she was sent to live in a house where she worked as a house cleaner and caregiver for an elderly woman and she could sleep there. She did not like the place; it was dirty and smelled foul. Her rescuer finally came—a woman who owned a restaurant where she started working. This woman noticed her constant sadness, disheveled appearance, listened to her story, and helped her find a new place where to work and live. Her journal ends with these words:

> Finally, that night I slept with bed sheets for the first time. I was 14 years old.

Unfortunately, I cannot say that her problems were resolved the night she finally had a bed with sheets to sleep in. Four years later, she got married—at a time when marriage was more of a duty to endure than a bond to cherish. Emotional instability became a constant companion in her life. The repeated trauma triggered a form of epistemic uncertainty that would leave her deeply disoriented throughout her life, making it difficult to discern when to trust the sincerity of what was said to her—even in expressions of affection from her own children. In my mother's case, madness became the most reasonable solution to keep herself sane and alive. It was the cleverest way for her *to be*, even if only for brief moments.

To me, as her daughter, she has never been mad. If anything, I saw her as someone desperately trying to find the words to describe what had happened and what was happening to her. As Virginia Woolf, another woman who endured sexual abuse at a young age from her half-brothers, wrote: "Nothing has really happened until it has been described. So, you must write many letters to your family and friends and keep a diary." (Nicolson, 2001, 2).

Lacking proper education, like many others of her generation, and without a network of people to connect with, it was as if nothing had ever happened to her. My phenomenological description here serves to show that, despite the complex traumas she endured, she could have had a better life if she had not been met with a reductionist environment that was numb to her story and eager to simplify the complexity of everyone's pain.

I believe the birth of her children initiated an intersubjective relationship of care that broke through the silence, even if only for brief moments. As I continue to analyze this form of reductionism, I will illustrate the intersubjective aspects of our story, with the hope of improving how we, as a society, relate to life and its difficulties.

Complex PTSD

In my mother's case, what was perceived as "madness" may well have been a rational response to reality shaped by complex PTSD. Baiasu and Collins (2026) call this "mad-sense," that is, a personal response to live creatively and resiliently beyond, or sometimes whilst, facing intense suffering.

As seen in Chapter 3, complex PTSD is, at best, a provisional label for a prolonged post-traumatic condition. It is likely that this term will evolve over time, as it does not fully capture the depth and complexity of the lived experience of someone who has survived a long sequence of traumatic events. CPTSD is a severe and enduring mental health condition that results from prolonged or repeated exposure to traumatic events, often of an interpersonal nature. These may include childhood abuse, domestic violence, captivity, or systematic oppression—experiences that involve sustained coercive control and an inability to escape. Different from my mother's time, CPTSD is now formally recognized as a distinct diagnosis in the 11th revision of the World Health Organization's *International Classification of Diseases* (ICD-11), where it is differentiated from standard PTSD by the presence of disturbances in self-organization. These disturbances include persistent emotion dysregulation, negative self-concept, and profound difficulties in interpersonal relationships. While PTSD centers on a limited set of fear-based responses to discrete trauma, CPTSD accounts for the more pervasive and cumulative psychological damage that prolonged trauma inflicts on identity and relational functioning (Cloitre et al., 2020; Maercker et al., 2022).

The prevalence of CPTSD varies across populations, estimated between 1% and 8% in the general population, but rising to as high as 50% in clinical mental health settings (Maercker et al., 2022). Such data suggest that CPTSD may be underdiagnosed or misdiagnosed under other labels, including borderline personality disorder or chronic depression, due to symptom overlap and a lack of awareness in diagnostic practices. CPTSD often presents with symptoms that exceed the boundaries of PTSD and can resemble a broader syndrome of affective instability, disconnection from the self, and chronic distrust or avoidance in relationships. These features can severely impair the individual's capacity for social belonging, occupational functioning, and emotional resilience.

As examined in Chapter 3, the symptomatology of CPTSD is rooted not only in the traumatic event itself, but in its relational context and developmental timing. Research consistently shows that trauma occurring in childhood—particularly when it involves a caregiver—is far more likely to result in CPTSD than trauma experienced in adulthood (Cloitre et al., 2020; Karatzias et al., 2019). The chronicity and cumulative nature of early trauma disrupt the development of core psychological capacities such as affect regulation, self-other differentiation, and secure attachment. Consequently, survivors often carry forward into adulthood a fragmented or unstable sense of self, persistent shame, and difficulty managing their emotional states in the face of interpersonal stress. These symptoms are not discrete but rather manifest as an interconnected pattern, leading to what has been described as a "complex" form of post-traumatic response (Herman, 1992).

Therapeutically, CPTSD presents unique challenges and often requires more than standard trauma-focused treatments designed for single-incident PTSD. Phase-based, multicomponent interventions, as those presented in the previous chapter, have shown the most promise. These approaches typically begin with a stabilization phase, focusing on safety, psychoeducation, and the development of self-regulatory skills, before moving into trauma-processing phases using methods such as cognitive restructuring, exposure therapy, interaffective exercise, or EMDR. The importance of a flexible, patient-centered approach has been emphasized by several studies, which suggest that individuals with a history of complex trauma may require longer and more varied treatment paths than those with traditional PTSD (Cloitre, 2015; Karatzias et al., 2019). Interventions that include both trauma-focused components and strategies for rebuilding relational trust and emotional regulation tend to yield the most favorable outcomes.

Further complicating treatment is the heterogeneity of trauma histories among individuals with CPTSD. While the ICD-11 offers a diagnostic framework that is increasingly validated across cultures and populations, it does not provide clear clinical guidelines for tailoring interventions to specific trauma types or individual needs (Cloitre et al., 2020). Factors such as ongoing stressors, comorbidities, and socio-cultural context all influence both the presentation of CPTSD and the appropriate therapeutic response. For example, war-affected populations and refugees may require different therapeutic emphases than survivors of childhood sexual abuse. Similarly, individuals with CPTSD related to systemic or institutional violence may face unique barriers to healing that go beyond the clinical setting (Keeley et al., 2016; Maercker et al., 2022).

However, diagnosis alone is not sufficient. A trauma-informed model of mental health must integrate developmental, relational, and socio-political understandings of suffering and recovery. Ultimately, the lives of people with CPTSD are shaped not only by the past trauma they have endured but also by the systems, relationships, and cultural narratives that mediate their recovery. As I will describe in this chapter, the systems surrounding these individuals often oversimplify the complexity of prolonged trauma and impose provisional labels that reduce the richness of their lifeworld.

Make It Simple: A Reductionist Approach

Chapter 1 has already addressed psychologism in connection with Husserl's work. In general, psychologism is a term that entered philosophical discourse to address a debated mistake, especially among German-speaking philosophers from 1880 onward. Originally coined by Johann Eduard Erdmann in 1870 to critique Eduard Beneke's position, the term was later translated into English to criticize those conflating psychological entities with non-psychological ones. For instance, identifying logical laws as psychological laws is seen as psychologism by those who believe the two are distinct. If the former equates to the latter, then what is logical depends on personal psychological points of views and understanding each other or getting over one's own mindset would be very challenging.

Psychologism is a form of reductionism that confuses the distinction between psychological processes and logical structures. It either incorrectly equates the essence of truth with psychological interpretations or makes it difficult to separate the psychological aspects of reasoning from its logical foundation. In day-to-day life, this results in an isolating condition where one attempts to perform reality checks based on what is happening around them, only to end up in a state of epistemological uncertainty. It becomes difficult to trust one's own instincts or to believe in a sense of truth that transcends the boundaries of individual beliefs.

Both are attitudes I commonly find reflected in my philosophical practice. In my office, it is quite easy to come in contact with clients who are convinced that the truth of an argument resides solely in their hands because they do not get emotional during a confrontation and are capable of maintaining a logical approach to the problem. Or, I have clients who tend to close themselves in the "I agree to disagree attitude"; convinced that everything is a matter of points of views; accordingly, they give up on any possibility of dialogue and true connection with their loved ones. If the psychological and logical are conflated, truth would either coincide with a flawless way to express oneself, or with points of views in which it would be hard to find a common ground. Both lead to different forms of isolation.

In the case of my mother's madness, both forms of reductionism equally hurt her chance to conduct a good flourishing life in the society. When people around her perceived her as a madwoman, there was no chance she could win an argument even when she was completely right. Her reasoning did not have enough structure to be acceptable from a logical oriented ear. From an emotional point of view, instead, her way to express herself was just too frightening; none would have wanted to meet her at the highs or lows of an argument. It would have been too intense. She was lonely and the society—the group of mothers at school, my teachers, the neighbors—seemed to confirm that she deserved to be so. As her child, especially at school, I remember being surrounded by a halo of pity and judgment: "poor child, it must be hard with that mother," "she (the mother) shouldn't have what she has (i.e. a seemingly normal life with a job and children)." A reductionistic attitude was constantly applied to our lives: she could not make sense and even worse she did not have the right to make sense. Moreover, no one took a few minutes to understand what our lives were truly like; instead, without realizing it, their assumptions became the implicit conditions of reality in our lifeworld.

On my side, since she was my reference point for what I considered normal, everything she did and said made sense to me. I took her every word as valid, which, of course, had its downsides, especially when she was emotionally distressed. Perhaps this tendency to accept her perspective was what made me a phenomenologist even before I encountered the discipline formally.

In the following sections, I will illustrate how the two reductionist attitudes complicate the search for meaning—a search to which all of us are entitled.

The Immediate Damages of Reductionism

In his *Prolegomena*, Husserl challenges both logicism and psychologism in his effort to establish a pure logic—a science of truth that is independent of how human beings happen to think. The rejection of reductionism in general would later allow him to develop his theory of intentionality, as it makes room to consider the essence of lived experience not merely as what an individual is undergoing from a societal perspective, but as a core sense constituted through an intersubjective system of validations occurring on both the subjective (noetic) and objective (noematic) sides of living consciousness. He insists on a sharp distinction between psychology and logic, grounded in the is-ought difference (Hua XIX/1, *Prolegomena*, §17). While proponents of psychologism argue that the way thought ought to occur (normatively) is simply a generalization of how it actually occurs (empirically), Husserl rejects this view. He contends that psychology deals with how people in fact think (the *is*), while logic concerns how thinking should be conducted in order to be valid (the *ought*), and the two should not be conflated.

For example, someone might believe that if most people tend to reason inductively from habit, then inductive reasoning must be logically valid. But Husserl would object: just because people *do* reason in a certain way, it does not mean they *ought* to. Logic must remain a normative discipline that evaluates the validity of inferences regardless of how thinking happens to manifest in psychological processes. Preserving the distinction between the two enlarges our world, as the essential truth we try to reach through our lived experience can always be explored anew in a recursive way—using the very tools that our previous grasp of that essence has already provided us.

In that sense, psychological logicism must be rejected as a form of reductionism, because it treats logic as a set of cognitive performances—how people in fact tend to think or arrive at truth—thereby collapsing the normative dimension of what *ought* to be into mere descriptions of what *is*. According to Husserl, instead, "each proposition expresses the idea of a relationship of commensuration between the norm and that which is regulated normatively" (Hua XIX/1, 48). In this context, Husserl specifically critiques John Stuart Mill's psychological account of logic (Mill, 1963–1991; Nordquest, 1979), Lipps' interpretation of logical laws as natural laws of thought, and Sigwart's conception of truth as the immediate experience of consciousness. These views reduce logic to a form of cognitive technology—a practical tool based on how people happen to reason—rather than treating it as a discipline governed by ideal, normative laws (Hua XIX/1 §18). As Husserl states, "logic cannot derive its laws from the accidental use of reason" (Hua XIX/1, 53). If it did, what counts as true and valid would be determined by majority consensus or prevailing habits of thought, rather than by reason's intrinsic norms. I would add that if this overlap were accepted as valid, it would leave no room for a personal quest for truth. "Yet,<according to Husserl>, each truth remains in itself what it is, it maintains its being ideal (…) it is a unity of validity in the atemporal domain of ideas" (Hua XIX/1, 130).

While Herbart's logical psychologism maintains to a certain extent the objectivity of the logical representation (Hua XIX/1, 215–17, §59), according to Husserl, Herbart's central failure lies in his inability to distinguish clearly between the ideal and the real, as he inevitably collapses the ideal into the real: "Herbart's basic mistake was more important: he located what is essential to the ideality of the logical concept in its normality, thus shifting the sense of true, genuine ideality, of unified meaning, into the dispersed multiplicity of experiences" (217). A second error arises from Herbart's conception of logic as a "moral of thought," which obscures logic's status as an autonomous, purely theoretical discipline. His third major error is his failure to recognize that reconciling "the subjective course of logical thinking with the real course of external actuality" (217) is not a genuine problem. These three errors lead to equating truth with the multiplicity of experiences—implying that if something is not experienced or reported as such, it is effectively denied the status of being true, or more troublingly, of being real and meaningful. That is precisely what happened to my mother—and to many others like her—who found themselves in a living hell, one so profound that words could not convey its boundaries to others.

The core problem with both psychological logicism and logical psychologism is their oversimplification of the complex quest for meaning, reducing it either to psychological abilities or to abstract logical symbols. The spheres of the ideal and the real, the ought and the is, are conflated. As a result, the essence of a certain experience may be confused with the way in which one individual—or a dominant group—experiences it.

This was evident in my mother's attempts to explain what was happening to the homeowners she worked for. Their truth and their way of validating experiences became the norm she should have adjusted to. She certainly needed someone to care for her, but not in the way they imagine care should look like. They took the quickest route—by speaking to her sister—instead, placing her in an even more difficult position.

Similarly, we often encounter this kind of attitude in our daily lives, such as when, at a doctor's office, one tries to honestly answer the question, "How are you doing?". We are expected to respond with as few words as possible. It is difficult to answer that question with honesty and depth because it takes time to fully explain, and rarely is there someone on the other side who is willing to give us that time or genuinely interested in hearing the complete answer. Truth is often reduced to a dichotomy: either "I'm feeling good" or "I'm not doing well." This reflects a normative expectation about what counts as a valid response. Personally—whether due to biographical reasons, this reductionist attitude, or a combination of both—I often find myself either unable or unwilling to express the complexity of my experiences to those who are supposed to care, such as my doctor, my colleagues, or even my friends. Being open to complexity is an attitude we can recognize in others and ourselves, but we frequently fail to give ourselves or others the time needed for that complexity to fully unfold.[4]

The reductionisms in logic and psychology tend to reduce the complexity of the given phenomenon in a conflated expectation of what the average experience would be considered valid and real. Psychological logicism would claim that those who are incapable of performing or are cognitively impaired do not make sense and are incapable of reaching out for sense. This reductionism serves as the basis for categorizing individuals who do not conform to the "logical norm" into more popular diagnostic labels, which ultimately results in their exclusion.

Equally dangerous are the consequences of logical psychologism, which would reduce the complexity of the psyche to the ability to combine symbols in correct grammar or use these symbols in acceptable sentences. In that sense, logical psychologism might provide the ground for developing "medicine" (psychopharmacy) to "alleviate" a person of the "wrong logic" and healing toward the correct logic.

This view would implicitly suggest that all those incapable of properly using grammar or conventional symbols are not capable of making sense. On the one hand, Herbart's psychology and pedagogy considered knowledge an assimilation and sum of ideas that entered consciousness, leaving it to the individual to learn how to associate and combine (Dunkel, 1969). On the other hand, Mill's psychology interpreted human beings according to empirical principles of utility and functioning; hence, the limits of functioning and being useful to each other made the human psyche somewhat broken.

Symbol, Reference, and Isolating Sense

How do we make sense of the bad that happens to us or that we do to ourselves? How do we make sense of our actions and their content? Is sense inherent in the expressions we use, or does it reside in universal symbols like numbers, letters, and punctuation? And does sense cease to exist when expressed by someone with cognitive or psychological impairments?

Reading my mother's short journal I realize that these are all luxury questions she might have never phrased in these terms. To a very minimal form, sense is attention. She just needed a life in which someone could pay attention[5] to her; as she writes about her experience as a nine-years-old:

> To get attention, I would pretend to have many ailments, but my family didn't understand anything. They didn't realize I had many problems. So, I punished myself by having my appendix removed, thinking they would be closer to me, but that didn't happen. Scrawny and thin, three days after leaving the hospital, they put me to work in the fields. We harvested chicory. It was so cold! In such small villages, we lived only off the harvest, and it wasn't enough for all of us. The cold, the rain… I was unwell.

Back in the 1940s, children and women hardly made sense as they were not recognized as peers in the world of adults. Nevertheless, today we have the opportunity to do better. While philosophy often operates through abstractions, these abstractions—like the questions I raised above—can lead to meanings that help us build a better society. At the heart of these questions is the fundamental right of every individual to be heard and supported in their search for meaning.

To address the questions above, Husserl reflects on the notion of attention, drawing on key concepts from Frege and Bolzano. From Bolzano, he adopts the notion that a symbol does not require a full sentence to denote meaning. A symbol can evoke a multitude of meanings without being part of a structured sentence or a set of symbols. This challenges the idea of logical psychologism, which argues that sense is derived from properly connecting sentences. Instead, Husserl suggests that it is the reference that bridges the symbol and its inherent sense.[6] Frege's work, on the other hand, serves as a key to distinguish between symbol, expression, and sense as three distinct elements. Symbols act as tools that make it possible to apply complex norms used to interpret sense. From that point of view, Husserl would call them a technology (Hua XIX/1, chapter 2, section 13) at the service of human ability to do science. Expression involves the combination of these norms (of grammar, logic, numbers) that, when applied correctly, enable someone or something to convey sense. However, the essence of sense itself exists independently of our ability to express it. As Frege notes, "The North Sea covers an area of 220,000 square miles" (1956, 20) is an objectively true statement, even though no two individuals associate this statement with exactly the same ideas, images, or mental experiences. Similarly, to come back to the practical application of this remark, the sense of truth that informs the actions of a person suffering from CPTSD exists independently of their ability to communicate it in flawless sentences to the people involved in their lives. Nevertheless, the impression I have, at least from looking at my mother's journal, is that her truth could never be shared because it could not be communicated as it was unacceptable for the society and too demanding to manage for those who listened to it.

> I tried to tell my story to my employers who lived in Monteverde, but they made things worse by calling home and telling my sister that she was misbehaving. This only made the situation even worse. Naturally, he told me that I shouldn't talk about it with anyone.

The truth can become a very cumbersome lie for the person who lives it when its expression is not validated in their immediate interaffective network. Holding especially a reductivist attitude that negates the difference between the three, that is, symbol, expression, and sense, leads to a progressive process of alienation from one's own core self. We tend to conflate the sign that nothing is happening with our inability to express it until its sense with its pressing evidence becomes further and further from us. Recognizing these three layers—symbol, expression, and sense—helps us avoid reductionism and remain open to the unexpected moments of sense that life, in all its forms, can present. My mother's employers did not pay attention to the symbols, that is, how disheveled and scared she was but took her expression seriously. They decided to call the source of the problem, dismissing the sense of what she was trying to convey. She was scared of that very person they made contact with, her sister. Even if she was young and maybe incapable of expressing herself with clarity, their choice (to call her sister) took away from her even more agency and self-determination for her future.[7] Conversely, the woman who eventually helped her had spent a long time simply observing, choosing not to intervene until she felt she could truly offer meaningful support. She took the time to get to know her, to understand how her world was structured. She tried to see life from her perspective, seeking ways it might gain a renewed sense of meaning—one that could genuinely enhance its quality.

Being able to see the complexity of these three layers empowers individuals to persist in their efforts to make sense of their lived experiences without giving up on making sense of what might seem absurd to everyone (even to those experiencing it). Unfortunately, reductionism, whether logical or psychological, often influences what is deemed acceptable sense within our communities, even affecting our personal relationships and creating barriers where understanding and support could otherwise flourish. Once again, the abuse my mother confided to her employers was, rightly, deemed unacceptable. However, they wanted it to end immediately—without giving much thought to how such a result could be effectively achieved or involving the person actually living through the experience in the process of finding a solution. This, and similar choices, generated that sense of affective instability, disconnection from the self, and chronic distrust or avoidance in relationships, typical of CPTSD, that severely impacted her sense of social belonging for her life. Furthermore, this reductionistic attitude often permeates educational systems, setting rigid standards for what is considered meaningful, and fostering environments that stifle the diversity of sense-making processes, encouraging even more traumatic experiences to come. This can inadvertently create isolating walls, even in spaces where care and mutual understanding are possible.

First Approach, Evidence: Sense for All

In this section and the one that follows, I will draw on Husserl's phenomenological theory to propose three ways of accessing sense that help us avoid reductionism in its psychological or logical forms—specifically those rooted in evidence, axiology, and representation. These approaches aim to preserve the distinction between sense, expression/reference, and symbol in the ongoing quest for truth. The first approach will focus on the Husserlian notion of evidence.

In Hua-Mat IX, text 32, Husserl writes that our best approach to understanding sense is through evidence—felt both in our biological (*Körper*) and living (*Leib*) bodies. Evidence, as Husserl describes, is the *via regia* that leads us to a truth deeply felt capable of guiding our life choices and resonating with us universally. Pain, for example, although the experience of pain is deeply personal and can manifest under various circumstances that may not align with common perceptions of pain, when this sensation surfaces, it is recognized in its universal characteristics because it speaks to us as human beings. These universal features resonate with what we feel in our bodies, allowing us to identify and understand the essence of pain, even when its external expression does not match the typical expectations.

In Prolegomena section 16, Husserl presents sense as a necessity (*Notwendigkeit*), explaining it as a theoretical core—a *Sollen* or ought—that dictates how things must be for them to exist as they are. For example, a triangle must have three angles to be perceived as a triangle. Sense, at its most basic level, is a legality that regulates how phenomena should be organized in order to appear to us as this specific phenomenon. Take, again, the experience of pain: a person who is high functioning and looks healthy might not seem entitled to claim they are in pain, yet this pain resonates as a visceral truth within them every time they experience it. To make sense of this feeling, they must find the core of it and use proper words to describe it, a process that is deeply intersubjective. In fact, we can see this theoretical core only if we have the necessary symbols and structures to refer to it. Often though we lack these tools because the society around us does not see us entitled to this feeling. As a case in point, pain in minorities and women, in particular, is dismissed as a psychosomatic problem (Hoffman et al., 2016).

In my mother's case, our interaffective bond was so strong that especially in early childhood I am quite sure I could feel her pain through my body; I could even have hallucinations consistent with hers.[8] Through our intersubjective connection, I could be in contact with that necessity to make sense although we were both dismissed as irrational. Unlike her, I was a child, and the other kids would sit with me, listening to my stories with very open minds. I vividly remember waiting in my elementary school homeroom and sharing with my closest friends what I had experienced the day before. They looked at me with wide eyes and accepted every word as true. I still recall how liberating and comforting those moments were for me.

For phenomena to be understood as they are, there must be space to accept them. Unfortunately, this space has not always been available. For instance, consider the historical condition where women were required to remain in abusive marriages or, to come back to the previous example, the present-day issue where the pain of African American women is often dismissed as a mental condition (Cousin et al., 2022).

To remain faithful to the complexity of sense and avoid reducing it to a personal invention or association of linguistic symbols, Husserl argues that we need a discipline that clarifies the structure in which sense manifests. A chair must allow people to sit on it to be recognized as a chair, a table must hold objects to be a table, and a warrior must be courageous to be a warrior (Hua XIX/1, chapter 11, section 60). There is an essential legality to the sense of each phenomenon that allows us to perceive it meaningfully. Phenomenology is the discipline and the method that allows us to describe this legality—which is why the struggle against psychologism and logicism lies at the heart of Husserl's philosophy.

When dealing with basic phenomena like a chair, a table, or a warrior, their sense is immediate and easy to grasp. However, when dealing with lived experiences like pain, anxiety, or fear, typical of CPTSD, understanding the inner legality of these phenomena becomes much more complex; It often becomes confused with societal expectations and assumptions about what is considered normal. Each layer of these experiences opens an infinite number of horizons that we must clarify, requiring keen observation and active listening to intersubjectively grasp the sense and maintain the legality of the structure. In this way, phenomenology, as Levinas suggests (1987), reactivates horizons of meaning, engaging with lived experiences to see how they make sense. It is crucial that this reactivation is intersubjective, as, according to Husserl, nothing occurs in a social vacuum.

Second Approach: See What I Mean?

A second key way to approach sense is through understanding how we form mental images and representations. This leads us closer to Husserl's definition of intentionality, which he describes in Ideas I, section 33, and in Logical Investigations V, section 82, as consciousness being a flow of intentional acts.

Intentionality is the structure that underlies life, where consciousness, as a living present, continuously engages with and reflects on being.

In the Logical Investigations, Husserl advances his exploration of sense by analyzing the intentionality of consciousness. In the first investigation, he examines linguistic entities (symbols) as tokens for expressing and referring to sense; in the second, he treats logic as a form of ontology, allowing us to penetrate the sense of being; and in the third investigation, he explains how Being is given to us—how something concrete that we can touch becomes an abstract meaning we hold in our minds. For example, the table I am writing on exists both as a physical object I can touch and as a representation of a table in my mind. How do we abstract this representation from the concrete table?

The answer lies in understanding the structure of intentionality, as described in the following three investigations. To avoid the reductionism discussed earlier, Husserl shifts the focus to the concept of representation. Representations, the mental images we create of what we perceive, cannot be reduced either to mental symbols (leading to logicism) or to feelings (leading to psychologism). In the former, a table would be merely a symbol of a surface with four legs; in the latter, a table would only be a table if I can perceive and attach sensations to it. Thus, the fifth and sixth Logical Investigations explain how our engagement with reality translates into mental representations. The adequacy of this representation to the real object depends on our perception gathering sensuous data and our intuition abstracting a categorial sense from it. My axiological reason then validates the association of sense data and categories by confirming that: "This is a table," and "Yes, I validate the sense of this statement." It is neither our logical nor perceptive skills alone that create an adequate mental image, but the axiological way our experience integrates with our epistemological ability to create logical categories. In the case of my mother, her axiological reason rarely validated her mental images with the meaning that was commonly associated with them. She rarely gave herself a chance to validate her feelings. As it is typical of individuals suffering from prolonged traumas, she was committed to a continual, self-sacrificing stance that permeated both her physical and cognitive life. For instance, her third pregnancy took a severe toll on her mental health, but those around her continued to convey the opposite message. She was told, "You're a mother; you must care for your child and have no time to be ill and complain." This attitude further isolated her and her young children, cutting them off from the support they needed to heal and maintain a decent quality of life.

Thus, our inner sense of the outside world, if you want mental images, cannot be the result of psychological perception alone or categorial intuition alone; they must encompass both from an axiological stance. The sense of social belonging, missing in people suffering from CPTSD, comes exactly from this complex mix of perceptions, personal ideas, and validations. In the third Logical Investigation, Husserl explains that the general categories we use in language may begin with our senses, with the perception of concrete elements of reality. Concreta, such as the wood of the table I touch, are non-independent objects that intuition associates with universal forms, like "this white table." While abstracta are independent (I can think of the table as a unit), concreta are the sensuous parts that make the table this specific table. In the categorial foundation of sense, we begin with general intuition—"this table"—and confirm it with sensuous data to achieve evident adequacy with reality, allowing us to say, "This is a table!" Both categorial meanings and sensuous data are essential for confirming the horizon of sense that a phenomenon generates. From here, it is easy to gather how challenging it is in the experience of CPTSD to achieve full adequacy. Even though the adequacy comes from a feeling of inner evidence, if the validation of one's own percepta is continuously dismissed, it becomes hard to make sense. The representation of what we live becomes nebulous and even unreal.

This illustrates how even simple experiences, like touching a table, although strongly embodied, might cease to make sense if they are not validated in full adequacy. Or, the sincerity of a compliment might come across as a threat when unexpected. The complexity increases when the experience involves the inner image we build of ourselves in the world. Relationships, bodily connections, feelings, and the way we abstract categorial symbols and words from these interactions shape how we move in the world. The representation that translates our concrete engagement with the real world into an embodied image is adequate to reality when its categorial form—"this table," "this person"—is fulfilled by its material concreteness. Unfortunately, not sufficient intersubjective space is made for this material fulfillment to occur in human relationships especially those of care in case of madness, especially when childhood traumas are so far away from the present affective perception of the majority of people around. In my personal case, I think that the intersubjective and interaffective relationship I had with my mother as her daughter has been to a certain extent healing because in our in-between-world it was possible to find this adequacy and accordingly sense. The problems though started when I grew up and I had to challenge that world without knowing that I was already part of it. This is the healing path that philosophy, and in particular phenomenology, can offer, challenging assumptions of normality to reveal as many horizons as possible on the same lived experience.

In the fifth Logical Investigation, section 44, Husserl provides at least 13 definitions of representation to emphasize the importance of keeping categorial and sensuous aspects distinct. Conflating the two leads to reductionism. Influenced by Twardowski, Husserl describes representations as a quasi-picture that is analogous to real content. "Analogous" here means proportionally similar, a form of evident or analogous reproduction of the content (Hickerson, 2007, 44, 53). Limiting individuals' freedom to feel their experience and find an image analogous to what they perceive leads to silence, where they may feel numb to their bodies and to the network of people around them. If a person is repeatedly denied this freedom, an inner attitude would develop which could be exemplified by the sentences: "It's not worth talking. I'll keep this to myself. It's too much effort to express to someone who doesn't want to hear." This generates a form of uneasiness or asymmetry with one's own embodied life. In definition 8 (Hua XIX/2, Logical Investigation V, 44), Husserl describes representation in a twofold sense: "Representation in the double sense of provoking presentations and doing duty for them" (Hua XIX/2, 173). On one hand, representation participates in the givenness of real being provided by instantiations, enabling the recognition of different kinds of states of affairs and grounding sciences like logic or ethics. On the other hand, representation is an abstraction or determination of sensuous data. When suffering from CPTSD, it can happen that the givenness of concrete life is suppressed or censored. In its place, abstraction—namely, ideas or concepts that should emerge from lived experience—begins instead to reflect the expectations of others, rather than what is directly and authentically experienced.

Intentional Essence: This Is What I Meant

Representation is a fundamental aspect of intentionality. Without it, intentional acts would be challenging to conceptualize because intentionality involves our capacity to reflect on phenomena. Things manifest to us through an intentional essence that animates the perceptive matter with a categorial form (Hua XIX/2, Logical Investigation V, sections 20–22), which we then recognize as something familiar and meaningful. This vast matter becomes a visible phenomenon when it appears to us with a specific how and what—such as the table I am touching. The correlation of how and what forms the core of the intentional essence, which allows an act to be objectifying, meaning that the object is presented to us in a way that makes sense because we can determine its content (what) according to a specific form (how). An act is objectifying when the matter it refers to is determined in a representable content that makes sense for us.

The primary structure of an intentional essence consists of a correlation between matter and quality, which are inseparable (Hua XIX/2, 416). Quality is how matter presents itself, and matter is what the quality presents. Husserl states that "act quality is undoubtedly an abstract aspect of the act" (Hua XIX/2, 43), while the matter is its concretum. For instance, a particularly painful experience may require more categorial effort to make sense of it, especially when those around us deny its validity. What my mother experienced, and what I experienced as my mother's child, was a concretum that hardly found its word shape but that does not mean that it never existed. The task of philosophy, in the form of epistemological logic, is to give expression to all aspects of that experience.

Sense is an inexhaustible unknown that can be determined by infinite correlations of how and what that may not yet be visible to us. Therefore, Husserl's phenomenology, especially in psychological and psychiatric contexts, cautions us that the most meaningful sense might be the one that lacks the words to be expressed and remains invisible. This visibility, which Husserl in Logical Investigations calls intentional essence and can be expressed in symbols, is our best means of approaching sense in itself.

A final, subtle challenge to our constitution of sense is axiological reason, the process that validates the categorization of specific data—the what according to the how. Axiological reason, as the Greek word *axios* suggests, refers to the value-category under which specific content is organized.

Third Approach: The Axiological Reason and Its Malfunctioning

The axiological reason, or the values we assign to what we perceive and categorize, presents a challenging moment in the meaning-making process. When we attempt to express the meaning of something, we use references to assign values that help gauge the concreteness of our experience and give form to its presence in the world. We can think of it as a footprint in the sand, which varies according to the weight, height, and posture of the person who made it. Influenced by Lotze (1885, Logik sect. 20), Husserl adopts the idea that axiological acts validate contents through *ratio* and *proportio*, meaning that the concreteness of being is expressed into a legality (the necessity I referred to in V.1) made present in intuition. For instance, when I perceive this table (concretum, matter), I accept (through an axiological/validating act) the awareness that these perceptual data are connected to this category (abstractum, form). Axiological acts are responsible for generating that quasi-picture, which, as previously mentioned in reference to Twardowski's influence, is proportional and analogous to what the senses have grasped.

One way to explain this is, again, through the analogy of a footprint in the sand. The representation provided by the axiological reason for our intuition is the cast left by the footprint. The axiological reason is the mode of consciousness that assigns a yes/no value to our intuitive capacity to grasp the concreteness of life; it determines the legality of what is given to us. For example, it recognizes that a footprint in the sand is a footprint, not a face print, because the sense data gathered match what we perceive.

When the impressions of our experiences—especially those related to prolonged trauma and the emotional pain it generates—are denied or dismissed as defects of the mind or mismatched with more conformist representations, we accumulate important *concreta* that fail to form mental images, yet they still influence the individual's sense of self. The footprint we once saw either ceases to exist or is renamed, until we too forget how those *concreta* once felt to us.

In Ideas I, section 40 (Hua III), Husserl introduces the notion of noematic *Sinn* to clarify this problem further. When we engage with life, we encounter the concreteness of being, which carries a sense that must be recollected and is not fully given to us, at least not in its formal meaning. This noematic sense requires understanding and determination before it can be expressed. Initially, when something appears to us, we may determine its meaning through a series of guesses. For example, I see a cup but only from the front. Is this a cup? As I move around it, my axiological reason continually validates the horizon of legality that tells me how a cup should appear to be recognizable as a cup.

Applying this to trivial objects, we can see how challenging it might be to truly understand what is in front of us. However, we do not feel hopeless because, eventually, we can determine what the object is. The situation is different when determining the noematic sense of certain psychological lived experiences, particularly in psychiatric patients, especially when a unique experience has been normalized by those around according to unfit representations. A state of abuse, sadness, and vulnerability might be simplified as a condition of abnormalcy and hypersensitivity.

In my mother's case, her emotional states have been rarely validated by her interaffective community and later on even by herself. The affective necessity that should bring forth the good value (Gutwert) or existence value (Daseinswert) of her life (Husserl, 2014) often became distorted, clouding or even preventing the being of *concreta* from becoming prominent in her lifeworld. Her existence as such was hardly ever valid as it was and her life was perceived by herself and others as wrong. She lost the references that could have made the expression of herself felt meaningful.

It was extremely hard for me to be a constant presence in her interaffective network. Although I loved her madly and I never felt separated from her, little gestures from me might have been interpreted by her as highly offensive thus she would exclude herself from the connection we had. Walking in a room and seeing me laughing with someone else could have meant that I was not paying attention to her, hence disrupting her interaffective resonance with me (Fuchs & Koch, 2014). Such an encounter could have compromised the meaning my existence would hold in her interaffective lifeworld. That is one of the areas where CPTSD and BPD seem to overlap and I will discuss this point in more depth in Chapter 9. Even though I was there for her, my same presence in her lifeworld could have been disturbed, losing its meaningfulness according to the unpredictable. That was maybe the most emotionally hurtful aspect of my relationship with her—having to accept that at times she would refuse my love because she would cease to believe in it. After all, if the interaffective environment taught her to believe that the most traumatic events of her life were not valid, and she could not trust the felt-sense they left behind, then why should my love—or anything good in her life—seem any more believable or acceptable?

Keeping up with the tides of her interaffective resonance in our shared world both in a physical and emotional way was hard. However, her consistent authenticity with me helped establish a strong foundation for our shared intersubjective world. Our lifeworld remained untouched even if the affections of the moments would have not allowed the expression of this love to come to the surface. Through time, we built an authentic place where we could always come back and meet.

Hence, the axiological problem lies in the intrinsic reference connecting how and what; it is in this connection that expression becomes possible. For instance, saying, "This is a table," "Is this a table?" or "What a table this is!" alters the sense of the table from an observation to a question or an exclamation. Changing the matter is even more apparent: "This is a scarf," "Is this a cat?" "What a gentleman." When habitual combinations that pair matter and form consistently fail, individuals may experience ongoing distress, leading to interaffective disorders, distrust in their intuitions, and a deep sense of alienation. That would explain the hypersensitivity my mother suffered from which would cause discontinuity in our interaffective world, where missing a call becomes a sign of rejection, or an intimate spending time with others signals abandonment. The intentional essence that such an individual builds constitutes a meaning that is not conducive to a fulfilling life. Being mindful of the axiological reason in how it validates the pairing of what and how and being open to infinite possibilities of pairing might help to keep each one's quest for sense open and eventually educate each other to more fitting pairing.

Conclusion

As Virginia Woolf's quote says at the beginning of this chapter in order to make this nothing something, we need to be able to describe it. The long-lasting effects of trauma, especially in childhood, can significantly compromise the quality of life for individuals who have already been exposed to injustice, as evidenced by the symptoms associated with CPTSD.

Reductionist approaches such as those described in this chapter would undermine any attempt to connect with the complexity of feelings generated by such experiences and accordingly be at home in one's own skin. As discussed in this chapter, approaches, such as logical psychologism and psychological logicism, devalue the complexity of sense because they conflate the role of psychology with that of logic and vice-versa. Being able to see the three layers through which we make sense of our lived experience, that is symbols, reference, and expression, is an important starting point to avoid creating isolating walls between one another. In this chapter, using the intersubjective bond between my mother and I, I showed how the experience of madness might become the most reasonable answer to a dismissive behavior that negates individuals the ability to connect with the sense of their experience through inner and external validation of the concreteness of their lived experience. Making intersubjective and interaffective space for sense, for how difficult it can be, is an ongoing work that can help our community to thrive not only in cases of CPTSD.

By employing these three approaches, that is, focusing on questions about how evidence is experienced, how mental representations are formed, or how self-validation is emphasized, we can reinforce the distinctions between symbols, expressions, and sense. This approach allows greater space for each individual's quest for meaning.

Notes

1 My deep gratitude goes to Magnus Englander and Zsuzsanna Chappell for reading this chapter and sharing their valuable insights with me.
2 Here, I openly use the term madness to remain loyal to the lived experience. For more references on critical madness in femininity, you can read Schlichter (2003).
3 It is important to note that this chapter also challenges social forms of reductionism that equate these issues solely with poverty. Unfortunately, significant social challenges affect various levels of socioeconomic status alike.
4 We can recall Eugene Minkowski's (1958) therapeutic approach, which consisted in "moving in" with patients—giving them the necessary time and space to naturally reveal and explore their issues. This approach sought to facilitate healing by fostering a supportive, immersive environment that allowed problems to surface and resolve gradually.
5 Here, I use the word "attention" in a phenomenological sense, referring to the fundamental intentional and perceptive connection by which one person is bodily present in another's life. The fact that my mother sought attention for ailments she didn't physically suffer from doesn't justify dismissing all her suffering as psychosomatic. I believe mind and body are a unified whole; where anxiety and tension accumulate, physical suffering often follows. The attention she sought was the primary presence of another in her lifeworld, co-participating in her suffering.
6 While Husserl appreciates Bolzano's perspective on the denotative role of symbols, he critiques him for lacking "the epistemological clarification of the purely logical basic concepts and laws" (Hua XIX/1, appendix, chapter 10).
7 Helpful here is also the distinction that Jaspers makes between content and meaning. They tried to help my mother based on the content of the story and not the meaning she was trying to convey.
8 Several scholars have emphasized that delusions and hallucinations may hold meaning and serve a psychological function for those who experience them (Baiasu & Collins, 2026; Bortolotti, 2022; Ritunnano et al., 2022).

References

Baiasu and Collins (2026). Sense and madness. In S. Ferrarello (Ed.), *The Bloomsbury handbook of phenomenological bioethics* (pp. TBD). London: Bloomsbury.

Bhugra, D., Smith, A., Liebrenz, M., Ventriglio, A., Gnanapragasam, S. N., Buadze, A., & Poulter, D. (2023). "Otherness", otherism, discrimination, and health inequalities: Entrenched challenges for modern psychiatric disciplines. *International Review of Psychiatry*, *35*(3–4), 234–241.

Bortolotti, L. (2022). *Why delusions matter*. London: Bloomsbury Academic.

Cloitre, M. (2015). The "one size fits all" approach to trauma treatment: Should we be satisfied? *European Journal of Psychotraumatology*, *6*(1), 27344. https://doi.org/10.3402/ejpt.v6.27344

Cloitre, M., Garvert, D. W., Brewin, C. R., Bryant, R. A., & Maercker, A. (2020). Evidence for the coherence and integrity of the complex PTSD (CPTSD) diagnosis: Response to Achterhof et al. *European Journal of Psychotraumatology*, *11*(1), 1739873. https://doi.org/10.1080/20008198.2020.1739873

Cousin, L., Johnson-Mallard, V., & Booker, S. Q. (2022). "Be strong my sista'": Sentiments of strength from Black women with chronic pain living in the Deep South. *ANS: Advances in Nursing Science*, *45*(2):127–142.

Davidson, A. C., & Moss, S. A. (2008). Examining the trauma disclosure of police officers to their partners and officers' subsequent adjustment. *Journal of Language and Social Psychology*, *27*(1), 51–70.

Dunkel, H. B. (1969). *Herbart & education*. London: Random House.

Frege, G. (1956). The thought: A logical inquiry. *Mind*, *65*(259), 289–311.

Fuchs, T., & Koch, S. C. (2014). Embodied affectivity: On moving and being moved. *Frontiers in Psychology*, *5*, 508.

Herman, J. L. (1992). *Trauma and recovery: The aftermath of violence—From domestic abuse to political terror*. New York: Basic Books.

Hickerson, R. (2007). *The history of intentionality: Theories of consciousness from Brentano to Husserl*. London: Continuum.

Hoffman, K. M., Trawalter, S., Axt, J. R., & Oliver, M. N. (2016). Racial bias in pain assessment and treatment recommendations, and false beliefs about biological differences between Blacks and Whites. *Proceedings of the National Academy of Sciences*, *113*(16), 4296–4301.

Husserl, E. (1983). *Ideas pertaining to a pure phenomenology and to a phenomenological philosophy: First book*. F. Kersten (Trans.). Dordrecht: Kluwer Academic Publishers. (Original work published 1913) (Hua III).

Husserl, E. (2001). *Logical investigations*. J. N. Findlay (Trans.). London: Routledge. (Hua XIX/1, XIX/2).

Husserl, E. (2014). *Grenzprobleme der Phänomenologie: Analysen des Unbewusstseins und der Instinkte. Metaphysik. Späte Ethik*. R. Sowa & T. Vongehr (Eds.). New York: Springer. (Hua Mat IX).

Karatzias, T., Shevlin, M., Fyvie, C., Hyland, P., Efthymiadou, E., Wilson, D., … & Cloitre, M. (2019). Psychological interventions for ICD-11 complex PTSD symptoms: Systematic review and meta-analysis. *Psychological Medicine*, *51*(8), 1263–1273.

Keeley, J. W., Reed, G. M., Roberts, M. C., Evans, S. C., Robles, R., Matsumoto, C., & Maercker, A. (2016). Disorders specifically associated with stress: A case-controlled field study for ICD-11 mental and behavioural disorders. *International Journal of Clinical and Health Psychology*, *16*(2), 109–127. https://doi.org/10.1016/j.ijchp.2015.09.002

Levinas, E. (1987). Meaning and sense. In *Collected philosophical papers* (Phaenomenologica, pp. 75–107, Vol. 100). Dordrecht: Springer.

Lotze, H. (1885). *Microcosmus: An essay concerning man and his relation to the world*. E. Hamilton, & E. E. Constance Jones (Trans.) (Vols. 1–2). Edinburgh: T. & T. Clark.

Maercker, A., Cloitre, M., Bachem, R., Schlumpf, Y. R., Khoury, B., Hitchcock, C., & Bohus, M. (2022). Complex post-traumatic stress disorder. *The Lancet*, *400*(10345), 60–72.

Mill, J. S. (1963–1991). *The collected works of John Stuart Mill* (Vols. 1–33). J. M. Robson (Ed.). Toronto: University of Toronto Press.

Minkowski, E. (1958). Findings in a case of schizophrenic depression. In R. May (Ed.), *Existence: A new dimension in psychiatry and psychology* (pp. 127–138). New York: Basic Books.

Nicolson, N. (2001). *Virginia Woolf*. New York: Penguin.

Nordquest, D. A. (1979). Husserl and Mill's 'psychologism'. *The Mill News Letter*, *14*, 2–9.

Ritunnano, R., Humpston, C., & Broome, M. R. (2022). Finding order within the disorder: A case study exploring the meaningfulness of delusions. *BJPsych Bulletin*, *46*(2), 109–115. https://doi.org/10.1192/bjb.2020.151

Schlichter, A. (2003). Critical madness, enunciative excess: The figure of the madwoman in postmodern feminist texts. *Cultural Studies ↔ Critical Methodologies*, *3*(3), 308–329.

5

HUSSERL'S ETHICS AND SCHIZOPHRENIA[1]

Introduction

In this chapter, I will explore the potential application of Husserl's ethical framework in psychotherapy and psychiatry, specifically focusing on his concept of the volitional body as it relates to time and society. This framework would offer an alternative to the forms of reductionism discussed in the previous chapters. As argued in my previous work (Ferrarello, 2015), Husserl's ethical phenomenology is rooted in the ontology of the volitional body and experienced through practical intentionality. This ethical phenomenology, when considered as a science, provides therapists and psychiatrists with tools to empathetically understand the client's worldview. From a practical perspective, it offers an ethical approach that social workers can adopt to engage more deeply with their clients. These dual aspects of Husserl's ethics—both as a scientific method and an ethical stance—can expand our understanding of how concepts of "normality" or normativity are constructed within society, fostering greater ethical awareness in both social practice and daily interactions.

In the first part of this chapter, I will present an overview of what phenomenological psychopathology writes about schizophrenia. Then, I will draw upon the work of Rogers (1957) and Gendlin (1961a, 1961b, 1962) on schizophrenia to demonstrate the relevance of Husserl's ethics in this context. These scholars emphasize that mental illness often reflects a natural response to a diseased

1 This is modified version of the chapter that was published in Englander, M. (Ed.). (2018). *Phenomenology and the social context of psychiatry: Social relations, psychopathology, and Husserl's philosophy*. Bloomsbury Academic.

DOI: 10.4324/9781003665557-5

environment and that the client's language should take precedence over that of the therapist. From this perspective, effective treatment does not rely on diagnostic labels but rather on the therapist's willingness to engage with the client's ethical environment. Through an empathetic approach that suspends pre-existing ethical judgments, the therapist can explore the client's sense of normality within their own ethical worldview. This approach requires both therapist and client to develop an awareness of their ethical assumptions and understand how these assumptions limit their actions.

In the second part of this chapter, I will delve into Husserl's notion of the volitional body in relation to time and society and discuss how this concept can be utilized in phenomenological practice to avoid reductionism. By examining the temporal and social dimensions of the volitional body, I will illustrate how Husserl's framework offers a valuable lens through which therapists can better understand the lived experiences of their clients, particularly in addressing ethical and existential concerns. This phenomenological approach not only deepens the therapeutic process but also promotes a broader ethical engagement in clinical settings.

Phenomenological Psychopathology on Schizophrenia

Phenomenological psychopathology offers valuable insights into schizophrenia, particularly by focusing on the disruptions in subjective experience. Scholars such as Louis Sass, Josef Parnas, Tudi Gozé, Eugène Minkowski, and Thomas Fuchs have contributed to a nuanced understanding of this condition, emphasizing the profound impact schizophrenia has on one's lived experience of time and selfhood.

Thomas Fuchs, in particular, has emphasized the disordered experience of time as a core feature of schizophrenia. Fuchs (2013) argues that schizophrenia entails a "disruption of temporal structure," leading to a fragmented experience of time. Individuals may feel that time either moves too slowly, too quickly, or is suspended altogether, resulting in a lack of continuity in their subjective experience. This disruption in temporal flow contributes to feelings of alienation from both the self and the external world. Fuchs links this temporal disruption to a disturbance in bodily experience, where patients feel as though their actions are disconnected from the present moment, further intensifying their estrangement from their environment and others.

This view builds on earlier work by Minkowski (1927), who described schizophrenia as involving a "loss of vital contact with reality." He focused on how patients seem detached from the natural flow of life, resulting in a disconnection from time and space. These alterations make it difficult for individuals with schizophrenia to engage spontaneously with their surroundings, leading to a rigid, abstract existence.

Fuchs' analysis, alongside the work of Sass and Parnas (2003), who describe schizophrenia as a disturbance in ipseity or basic selfhood, highlights how phenomenology offers a profound understanding of the disorder's core features. Schizophrenia, in this framework, is not simply defined by hallucinations or delusions but by fundamental disruptions in how patients experience time, space, and selfhood. These existential disruptions create the conditions for the symptomatic manifestations typically associated with the disorder.

Such a phenomenological approach also has significant implications for treatment. Fuchs (2013) suggests that therapy should aim to restore a patient's ability to experience time as a continuous, flowing phenomenon. Traditional symptom-focused approaches might miss these deeper existential disruptions, making it critical to develop therapeutic methods that attend to the patient's subjective experience of time and self.

Ethics in Practice

Spiegelberg's (1972) work on phenomenology and psychiatry provides a valuable exploration of the intersection between these two fields, offering insights into how phenomenology has shaped the understanding and treatment of mental disorders. He highlights a number of thinkers, psychologists, and therapists who have integrated Husserl's phenomenological methods not only to deepen their comprehension of mental illness but also to refine their clinical practices.[2] Among these,

2 Phenomenological psychology and psychiatry first took root in the German-speaking world, primarily through the work of Edmund Husserl's students and collaborators. Figures such as Alexander Pfänder, Max Scheler, Moritz Geiger, and Adolf Reinach extended Husserl's insights into areas such as psychology, affectivity, motivation, and values. Karl Jaspers, while distancing himself from transcendental phenomenology, incorporated phenomenological description into psychiatry in his seminal *General Psychopathology* (1913/1983), emphasizing subjective experience and empathic understanding as central to psychiatric assessment. Ludwig Binswanger, drawing from both Husserl and Heidegger, developed *Daseinsanalyse*, an existential-phenomenological approach that prioritized the patient's being-in-the-world over discrete symptomatology. Meanwhile, Erwin Straus and Viktor von Weizsäcker introduced phenomenology into neurology and medical anthropology, offering richly embodied accounts of perception and illness. Eugène Minkowski, shaped by both Husserl and Bergson, contributed a phenomenology of the lived world, especially in his explorations of temporal disturbance in schizophrenia. Collectively, these thinkers challenged objectivist trends in psychiatry and foregrounded the subjective structures underlying mental illness. In France, phenomenology took on an existential orientation, particularly through the works of Jean-Paul Sartre and Maurice Merleau-Ponty. Sartre, influenced more by Heidegger than Husserl directly, reinterpreted intentionality within an existential-psychoanalytic framework, developing foundational ideas such as the gaze, freedom, and bad faith. Merleau-Ponty's *Phenomenology of Perception* (1945), influenced by *Ideas II* and *The Crisis*, reconceived perception as a pre-reflective, embodied mode of being. His Sorbonne lectures on child psychology and language further expanded phenomenology's psychological dimensions. In French psychiatry, Henri Ey attempted to synthesize phenomenology with neuropsychiatry, while Jacques Lacan—partly through Alexandre Kojève's Hegelian

Gendlin and Rogers are of particular significance for the focus of this chapter. Although they were not directly acquainted with Husserl's ethical manuscripts, Gendlin recognized the ethical dimensions embedded in Husserl's *Logical Investigations* (Spiegelberg, 1972, 155). As shown in the previous chapters, Husserl's phenomenology involves not only an intellectual effort to apprehend the world but also an affective and emotional engagement with it that goes beyond the simplifications of any reductionism. The approaches of Gendlin and Rogers serve as practical examples of how this dual intellectual and affective orientation in Husserl's phenomenology can be effectively applied in clinical settings.

Gendlin and Roger's Client-Oriented Approach

In a 1962 article, Gendlin summarized a study conducted with Rogers on hospital patients diagnosed with schizophrenia, using a client-centered therapeutic

reinterpretations of Husserl and Heidegger—incorporated phenomenological motifs into psychoanalysis. Elsewhere, phenomenology shaped psychiatric and psychological discourse in Italy, the Netherlands, and Latin America. In Italy, figures like Enrico Morselli and Emilio Servadio engaged existential dimensions of therapeutic practice. Dutch psychiatrist H.C. Rümke and others applied phenomenological insights to diagnostic and therapeutic refinement. In Latin America, especially Argentina and Brazil, Husserlian thought intersected with psychoanalytic and existential traditions, deepening reflections on embodiment and subjectivity in clinical contexts. In the United States, the initial reception of phenomenology was largely philosophical, but key figures soon bridged the divide between phenomenology and psychology. William James—though preceding Husserl chronologically—exerted a proto-phenomenological influence that Husserl himself admired, especially for his focus on lived experience and introspection. Conversely, Wilhelm Wundt's followers in America, as Spiegelberg observed, largely missed the philosophical core of Husserl's project. By the mid-20th century, humanistic and existential psychologies became fertile ground for Husserlian ideas. Carl Rogers, in developing client-centered therapy, increasingly aligned his emphasis on empathy and the primacy of subjective experience with phenomenological principles. Rollo May drew explicitly from Binswanger and Heidegger in shaping existential therapy. Eugene Gendlin, a student of Rogers, developed "Focusing," a therapeutic method centered on pre-conceptual felt meaning—arguably a deeply phenomenological concept. Although based in Switzerland, Medard Boss's collaboration with American analysts helped spread *Daseinsanalyse* across the Atlantic. Academic psychology also felt the influence of phenomenology through thinkers such as Aron Gurwitsch, Alfred Schutz, and Amedeo Giorgi. Gurwitsch elaborated a field theory of consciousness grounded in Husserl's unpublished work. Schutz introduced phenomenological concepts into sociology, founding the interpretive paradigm of the social sciences. Giorgi formalized a phenomenological method for psychological research that significantly influenced qualitative studies in psychology, nursing, and education. As Spiegelberg's historical analysis shows, phenomenology did not yield a single "Husserlian psychology," but rather inspired a range of innovative approaches across disciplines and cultures. These included methodological revolutions, privileged description and eidetic insight over reductionism, ontological shifts that recast psychiatry and psychology as sciences of meaningful experience, and therapeutic innovations—from client-centered therapy to existential analysis—firmly grounded in the person's lived world. While Husserl never set out to create a psychology or psychiatry, his call to return "to the things themselves" laid the groundwork for a more reflective, humane, and context-sensitive understanding of mental life, whose legacy continues to unfold across both European and American traditions.

approach. This approach is grounded in three main tenets: first, the focus on cultivating a deep personal relationship with the client, characterized by empathetic understanding; second, the therapist's spontaneity and genuine emotional expressiveness; and third, the recognition of the sub-verbal, affective, and pre-conceptual aspects of communication (Rogers, 1957, 1959a, 1959b). These principles, as Gendlin and Rogers proposed, are not merely therapeutic tools but reflect an underlying ethical stance that guides the therapist in their interactions with the client. For example, a therapist adopting such an approach is ethically required to reflect critically on their assumptions, asking, "Am I engaging with the client's worldview, or am I interpreting their experiences through my unrevised ethical and moral lenses?" Such questions emphasize the importance of suspending through epoché and reduction preconceived notions to ensure that the therapist genuinely connects with the client's subjective experiences without imposing their own biases.

This client-centered approach also highlights that healing is an inherently intersubjective process, where the therapist's private and shared ethical observations significantly influence the client's lived experience (Gendlin et al., 1960). The more self-aware and transparent the therapist is about their assumptions, the greater the potential for the client to explore their emotional experiences. Rogers and Gendlin stress that the therapist's pre-conceptual life—how they unconsciously bring their feelings and assumptions into the therapeutic space—plays as critical a role as their active, verbal communication. By embracing this awareness and communicating genuinely with the client, the therapist creates a trustworthy environment that fosters real empathy and understanding. Gendlin (1961a, 1962) observes that even if a therapist does not always reach deep levels of awareness, the client can often sense the therapist's feelings, making empathy an ongoing, dynamic process rather than a fixed outcome.

Additionally, Gendlin (1961b) identified common reactions among schizophrenic clients, including non-motivation, silence, non-exploration, and intense sub-verbal interaction. These responses, though challenging, require the therapist to maintain genuine engagement and unconditional positive regard, listening to the client's sub-verbal expressions as well as verbal ones. Gendlin and Rogers emphasized that therapists should resist interrupting silences or demanding verbal responses that conform to preconceived therapeutic parameters, which could disrupt the patient's self-expression and inner processing (Betz & Whitehorn, 1956). Instead, they advocate for a more flexible approach, where therapists honor the client's passive and active experiences, understanding that meaningful communication may not always occur through words. This stance emphasizes the importance of recognizing and working with the client's pre-verbal, affective experiences, which can deepen the therapeutic relationship and foster a more comprehensive healing process. In exploring these ideas, I will later address how Husserl's notion of the volitional body and its relation to time and society can provide additional tools for accessing the pre-verbal realm in therapy.

Ethics as a Science

In 1889, Husserl initiated a reflective project aimed at establishing a science of ethics, envisioned as a parallel to the science of logic. Throughout his life, he worked toward integrating logic and ethics as complementary components within the broader framework of phenomenology, where both conceptual and emotional lived experience were regarded as mutually enriching aspects of consciousness (Hua XXVIII). According to Husserl, as articulated in Logical Investigations, Ideas, and later in Crisis, science should be understood as a "unity of foundational connections" (Hua XIX/I, 14; En. tr. 18). This unity demands systematic coherence in a theoretical sense, achieved through grounding knowledge and organizing such foundations in a structured sequence (Hua XIX/1, 14–15; En. tr. 18). For Husserl, this foundational coherence is both emotional and practical, grounded in the notion that life itself represents an organized conceptual order overlaying our felt experiences. Knowledge, in Husserl's framework, emerges from sorting inner feelings and perceptions through temporal and causal relationships, ultimately constructing a unified system of meaning and value.

Husserl positioned ethical science within this larger phenomenological structure, considering ethics to be grounded in what he referred to as an "ontological region"—specifically, the region of the volitional body (Hua XXXI, 478). Just as physics and biology pertain to specific ontological regions of being, ethical science systematically explores human actions, grounding them in what constitutes the essence of action itself. Ethical praxis, in Husserl's view, is thus oriented toward clarifying the meaning inherent in human actions. Consequently, ethics becomes a science of the volitional body, providing methods for elucidating its contents and guiding principles for action.

The challenges identified by Gendlin and Rogers regarding sub-verbal communication, particularly in their third tenet, point directly to the difficulty in accessing the client's volitional body. Pre-verbal lived experience, which forms the scientific basis of Husserl's ethics, is central to understanding the core of client-oriented therapeutic approaches. The volitional body, as Husserl conceptualized it, relates to both action and temporality, offering key ethical insights for living a fulfilling life. These principles include owning one's volitional body and taking responsibility for one's experience of time. In the following sections, I will delve deeper into Husserl's notion of the volitional body and its ethical implications, examining how these principles can inform both philosophical and therapeutic practices.

The Agency of the Volitional Body

In this section, I will discuss the process through which the client becomes the subject of her own body and develops a meaningful relationship with it. Husserl conceptualizes the volitional body as a vital connecting bridge (*verbindende Brücke*, Hua-Mat IV, 186) between nature and spirit, matter and reflection. It functions as the ontological region in which an ego, or subject of actions (*Handlungen*), emerges and engages in creative acts (*poietische Akte*) that generate habits and, consequently, form ethical layers (Hua-Mat IV, 104). This volitional dimension enables the constitution of an ethical subject—an *en-worlded* person who exercises will and makes choices.

By grounding ethical development within the volitional body, Husserl offers a model for understanding how individuals can progressively establish ethical subjectivity through their lived experiences and bodily actions. This process, in turn, shapes how one navigates ethical decision-making and personal responsibility, as the individual is not merely reacting passively to external forces but actively participating in the shaping of their ethical identity. As a result, the volitional body serves as the locus where the convergence of physical, mental, and ethical dimensions of the self occurs, promoting a unified experience of personal agency and responsibility in relation to both self and the surrounding world.

The Layers of the Volitional Body

The volitional body, as Husserl elaborates, is a locus where natural and spiritual aspects intersect. It is through this body that individuals transform themselves from mere physical entities (*Körper*) into ethical agents. The process begins with recognizing the body as a physical object among other objects, a state Husserl refers to as a pre-subjective condition. In *Ideas II* (Hua IV, §36), Husserl describes the physical body as a composite of *hyletic* syntheses—primitive elements of otherness (Hua IV, §44)—on which the unclarified traits of the ego rely. The client, in the studies by Gendlin and Rogers, often inhabits this material, pre-subjective state, struggling to recognize their bodily experiences as truly their own.

This creates a challenge for therapists, as the client's verbal and intentional language can feel artificial and restrained, with the authentic language residing in the unspoken experiences of the body. According to Gendlin and Rogers, the role of the therapist is to facilitate a shift where the client moves from perceiving their body as mere undifferentiated matter to acknowledging it as their own lived body (*Leib*). As Husserl explains in *Cartesian Meditations*, the physical body initially appears as "there-for-me" (*da-für-mich-sein*, Hua I, 124)—an object that can become an instrument of self-awareness but is initially experienced as alien. It is through the therapist's empathetic engagement that the client can bridge the gap between the alienness of their physical body and the sense of ownership over their lived body.

In this dynamic, the therapist's own feelings and responses serve as tools to help the client move beyond the initial shock of recognizing herself as both subject and object. Through this empathetic engagement, the therapist enables the client to re-establish a connection with their body, transforming it from an inanimate object into a subjectively lived experience. Husserl's notion of the *volitional body* becomes central in this process, as it helps frame the transition from bodily alienation to subjective ownership. By fostering awareness of sensations, pain, pleasure, and other embodied experiences, the client begins to reclaim their body as their own, ultimately laying the foundation for ethical subjectivity and meaningful interpersonal connections.

This process is further illuminated by Husserl's distinction between the physical body (*Körper*) and the lived body (*Leib*). As Biceaga (2010) points out, Husserl introduced this distinction to highlight the constitution of objective nature while securing a region of *ownness* within which the subject is intersubjectively constituted. The client's journey toward healing begins when they draw the first boundary between their physical body and their subjective sense of self, leading to a deeper engagement with both their own body and the world around them.

By working with the body's functioning, therapists can help clients awaken their volitional sense of *ownness*. Engaging in physical activities such as exercise, music, or art can be instrumental in facilitating this awakening. As Husserl asserts, the birth of the volitional body marks the moment when an inanimate entity becomes a subject, allowing it to live out its goals in a more awakened and integrated manner (Hua XXXI, 478). Thus, reconnecting with the volitional body not only enhances self-awareness but also fosters the ethical responsibility essential for living a fulfilling life. Losing awareness of our own body is often the first sign of dysfunction, regardless of the level at which it occurs. The foundation of agency, in a way that is ethically coherent with one's own values, is rooted in the emergence of the volitional body—where affection (*Gemüt*) animates what was previously inert, transforming it into a conscious, self-aware subject. This awakening prompts the subject to actively pursue a goal that was previously only experienced at a sub-personal or material level (Hua XXXI, 478).

The Agency of Time

Taking ownership of lived time is fundamental to inhabiting one's lived experience, a process that significantly contributes to psychological and ethical integrity. In phenomenological terms, the challenge of owning one's lived time is a continuous task, much like mastering one's embodied existence. Time is not merely a background condition for our actions but is an intrinsic aspect of lived experience, one that demands constant attention and engagement. In Husserl's framework, this ownership begins with the application of the phenomenological epoché and reduction, through which the stream of experience, often referred to as the "sphere of irritability," becomes accessible (Hua III, §43). This sphere represents a primal layer of experience, where affections, drives, and sensuous tendencies converge, forming the foundation from which the ego emerges.

At this early stage, consciousness exists in an ego-less state where a pre-temporal, undifferentiated flow of experience unfolds. Husserl emphasizes that this original stream of consciousness operates beneath the level of intentional thought and cognitive acts, forming what he calls a "living present" (*lebendige Gegenwart*) (Hua XIV, 45, 301). This living present is the substratum of all experience and serves as the ground from which meaningful experiences arise, functioning as a "creative primal presenting" (Hart, 1992, 25–26). It is this flow that sustains the ongoing intentional activity of the ego, but it is not yet intentional itself. Husserl stresses that this pre-temporal flow is absolute, meaning it exists outside of the ordinary, linear temporality of "befores" and "afters" that typically structure human experience. This foundational layer is not accessible through conventional reflection or explanation because it exists prior to any structured engagement with the world. As such, it remains elusive to the ego until it is brought into alignment with the higher layers of intentional time.

Husserl identifies three layers of temporal experience, each contributing to the overall structure of consciousness. The first layer is a pre-temporal and ego-less stream, the second layer involves immanent experiences such as sensory data and passive synthesis, and the third layer constitutes world-time, the time of intentional acts and lived experience in the world (Hua I, 128). In the third layer, consciousness engages actively with the world, structuring events according to causal sequences and temporal orders. These layers interact to form the basis of one's temporal life, and in a well-integrated individual, they flow together in a more or less harmonious way. However, this harmony is often disrupted in cases of psychological disintegration, as seen in the study of schizophrenic clients by Gendlin and Rogers. Clients with schizophrenia often become stuck between the first and second layers of temporal flow, leading to a breakdown in the continuity of their personal stream of time.

The disruption of temporal experience in such cases illustrates the importance of *practical intentionality*. In Husserl's ethics, practical intentionality links the volitional body with the unfolding of time (Hua VIII, 34; Hua XI, 61; Hua XIV, 172). Practical intentionality refers to the way in which the volitional body of the ego interacts with the flow of hyletic data—sensory and emotional stimuli that form the raw material of experience. In cases where individuals are stuck in the pre-temporal layer, this interaction between the ego and the sensory flow is impaired, preventing them from fully inhabiting their lived time. The result is a sense of alienation from one's own experiences, a feeling that time is slipping away or is disconnected from one's subjective life.

For Husserl, the process of reclaiming ownership of time begins with the ego's decision to engage actively with its own temporal flow. The transition from passive receptivity to active intentionality marks a fundamental shift in the individual's relationship to time. As Husserl explains, this shift involves a movement from a state of "Ichfremd" (alien to the self) to one of full intentional engagement, where the ego takes responsibility for its temporal life (Hua XXXIII, Text 15, 277–278). The individual must confront the pre-temporal, undifferentiated flow of experience and transform it into a coherent stream of lived time through the exercise of will and intentionality. This process, however, is fraught with difficulty, as it requires the individual to navigate the tension between the pre-egoic stream and the intentional acts that constitute world-time.

In the therapeutic context, practical intentionality serves as a crucial tool for helping clients reclaim their sense of time and self. As demonstrated in the work of Gendlin and Rogers, clients who are unable to align their temporal streams often struggle with a loss of selfhood and agency. By guiding clients through the process of reconnecting with their pre-temporal experiences, therapists can help them regain a sense of ownership over their lived time. This involves helping clients move from passive receptivity to active engagement, encouraging them to take responsibility for their temporal existence and the meaning they ascribe to their experiences. The therapist, in this process, must also be attuned to the client's temporal disruptions, using their own practical intentionality to model the process of time ownership for the client.

Thus, practical intentionality provides a framework for understanding how individuals can reclaim their temporal lives and, by extension, their psychological integrity. This reclamation is not a one-time event but an ongoing process that requires constant epoché, reduction, and attention to the flow of experience. As Husserl's ethics suggests, the alignment of the three temporal streams—pre-temporal, immanent, and world-time—is essential for a fulfilling and integrated life. The role of the therapist in facilitating this alignment is crucial, as it helps clients move from a fragmented experience of time to one that is coherent and meaningful. Through this process, clients can begin to see themselves not as passive recipients of time but as active participants in the creation of their own temporal lives.

By taking ownership of their lived time, individuals can achieve a deeper sense of psychological and ethical wholeness, as they align their pre-temporal, sensory experiences with the intentional acts that define their engagement with the world. This process of temporal integration is central to Husserl's ethics and offers valuable insights for psychotherapy and psychiatry.

Existing as a Volitional Body

This section focuses on Husserl's concept of *Daseinswert* (value of being), which is central to understanding how individuals come to fully inhabit and take ownership of their bodies in lived time. I discussed this concept also in Chapters 2 and 9 as it is essential to individuate that point of well-being and ease that the individual feels with their own lives. Literally, the term refers to the value we have in just expressing our existence. Husserl links the concept of *Daseinswert* (value of existence) to practical intentionality, which refers to the way the volitional body instinctively engages with values and performs meaningful actions. This pre-reflective axiological functioning occurs before an individual becomes fully aware of themselves as a reflective subject, yet it remains crucial in the emergence of the "I" as an agent capable of actions and desires (*Ich kann* and *Ich wille*) (Hua-Mat IX, 137–143). At this stage, the human being operates in a self-less, undifferentiated mode, which means that the embodied personhood has not yet been fully claimed by the subject. Through the condition of *Daseinswert*, an individual begins to recognize themselves as an ethical subject, capable of intentional actions and self-directed choices, and thus lays the groundwork for ethical life.

Husserl also describes *Daseinswert* as a "good-value" (*Gutwert*), which refers to the original ontological stratum that exists for us. In therapy, as seen in Gendlin and Rogers' studies, this concept manifests when the therapist allows the client space to recognize their inherent worth as human *beings*. The therapist helps the client discover and inhabit their *Daseinswert* by providing an open space for the client to assume their full humanity and become a subject with the ability to make choices. The *Daseinswert* creates the ethical space for the client to assemble their previously scattered hyletic (sensory) matter into a coherent sense of self. This process is crucial in enabling the client to perceive their existence as meaningful and valuable, laying the foundation for them to take ownership of their lives and the values that guide their actions.

The *Daseinswert*, as an axiological core, calls for the constitution of units of axiological meaning that are fundamental to the individual's ethical development. This process involves the individual's will (*Ich kann* and *Ich wille*) directing bodily and emotional functions toward specific life goals (*Lebensziele*), such as becoming a professional, a parent, or a caregiver. These goals are shaped by the individual's inner vocation (*Beruf*), which is propelled by the affective force of the *Daseinswert* and expressed in action. Husserl emphasizes that the primitive "I can" is essential for the formation of the "I" as an ethical agent and that this foundational moment of being (*Dasein*) is directly connected to the flow of time (Hua-Mat IX, 133). Through full engagement with their embodied experiences and the temporal horizon in which they exist, an individual can become a responsible subject, aware of their ethical potential and guided by their affective drives toward their personal vocation.

In therapy, the therapist's role is to facilitate this transition from dormant, scattered matter to a fully realized, responsible subject. This is achieved by stimulating the client's ethical awakening, helping them recognize the affective force of their organic body, and guiding them toward fulfilling their life's vocation. This therapeutic process is largely pre-verbal, addressing the underlying structures of the self that precede fully articulated subjectivity. By helping the client attend to the affective dimensions of their existence, the therapist enables the individual to assume responsibility for their lived time and lived body, ultimately guiding them toward a more integrated and meaningful life.

The Role of the Society

In this section, I analyze the concept of ownership over body and time in relation to one's community, drawing heavily on the ideas of empathy discussed in Chapter 2, particularly as developed by Edith Stein (1917/1989) and Edmund Husserl. The process of taking ownership of one's lived experience—both of the body and of time—is complicated by the pre-existing interpretations imposed by the community in which an individual lives. This communal influence, while often necessary for social functioning, can cause a disconnection from an authentic sense of self when an individual struggles to align their own experiences with communal norms. Gendlin and Rogers' therapeutic approach emphasizes the role of empathy in bridging this gap between self and community.

Stein's notion of *iterated empathy*, where a person imagines themselves in the position of the other, is pivotal in therapy. The therapist must step into the client's perspective to help them see how their experiences are shaped by their community. Husserl's concept of the natural attitude—where individuals see themselves as part of a community rather than as distinct subjects—underlines the importance of helping clients recognize the influence of their social environments on their personal identity. This natural attitude can sometimes obscure the client's ability to take ownership of their body, time, and being, which Gendlin and Rogers address through the therapeutic relationship.

The concept of *communalization* (*Vergemeinschaftung*) in Husserl's phenomenology describes how an individual may gradually recognize themselves as part of a "we," through a process of *pairing* (*Paarung*), where the individual comes to see the other as both similar and distinct from themselves. This analogy-based apprehension is the basis of Husserl's *harmonious synthesis* (*Einstimmigkeitssynthese*), according to which individuals can experience a coherent sense of self within their community. In Laing's work (1960), this dynamic is critical to understanding the societal roots of mental health disorders like schizophrenia. The community can contribute to, or even be the source of, a client's psychological challenges. In such cases, therapy aims to realign the client's sense of self in relation to a healthier community.

Laing (1960) argued that, in the case of schizophrenia, it is often the community itself that is the root cause of psychological problems attributed to the individual. According to Laing, mental illness can be viewed as a healthy response to a toxic system. Within a dysfunctional family system, the schizophrenic is not seen as an individual who is reacting authentically to their environment but is instead labeled as the sick one. They are considered ill because they do not allow the expected *harmonious synthesis* of the group to occur. Even a healthy person can be perceived as ill if they disrupt this expected synthesis by resisting the roles or norms imposed by the group. In such cases, the individual's stance appears pathological to others because it diverges from the communal expectations.

From a Laingian perspective, it is the alter egos within a toxic environment that contribute to the individual's mental distress. The empathy of a therapist is crucial in helping the client regain a healthy sense of otherness and self. Through empathetic engagement, the therapist enables the client to reconstruct a new sense of self within a community. In particularly harmful family dynamics, such as cases of child abuse, the child may be treated as an object rather than as a sentient human being. This dehumanization exacerbates the psychological distress.

The objective world and the mutual existence of others are achieved through what Husserl called a *harmonious confirmation of an apperceptive constitution.* This means that we understand and relate to others by continuously confirming or adjusting our perception of them through intersubjective experiences. Harmony is maintained when these experiences do not conflict with the larger group's synthesis of reality and aims and when they can be emotionally sustained over time. However, when harmony erases an individual's identity, it creates a pathological system that requires therapeutic intervention to restore healthy relationships. A therapist's role, therefore, is to help re-establish new relational norms within the family system, allowing the client to function more authentically and harmoniously, in line with Husserl's concept of harmonious synthesis.

Additionally, Husserl's concept of *objectivating equalization* (*Gleichstellung*) (Hua I, §56, 129) emphasizes the mutual constitution of the ego and the community. The mutual relations linking the members of a community involve an "objectivating equalization" (Gleichstellung) (Hua I, §56, 129) of the existence of the ego and the others. "I, the ego, have the world starting from a performance (Leistung), in which… constitute myself, as well as my horizon of others and, at the same time (in eins damit), the homogeneous community of 'us' (Wir- Gemeinschaft)"; this constitution is not a constitution of the world, but an actualization which could be designated as "monadization of the 'ego' – as actualization of personal monadization, of monadical pluralization" (Hua VI, 417). The ego, through its actions and performance (*Leistung*), constitutes itself along with its horizon of others and the larger communal framework. This process, which Husserl refers to as the *monadization* of the ego, involves the actualization of the self in relation to others. The therapist's task is to guide this process of actualization, ensuring that the client can establish a more balanced and harmonious function within their social system, thus restoring psychological well-being.

Conclusion

In the first part of this chapter, I explored Gendlin and Rogers' approach, emphasizing its three core tenets. Gendlin highlighted that the third tenet, which pertains to the sub-verbal, affective, and pre-conceptual nature of therapeutic communication (Rogers, 1957, 1959b), presents the most significant challenge. To address this, I utilized Husserl's descriptions of the volitional body, practical intentionality, and the three layers of time to demonstrate how phenomenology can help explore these pre-conceptual, affective dimensions in human relationships.

From a phenomenological perspective, the primary goal of therapy is to encourage the client to recognize themselves as *Daseinswert*—a being with intrinsic value who can take ownership of her body, time, and existence, fully inhabiting the human role made possible by the therapist. The therapeutic process should foster this constitution of *Daseinswert*, allowing the individual's will to find its place within the community of wills (*Willensgemeinschaft*; Hua-Mat IX, 111–114). Of course, this process is often challenged by the structures of the family or political community, much like in Husserl's phenomenology, which views full harmony as an endless pursuit of relative accomplishments.

The broader aim of Husserl's ethics is the continuous clarification of interconnected lives within a community, reawakening the authentic meanings buried in *ego-less* habits (habits performed without conscious intention). A phenomenologically trained therapist should employ practical intentionality to analyze both the passive, ego-less dimensions of personal life and the active meanings that need to be revealed in the client's life. Importantly, therapists must be aware of their own role in this cycle, understanding that their language, expectations, and normative attitudes may unconsciously contribute to the client's difficulties.

Mental illness, in this context, becomes an opportunity for all of us—clinicians, scholars, and individuals—to expand our understanding of normativity and the community's dynamics. Often, society labels "insane" responses to systemic pressures, but as Laing famously argued, it is the system, not the individual, that may be truly pathological. In fact, as Laing suggests, the response of a person suffering from schizophrenia to an insane system may be the most rational. The clinician's task, therefore, is to see these hidden layers of human experience and find the appropriate means—whether through words, actions, or images—to name them, thus helping others recognize what remains unseen.

The concept of *formless matter*, which calls for recognition in an appropriate form, mirrors this therapeutic challenge. Until this form is articulated in the client's life, all forms remain possible yet inconceivable. Mental illnesses represent *formless matter* that demands acknowledgment in new, acceptable forms. They are not necessarily pathological but signal new shapes that require new meanings. Foucault's analysis of the history of madness and conditions once deemed mental illnesses, such as homosexuality, demonstrates the shifting relationship between form and matter in society. The alignment of form and matter that results in emotional and cognitive resonance is often what is labeled as "normal." To attain this, we must cultivate empathy and the capacity to perceive the infinite possibilities within these correspondences.

References

Betz, B., & Whitehorn, J. C. (1956). The relationship of the therapist to the outcome of therapy in schizophrenia. *Psychiatric Research Reports of the American Psychiatric Association*, *5*, 89–106.

Biceaga, V. (2010). *The concept of passivity in Husserl's phenomenology*. Springer.

Englander, M. (Ed.). (2018). *Phenomenology and the social context of psychiatry: Social relations, psychopathology, and Husserl's philosophy*. Bloomsbury Academic.

Ferrarello, S. (2015). *Husserl's ethics and practical intentionality*. Bloomsbury.

Fuchs, T. (2013). The phenomenology of affectivity. In K. W. M. Fulford, M. Davies, R. G. T. Gipps, G. Graham, J. Z. Sadler, G. Stanghellini, & T. Thornton (Eds.), *The Oxford handbook of philosophy and psychiatry* (pp. 612–631). Oxford University Press.

Gendlin, E. T. (1961a). Experiencing: A variable in the process of therapeutic change. *American Journal of Psychotherapy*, *15*, 233–245.

Gendlin, E. T. (1961b). Initiating psychotherapy with 'unmotivated' patients. *Psychiatric Quarterly*, *35*, 134–139.

Gendlin, E. T. (1962). *Experiencing and the creation of meaning*. The Free Press of Glencoe.

Gendlin, E. T., Jenney, R. H., & Shlien, J. M. (1960). Counselor ratings of process and outcome in client-centered therapy. *Journal of Clinical Psychology*, *16*, 210–213.

Hart, J. (1992). The entelechy and authenticity of objective spirit: Reflections on Husserliana XXVII. *Husserl Studies*, *9*, 91–110.

Husserl, E. (1956). *Erste Philosophie (1923/4). Erste Teil: Kritische Ideengeschichte* [First philosophy (1923–24). First part: The critical history of ideas]. The Hague: Martinus Nijhoff (Hua VIII).

Husserl, E. (1960). *Cartesian meditations: An introduction to phenomenology*. D. Cairns (Trans.). The Hague: Martinus Nijhoff. (Original work published 1931) (Hua I).

Husserl, E. (1966). *Analysen zur passiven Synthesis. Aus Vorlesungs- und Forschungsmanuskripten, 1918–1926* [Analyses of passive synthesis. From lectures and research manuscripts, 1918–1926]. M. Fleischer (Ed.). The Hague: Martinus Nijhoff (Hua XI).

Husserl, E. (1970). *The crisis of European sciences and transcendental phenomenology: An introduction to phenomenological philosophy*. D. Carr (Trans.). Evanston, IL: Northwestern University Press. (Original work published 1936) (Hua VI).

Husserl, E. (1973a). *Phänomenologie der Intersubjektivität. Texte aus dem Nachlass. Zweiter Teil. 1921–28*. I. Kern (Ed.). Martinus Nijhoff (Hua XIV).

Husserl, E. (1983). *Ideas pertaining to a pure phenomenology and to a phenomenological philosophy: First book*. F. Kersten (Trans.). Dordrecht: Kluwer Academic Publishers. (Original work published 1913) (Hua III).

Husserl, E. (1984). In U. Panzer (Ed.), *Logische Untersuchungen* [*Logical Investigations*]. Den Haag: Martinus Nijhoff (Hua XIX/1, XIX/2).

Husserl, E. (1988). *Vorlesungen über Ethik und Wertlehre. 1908–1914*. U. Melle (Ed.). Kluwer Academic Publishers (Hua XXVIII).

Husserl, E. (1989). *Ideas pertaining to a pure phenomenology and to a phenomenological philosophy: Second book*. R. Rojcewicz, & A. Schuwer (Trans.). Dordrecht: Kluwer Academic Publishers. (Original work published 1952) (Hua IV).

Husserl, E. (2001a). *Analyses concerning passive and active syntheses: Lectures on transcendental logic*. A. J. Steinbock (Trans.). Dordrecht: Kluwer Academic Publishers (Hua XXXI).

Husserl, E. (2001b). *Die 'Bernauer Manuskripte' über das Zeitbewußtsein (1917/18)* [The 'Bernauer manuscripts' on time-consciousness]. R. Bernet, & D. Lohmar (Eds.). Dordrecht: Kluwer Academic Publishers (Hua XXXIII).

Husserl, E. (2002). *Natur und Geist. Vorlesungen Sommersemester 1919*. M. Weiler (Ed.). Kluwer Academic Publishers (Hua-Mat IV).

Husserl, E. (2012). *Einleitung in die Philosophie. Vorlesungen 1916–1919* [Introduction to philosophy. Lectures 1916–1919]. H. Jacobs (Ed.). Dordrecht: Springer (Hua-Mat. IX).

Laing, R. D. (1960). *The divided self: An existential study in sanity and madness*. Penguin.

Merleau-Ponty, M. (1945). *Phenomenology of perception*. New York: Routledge.

Minkowski, E. (1927). *La schizophrénie: Psychopathologie des schizoïdes et des schizophrènes*. Paris: Payot.

Rogers, C. R. (1957). The necessary and sufficient conditions of therapeutic personality change. *Journal of Consulting and Clinical Psychology, 21*, 95–103.

Rogers, C. R. (1959a). A theory of therapy, personality, and interpersonal relationships as developed in the client-centered framework. In S. Koch (Ed.), *Psychology: A study of a science* (Vol. 3, pp. 184–256). McGraw-Hill.

Rogers, C. R. (1959b). A tentative scale for the measurement of process in psychotherapy. In E. A. Rubinstein, & M. B. Parloff (Eds.), *Research in psychotherapy* (pp. 96–107). American Psychological Association.

Sass, L. A., & Parnas, J. (2003). Schizophrenia, consciousness, and the self. *Schizophrenia Bulletin, 29*(3), 427–444.

Spiegelberg, H. (1972). *Phenomenology in psychology and psychiatry*. Northwestern University Press.

Stein, E. (1989). *On the problem of empathy*. W. Stein (Trans.). ICS Publications. (Original work published 1917).

6

THE CRISIS OF MEDICAL SCIENCES AS A CRISIS OF MEANING

Introduction

I run a small YouTube channel where I post videos on various philosophical topics. One of my videos, an interview with James Giordano on neuroethics, gained significant attention and sparked thoughtful engagement from viewers. One comment, in particular, caught my eye:

> In my experience, when it comes to medical issues, those who talk about 'ethics' or identify as 'ethicists' are almost always on Team Anti-Human.

I found myself relating to this sentiment, as I have experienced it too—even though I am often positioned as the ethicist within bioethics and medical humanities. When ethics and science intersect, we often lose sight of the human beings who should be the central focus of our efforts. This raises several important questions, which will guide the theoretical exploration of this and the following chapters.

How often does it happen that the science meant to help us feel better and stronger actually makes us feel more vulnerable and insecure? How many times has science been used as a justification for cruel persecutions, as seen in the case of eugenics or the Tuskegee experiments? How did we reach the point where the immense progress of science mismatched with the wisdom we can apply to make sense of our lives? In this chapter, I will use Husserl's phenomenology to trace the divide that has grown between science and human life. At some point, human life and science stopped working in mutual aid in the process of meaning-making. Science became the primary tool for technological expansion,

DOI: 10.4324/9781003665557-6

and in doing so, human beings became objects of use rather than the inventors of their own future. Human beings were reduced to objects of sacrifice in the name of scientific progress.

This chapter will explore the widening gap between humanity and science, truth and utility, and meaning and function. While I fully believe in the progress and achievements of science, I also think we can improve in connecting scientific advancements with a deeper understanding of human lives, particularly when it comes to promoting societal well-being. Drawing on Husserl's later philosophy, with its focus on the lifeworld, intersubjectivity, and empathy, this chapter will shed light on the crisis of modern science and its implications for clinical practice. First, I will discuss Husserl's biography in the later years of his life to illustrate how his personal experiences intertwined with his philosophical message. Next, I will examine his critique of Western science and its effects on human well-being. Lastly, I will explore the implications of his ideas for clinical practice.

Concluding Notes on Husserl's Life

After retiring in 1928, Edmund Husserl faced increasing political and personal challenges, particularly as the political landscape in Europe shifted. Despite these challenges, Husserl continued his philosophical work while translations of his major works, including *Ideas*, were underway in English-speaking countries. During this period, Husserl deepened his phenomenological investigations—especially into empathy and intersubjectivity—examining how the Other is given in first- and second-person experience. In 1933, the rise of the National Socialist Party brought new restrictions. That April, a law was passed re-establishing a civil service that excluded non-Aryans from state careers. Husserl, who was of Jewish descent, was directly impacted by these laws.

In 1934, Husserl was not allowed to attend the International Congress of Philosophy in Prague due to these political developments. Despite his exclusion, he sent a paper to be read on his behalf, which was given more time than initially allotted, reflecting the enduring respect for his intellectual contributions. Later that year, in May, Husserl undertook private lecture trips to Prague and Vienna, meeting with influential figures such as Martin Buber, Ernst Cassirer, Thomas Mann, and Jan Patočka. Despite the political drawback, these intellectual engagements point to his ongoing commitment to "the burning need for an understanding of the Spirit." (Husserl, 1994, 481–482).

By 1937, Husserl had reworked much of the material from these trips and his ongoing reflections into what would become The Crisis of European Sciences. This seminal work was partially published in the journal Philosophia in Belgrade, though the final sections remained unpublished due to Husserl's declining health. Sadly, he fell ill and passed away before completing this work.

In 1935, just a few years before his death, Husserl's teaching license was revoked, an event that profoundly affected him. The *Kronik* records that this felt "like a bomb on his life" (Schuhmann, 1977, 467).

Following his death, Husserl's student Eugen Fink and father Herman van Breda, took great measures to preserve his philosophical legacy. Van Breda, in particular, played a critical role in rescuing Husserl's manuscripts from potential destruction under Nazi rule, ensuring that Husserl's contributions to phenomenology would survive for future generations.

Philosophy and the Crisis

As previously mentioned, *Philosophy and the Crisis of European Man* is an essay that was read aloud at a conference in Prague, which Husserl was not permitted to attend due to his race. These pages can be viewed as a testament to Husserl's work in phenomenology, as they revisit many of the key themes he explored throughout his career. For the sake of brevity, I will focus on the themes of the crisis of science and the concept of *Lebenswelt* (the lifeworld), which serve as a fitting conclusion to the conceptual overview of Husserl's work presented thus far. It is important to note, however, that these themes are grounded in earlier discussions of sense, its distinction from expression and language, and Husserl's critique of reductionism (whether in the form of logicism, psychologism, anthropologism, historicism, or naturalism). In addition, they emphasize the need for a deeper understanding of empathy, intersubjectivity, the structure of time, and the teleology of history.

Husserl's Review of the History of Science through Philosophy and Its Application to Clinical Work

The crisis of Western science, as Husserl observed in his presentation, remains as relevant today as it was then. The science that lays the foundation of our medicine is, according to Husserl, itself in a state of illness. The "well-known distinction between scientific medicine and naturopathy" (1965, 149) is an expression of this crisis and points to a deeper dichotomy within science. Weber, in 1922, had already highlighted the root of the problem, focusing on the lack of a unified meaning for science in relation to the human spirit. However, unlike Weber, Husserl remained optimistic. He believed that if we could trace the history of science back to the point where it became "ill," then philosophy could help heal science and restore its meaning for humanity. For Husserl, technological advancements alone cannot satisfy the profound human craving for meaning, and he passed away shortly before eugenics reached the height of its ethical atrocities.

In his critique of the history of science (1956), Husserl focuses on figures like Plato, Galileo, Descartes, and Kant, particularly in their dialogue with Hume.

In this analysis, Husserl demonstrates with great clarity how theoretical knowledge, which underpins the universal application of science, has led to a kind of mythical culture. This culture, he argues, distances human beings from the generation of meaning and purpose in life, especially in fields like medicine, where science has become overly mechanized.

Husserl emphasizes that the theoretical aspect of science has transformed its subjects into inanimate objects. The Greek *theorein*—the contemplation of the world's wonders—was originally meant to serve human beings, enabling them to live better lives, free from sickness, misfortune, and death (1965, 11). Yet, over time, this knowledge experienced a "sharp cleavage" (1965, 12) that separated *theorein* (contemplation) from *praxein* (action), and *episteme* (scientific knowledge) from *doxa* (opinion). Science and life became distinct, disconnected worlds, with science focusing on an objectivity that ultimately reduced the human being to an object within its framework.

I will briefly pause Husserl's review of the history of science to highlight the crucial significance of this distinction in contemporary clinical practice. This distinction between science and life is particularly relevant to clinical practice, where the gap between the objective, scientific understanding of disease and the subjective, lived experience of illness becomes evident (Carel, 2008, 2011, 2016; Toombs, 2001). In healthcare, the separation between *episteme* (interpreted as objective knowledge) and *doxa* (subjective opinion) can manifest in the way patients are treated: as biological objects rather than as human beings with unique, meaningful experiences of illness. The first-hand accounts patients provide about their symptoms or illness are often dismissed as bothersome interruptions that complicate the scientific evaluation of their condition. Husserl's phenomenological perspective calls for a reintegration of these two worlds, where clinicians take into account not just the objective data but also the patient's lived experience.

As modern science progressed, Husserl argues, it lost the connection to *aletheia*—the Greek notion of truth. For the Greeks, *aletheia* was a truth embedded in lived experience, a truth that could never be fully captured because of its dynamic, living roots. In contrast, modern science began to view truth as an ideal, an unreachable form separate from human experience (Husserl, 1965, 7). This shift led to the belief that human beings, with their subjective perspectives, could contaminate this ideal objectivity. Hence, scientific knowledge began to be regarded as abstract and detached from human beings. In this shift, Plato's notion of truth as *methexis*—a participation in the ideal—was lost. Whereas in Plato's view, the imperfection of the material world still allows for a partial participation in ideal forms—much like how circular objects partake in the essence of circularity—this new perspective treats any such participation as inherently disrupting the exactness of meaning. The imperfection of the real world distorts and contaminates the pure essence of the ideal form, preventing them from fully embodying the truth of the form. Science became detached from real life, adopting numbers and geometrical forms as its objective language. The scientific revolution initiated by Galileo placed truth as an objective construction, an ideal independent of human subjectivity.

In that sense, Husserl calls Galileo "the genius that discovers and conceals" (1970b, 51), because while Galileo attempted to establish an objective foundation for science, he also initiated a reductionistic approach. Galileo wrote during a time when much ancient and progressive knowledge had been lost—particularly following the destruction of the Library of Alexandria. Consider, for example, that Aristarchus of Samos had already proposed a heliocentric model of the universe as early as 310 BCE.

In the aftermath, monasteries and churches became the primary centers of literacy, with the Bible emerging as the dominant source of natural and supernatural knowledge. The scientific endeavors of figures like Bruno, Kepler, and Galileo aimed to carve out a space for knowledge independent of religious doctrine. Up to that point, subjects such as law, physics, medicine, and logic found their theoretical foundations in biblical teachings. In *The Assayer* (1623/1957), Galilei diplomatically explores the distinct spheres of influence between religion and science, the church and universities, and meaning and fact. He argues that nature communicates through a language decipherable via mathematical symbols and comprehensible through physical and geometrical forms. Galilei thus articulates a framework in which science investigates the natural world through methods distinct from those of theology, while the spiritual sphere of meaning and values remains the domain of the latter.

Even though Galilei's goal was to carve out a space for science independent of religious authority, he reduced the complexity of nature by equating its essence with the language used to describe it—mathematics and geometry.[1] As we saw in the first and fourth chapters, its complexity was reduced to the symbols we employ to refer to it. This reductionism can still be seen today in clinical practice, where the complexity of human health is often reduced to measurable metrics, like lab results or imaging scans, without taking into account the patient's subjective experience. While metrics are certainly important, we cannot think to fix medical problems without calling into question the actual life of the individual suffering from a certain disease. Life and its understanding are deeply intertwined; the tools we use to address problems should never overshadow the lived experience of the individual.

As we already mentioned in Chapter 4, Husserl criticizes this reductionistic approach, arguing that technology and scientific reasoning have come to dominate, transforming human understanding into a tool that is valued only when it is useful. As he explains in his *Prolegomena*, technology is only one layer of science, not the whole of it (1970a, 38). However, modern science has reduced itself to a technology, severing the Greek connection between *aletheia* (truth) and the pre-scientific world, or the world of lived experience, where any participation (*methexis*) with the truth is not only possible but ever required. In clinical settings, this means that the healing process becomes mechanistic, focusing on the body as an object rather than a lived experience. For instance, consider the increasing challenges surrounding breast cancer screening (Sidek et al., 2023). Although mammograms are an essential tool for the early detection of breast cancer, contributing to women's health and longevity, they can be difficult to interpret. Frequently, they result in false positives, leading women to undergo additional, often invasive procedures such as biopsies, fine needle aspirations, or tomosynthesis, as well as more frequent mammogram screenings. This can cause significant anxiety, which may deter women from attending these routine screenings, potentially leading to greater harm in their daily lives than the benefits offered by the exam (Sidek et al., 2023). As Ekpo and colleagues (2018) emphasize, mammogram errors cannot be resolved solely through technological advancements. Women's health requires a more holistic approach that goes beyond diagnostic tools and their interpretation. To restore a holistic view of health, clinicians must reconnect with the subjective, meaningful experiences of their patients, allowing them to generate new meanings and purposes in their lives.

Husserl's insight that "Opiates suppress the symptoms; they do not cure the disease" (1970b, section 2) is a critique that extends to modern medicine. Medicine, like science, risks becoming fact-minded, addressing symptoms without understanding or addressing the deeper human experience of illness. As Husserl writes, "European nations are sick and European sciences are sick" (1970b, 6) because they lack the understanding of nature's full scope, which includes both pre-scientific and scientific perspectives. Modern science has forgotten the human behind the science, reducing individuals to objects within the framework of technology and objective fact. "Merely fact-minded sciences make merely fact-minded people" (1970b, 6). If human health is reduced to mere numbers, it would become increasingly difficult for individuals to have agency over their own well-being, as humans are not just data points. This detachment could lead to a sense of alienation from one's health and body, with people feeling disconnected from the tools and processes designed to help them maintain well-being. In such a scenario, pseudo-sciences may gain traction, offering false solutions to serious illnesses like cancer, exploiting the gap left by an overly mechanistic approach to healthcare.

Husserl's work encourages a return to a holistic understanding of the human being, not just as a biological entity but as a person with subjective experiences that provide meaning. As the phenomenological approach to psychopathology shows (Fuchs, 2012; Stanghellini & Rosfort, 2013), rather than focusing solely on symptoms or biological dysfunctions, clinicians are called to consider the patient's lived experience, which includes emotions, relationships, and personal narratives. By integrating both objective and subjective perspectives, clinicians can offer more compassionate and effective care, fostering a healing environment that addresses not just the body but the whole person.

Should Truth Be Useful? The Utilitarian Principle

A fact-driven science produces fact-driven people, where utility becomes the guiding principle for evaluating scientific effectiveness. In this view, "truth must be useful, but not necessarily meaningful." Facts are only valuable insofar as they serve progress, which itself is oriented toward the next practical milestone. Modern science often suggests that human beings, like their sciences, must serve a purpose. Talents and abilities are valued only if they are deemed useful, and if not, they are considered to have no worth. This becomes problematic when "use" is equated with "profit," leading to the devaluation of anything related to the humanities, as it is often seen as unprofitable. Consequently, we continue to witness the crisis facing the humanities across various fields. What cannot be easily quantified or measured becomes difficult to transform into a profitable technology, thus diminishing its perceived value and utility. Knowledge, *episteme*, and *aletheia* (truth) are reduced by the logic of reductionism to mere measurements that render them ready for human use. When "the human being loses faith in reason" (Husserl, 1970b, 9), they also lose faith in the possibility of meaningful progress. Consider the increasing reliance on technology in medical practice and the corresponding decline in education focused on the humanities. Doctors are required to complete more and more online forms for each patient, to the extent that their attention often shifts away from the patient to focus, then, on the digital technology. The medical encounter between doctor and patient often happens with the doctor staring at the screen to gather all the information they need. This is problematic because professional liability now relies heavily on what is documented in these forms, while meaningful connections and medical progress often stem from direct interactions with the patient. Given that human energy is finite, it is reasonable to assume that this shift comes at the expense of doctors' ability to exercise empathetic presence toward their patients. This, in turn, creates a sense of detachment and carelessness, which ultimately benefits no one.

Galileo, and later Descartes, contributed to the formation of reductionism, in both its naturalistic and scientistic forms, which became a dominant system in modern thought. Both thinkers, according to Husserl, neglected the constitutive role of the transcendental ego, which is deeply rooted in the *Lebenswelt* (life-world) and fundamental to the generation of meaning. Descartes' system, with its separation of *res cogitans* and *res extensa* (mind and body) connected through the pineal gland, attempted to rationalize the division between the natural sciences and the human sciences that Galileo had first theorized.[2]

In *Science as a Symbolic Construction of Man* (1948), Hermann Weyl, a mathematician influenced by Husserl's critiques, refers to this separation as "the ridiculous circle" (1948, 56). Weyl critiques science for becoming empty of meaning, noting that philosophy, which Carr argues should function as a "community itself" (1948, 97), has been relegated to the role of cheerleader for science. The symbols used by science to explain reality—such as the discovery of DNA's double helix by Watson and Crick—offer little insight into the mystery of individual human lives, despite revealing significant biological information.

As Paci aptly states, "Nature is in itself what it is and is in itself mathematical no matter how much we know of mathematics" (1972, 264–265), but human beings are more than mathematical symbols. The attempt to explain the mystery of life solely through these scientific symbols leads to alienation (*Verdinglichung*), as human beings become disconnected from their *telos* (purpose), their personal story, and their role in the unfolding history of the world. The human subject is no longer seen as a meaningful contributor to the layers of sense that constitute the lifeworld; instead, they become reified in the language used to describe the technological application of being, whether through mathematics, geometry, or physics.

Husserl reminds us in the *Logical Investigations* that theoretical knowledge is distinct from technological application; *episteme* (knowledge) is not the same as *doxa* (opinion), and *aletheia* (truth) is not the same as *praxis* (action). Maintaining these polarities is essential because it is in the oscillation between them that meaning and a sense of purpose emerge, illuminating our lives. Bending concepts of worth and value to the utility they can offer leads to oversimplifications and impoverishes our lives.

In medicine, psychiatry, and clinical practice, the reduction of science to mere utility and fact can be particularly harmful. When human beings are treated as objects for clinical management, the deeper sense of healing, which is connected to their lived experience, is often neglected. European sciences, as Husserl states, are in crisis because human beings are no longer fulfilling their *telos*. The truths that animate life are reduced to facts—often financial or practical—that must be immediately useful. As a result, ethics in clinical practice risks becoming narrowly focused on the maintenance of utility rather than on the meaningful pursuit of health and well-being. In the pursuit of maintaining utility, the quality of service unexpectedly declines rather than improves, leaving us with a sense of betrayal that we are not adequately equipped to understand. Consider, for example, in Western countries, the crisis of emergency departments (ERs) closing (Duong, 2022) and the resulting challenges for doctors, clinicians, and nurses in providing care to those in crisis. Driven by profit-oriented logic, hospitals located in competitive markets or within a 15-mile radius of each other are shutting down. Furthermore, specialized doctors, who are more costly, are increasingly being replaced by nurse practitioners (Razavi et al., 2020), who, while skilled, cannot fully meet the demands of an underfunded ER lacking sufficient investment in personnel. Although this may seem like an efficient and convenient solution to manage societal health, it ultimately costs the healthcare system more in time and money.[3] The ERs still open are overcrowded and underfunded. A growing number of individuals in need of specialized care do not receive timely and adequate treatment. As a result, people feel betrayed by a system that becomes increasingly alienating.

This reductionism affects the very practice of healthcare professionals. Instead of fostering a reflective and empathetic approach, professionalism is often reduced to the blind application of guidelines, with professionals becoming detached and impersonal in their roles. Empathy, where it is allowed, is reduced to a mechanical form of mirroring the other, severed from the roots of the *Lebenswelt* (Englander, 2023; Englander & Ferrarello, 2022). This results in a healthcare system that operates on an unquestioned and naïve foundation, failing to engage with the deeper existential and ethical dimensions of care. Thus, truth becomes reduced to a mathematical or geometrical construct, with its ethical purpose largely tied to maintaining utility. In this practical application of science, there is little room for questioning or critical reflection. By embracing a more phenomenological approach, clinicians can reconnect with the lived experience of their patients, restoring the balance between the scientific and the human aspects of medical practice. This would allow for more meaningful patient interactions, where the goal is not merely utility but a deeper understanding of the patient's experience and an ethical commitment to their well-being.

Our Current Crisis

These premises lead inevitably to a crisis, much like the use of the term by Kant in his *Critique of Pure Reason.* The Greek word *krisis* refers to the Greek verb *krinein*, meaning "to judge" or "to decide" in front of a bifurcation; this highlights the necessity of making a choice while evaluating the limits of reason and its application to human life. If the guiding truths of our lives are reduced solely to empirical facts, then everything becomes "true," and those who speak the loudest are considered more "true" than others. This leads to a fragmented world where, for example, we rely on fact-checkers to navigate the chaos of information.

The problem of infinity, which Husserl left unresolved in *Philosophy of Arithmetic*, becomes even more urgent in this context. He argues that "objective truth is never explicable in itself" but rather emerges from an *Ur-evidenz* (a foundational self-evidence) that demands a transformation in human attitude to perceive it (Husserl, 2003, section 34). To overcome this crisis, we must return to the original sense of this living *Ur-Evidenz*, expressed as "the self-evidence of the I am" (Husserl, 1970b, 13). As Husserl states in *Logical Investigations*, section 29, "only transcendental phenomenology can solve the great riddle of the correlation between being and consciousness" (1970b, 40). This is why Husserl had to move beyond the impasse presented in his first volume of *Ideas*. Returning to "the things themselves" cannot mean returning to a static picture that can be disassembled into its parts. Instead, it involves engaging with the world as it is lived: "what is actually first is the merely subjective-relative intuition of a prescientific life-world" (Husserl, 1970b, section 34a). For example, Wittgenstein's use of the Jastrow duck/rabbit shows how the combination of experience and stimuli is essential in the process of meaning-making. Our life is the *Ur-evidenz* that in every living point opens a horizon of anticipations and expectations that are fulfilled through our experience. The world is the pre-given unitary horizon (Husserl, 2014, section 68) or noematic framework of sense against which we constitute and generate the sense and validity of what is (Husserl, Ms BII, 9).

The *Lebenswelt* (lifeworld), or the mundane, lived experience of the subject, is the prerequisite for our ability to come back to "the things themselves." In this lived engagement, we function as embodied beings. This is why Husserl's phenomenology is both static and genetic. The term "genetic" comes from the Greek *gignomai*, meaning mainly these three verbs: "to be born, to become, or to be." In perceiving the essence of a phenomenon, we not only observe its being but also how it transforms through our interaction with it. Our perspective and engagement are integral to this process of becoming.

For clinical practice, psychiatry, and medicine, this understanding of a dynamic, lived interaction between subject and world is essential. Clinicians need to recognize that patients' experiences are not static or reducible to symptoms or diagnoses. Instead, each patient's lived experience and subjective world are constantly evolving through interaction with their environment, relationships, and inner states (Oben, 2020). This dynamic approach opens up a more holistic understanding of mental health, where the aim is not just to treat symptoms but to restore meaning, agency, and coherence in the patient's lifeworld.

Lebenswelt

The concept of *Lebenswelt*,[4] or lifeworld, serves as the antidote to the crisis of European sciences. Husserl used this term in various ways (e.g., *Geistige Welt* [spiritual world], *Umwelt* [surrounding world], *Heimwelt* [home-world], *Interessenwelt* [world of interest], *Allwelt* [all-world], *Welthorizont* [world-horizon], *Weltvenichtung* [annihilation of the world], and *Verweltichung* [in-worlding]) to highlight its importance in giving meaning to our lives.

In medicine and psychiatry, the *Lebenswelt* can guide a more empathetic and holistic approach to care. For instance, when treating trauma or chronic illness, acknowledging the patient's lifeworld—their relationships, values, and the meaningful context in which they experience health and illness—is critical to effective treatment. The collapse of someone's lifeworld, such as after a traumatic event or the death of a loved one, can severely impact their ability to make sense of their experiences and reconstitute their identity. A lifeworld collapse occurs when a person's previously coherent framework of meaning, trust, and embodied routine is shattered, leaving them unable to orient themselves meaningfully within their world. This collapse can be temporal (loss of continuity), spatial (loss of anchoring), intersubjective (loss of recognition), or affective (loss of motivational tone).

Compelling cases on this point are found in Holocaust survivors, such as those documented in the works of Viktor Frankl (*Man's Search for Meaning*, 1959), where the death of loved ones and the extreme trauma of concentration camps often led to a collapse of their lifeworld. Survivors struggled to find meaning and identity in a world that had profoundly changed, often requiring a deep existential reconstitution of self in order to make sense of their altered realities. No matter how advanced medical tools may be in addressing specific issues, the collapse of a person's lifeworld often creates a deeper wound that requires more care and attention. Similarly, today, for example, the so-called Ulysses Syndrome (Ferrarello, 2021), which affects refugees and immigrants forced to leave their countries under distress, often leads to the development of chronic conditions that cannot be adequately addressed through a solely biochemical approach with medication (Essex, 2005). A Holocaust survivor or refugee with Ulysses Syndrome or a CPTSD survivor may report that "the world no longer feels real." This is not a delusion but a breakdown in the basic, taken-for-granted structure of experience. Similarly, a mother experiencing postpartum psychosis might describe feeling "outside of time" or unable to connect with the baby. These are examples of lifeworld collapse: when the ordinary world loses its familiarity, coherence, and sense.

Husserl's focus on *Lebenswelt* highlights the importance of understanding a patient's embeddedness in their world. This is not merely about treating biological symptoms but about addressing how patients find meaning in their experiences, relationships, and life goals. In psychiatric care, this approach encourages practitioners to understand mental health not just as a set of symptoms but as disruptions in how individuals engage with and make sense of their world. The patient's lifeworld, including their sense of time, relationships, and environment, forms the backdrop against which healing can occur. Husserl also connects *Lebenswelt* to time as a lived experience. As shown in the previous chapters, time, for Husserl, is not a static series of moments but a living present that opens a horizon of presence in the world. This temporal understanding is vital in clinical settings where patients often experience time differently—such as in depression, trauma, or terminal illness. Patients' perceptions of time may become fragmented or distorted, and recognizing this can aid in providing compassionate care that addresses not just the physical but also the existential dimensions of their suffering (Kidd and Carel, 2017; Toombs, 1990). For example, Toombs' notion of the temporality of illness is deeply influenced by Husserl's understanding of time and emphasizes the subjective experience of time that is drastically altered when a person becomes ill. In her work, Toombs (1990) explores how illness creates a distinct rupture in the patient's temporal experience, contrasting the linear, objective time of medical professionals with the lived time of the patient. For the patient, illness can result in a sense of "frozen" or slowed time, where the future becomes uncertain and plans are disrupted. Time is no longer experienced as a continuous flow but can feel fragmented or suspended. This disruption in temporal continuity reflects the existential impact of illness, where life is no longer predictable, and the patient's previous sense of self and future is often put into question. Toombs contrasts this with the time experienced by healthcare professionals, which is governed by schedules, treatment timelines, and measurable outcomes. The mismatch between the patient's subjective time and the professional's objective time can lead to miscommunication and a lack of understanding in the clinical encounter. Toombs argues that understanding the temporality of illness from the patient's perspective is crucial for healthcare providers. By recognizing that patients may experience time differently due to their illness, clinicians can foster a more compassionate and empathetic approach to care.

Intersubjectivity and Empathy in Clinical Practice

Husserl's exploration of intersubjectivity, the way in which we experience others as subjects like ourselves, provides an essential framework for empathy in clinical practice. Empathy, for Husserl, is not merely about reflecting or mirroring the emotions of others but involves deeply engaging with the lived experience of another person. In clinical settings, particularly in nursing and psychiatric care, this kind of empathy is crucial for building trust, understanding patients' subjective experiences, and offering care that is attuned to their needs (Yegdich, 1999).

Intersubjectivity also becomes a neutral metaphysical space where layers of meaning are generated. This neutral space allows for a more nuanced understanding of a patient's experience, where clinicians can navigate between the objective facts of medical science and the subjective realities of patients' lived experiences (Uljée, 2023). The clinician's role is not simply to apply standardized treatments but to co-construct meaning with the patient in a way that honors their lifeworld, experiences, and personal history.

When the lifeworld collapses—such as during trauma or the experience of grief—the sense of self, identity, and purpose can become destabilized. In these situations, the clinician's task is to help the patient rebuild their lifeworld by recognizing and validating the patient's experiences and guiding them toward healing through understanding, empathy, and meaningful engagement with their world. This process is central to effective psychiatric care, nursing, and bioethics, as it focuses not just on physical symptoms but on restoring a sense of coherence and meaning in the patient's life.

Levels of Self-Constitution: The Lived Body and the Lifeworld

Another level on which the consideration of the live-world is important is the understanding of our self-constitution in relation to our lived body. Self-constitution refers to the basic, pre-reflective awareness we have of ourselves. In everyday experiences, our sense of self is "given" through our interactions with other people and objects. As subjective beings, we engage with the world, reacting to stimuli and being passively affected by our environment. Cognitive research often attributes schizophrenic symptoms, such as thought insertion or hearing voices, to malfunctions in the brain's self-monitoring mechanisms (Frith, 1992). However, Husserl's phenomenology shows that pre-reflective self-awareness is not secondary to experience but is central to embodied perception. Husserl explains that objects and people exist within a self-centered framework, structured by factors like gravity and kinesthesia (Husserl, 2014, 144–161).

This idea is rooted in the distinction between *Leib* (the lived body) and *Körper* (the physical body) discussed already in the previous chapters. While the physical body is viewed from a third-person perspective and treated as an object, the lived body is experienced from a first-person perspective, through sensations such as pain, pleasure, and agency. This distinction is crucial in clinical practice, as it helps healthcare professionals grasp patients' experiences from their perspective, particularly when dealing with conditions like chronic pain or mental health disorders that disrupt their sense of self and agency (Straus, 1969).

Research following Husserl has expanded on these ideas, addressing aspects such as the sense of agency, ownership, emotional sensibility, and tactile experience (Fuchs, 2013; Jaspers, 1959; Merleau-Ponty, 1942; Ratcliffe, 2008; Scheler, 1980; Schneider, 1950). These insights have proven valuable in understanding the psychopathology of selfhood (Stanghellini, 2006), as those we will explore in the remaining chapters. For instance, Josef Parnas, Dan Zahavi, and their colleagues have developed the EASE (Examination of Anomalous Self-Experience) tool to measure disruptions in self-experience in patients at risk for schizophrenia (Parnas et al., 2005; Zahavi, 2000). This tool enables clinicians to capture disturbances in self-experience, enhancing their understanding of mental health conditions.

Conclusion

In this chapter, we explored the growing disconnection between human life and science, focusing on the tension between truth and utility, meaning and function, as illuminated by Husserl's later philosophy. Husserl's notions of the lifeworld (Lebenswelt), intersubjectivity, and empathy offer profound insights for understanding the crisis in modern science and its implications for clinical practice, medicine, and psychopathology.

Husserl critiques the fact-driven orientation of modern science, arguing that its focus on utility neglects the human experience and the generation of meaning. This reductionist approach to science, where "truth must be useful," leads to the objectification of both humans and their sciences. In clinical practice, this is reflected in the treatment of patients as objects of biological measurement, rather than as whole beings with subjective experiences. This utilitarian principle flattens reason, *episteme* (knowledge), and *aletheia* (truth) into mere measurements that ignore the deeper, lived realities of human existence.

The crisis of science, as Husserl identified, stems from its detachment from the lifeworld, the pre-scientific domain of lived experience. In clinical settings, this manifests as the gap between the objective data of medicine and the subjective experience of patients. Husserl's work calls for the reintegration of these two perspectives, advocating for an approach to healthcare that considers both the objective and subjective dimensions of illness.

His insights on temporality, particularly the subjective experience of time in illness, provide valuable frameworks for understanding the disruption of temporal continuity in patients' lives. This is especially relevant in conditions like chronic illness, trauma, or terminal disease, where patients' lived time diverges from the objective time of medical practice. By acknowledging these subjective experiences, clinicians can offer more empathetic, personalized care that addresses the existential dimensions of health.

Husserl's exploration of intersubjectivity further emphasizes the importance of empathy in clinical practice. Empathy, as Husserl presents it, goes beyond mere reflection; it involves deeply engaging with another's lived experience. This is crucial in therapeutic and nursing settings, where establishing meaningful, empathetic connections can help patients rebuild a fragmented sense of self, especially in cases of mental health disorders. The discovery of mirror neurons supports this phenomenological perspective, underscoring the biological and psychological significance of empathy in social interaction and patient care.

In conclusion, Husserl's philosophy offers a vital critique of the reductionism prevalent in modern science and medicine, advocating for a more holistic approach that considers the subjective, lived experience of individuals. His work provides valuable insights for clinicians, psychiatrists, and bioethicists, encouraging them to balance the objective demands of science with the ethical and existential needs of their patients. By embracing a phenomenological perspective, healthcare professionals can bridge the gap between fact and meaning, offering more compassionate and effective care that honors the full complexity of human experience.

Notes

1 In *The Origin of Geometry*—much like in his earlier work on *Philosophy of Arithmetic*—Husserl critiques the reductionist use of geometry and, more broadly, mathematics to explain the being of the world as an object independent of human experience.

2 An anecdote illustrates the enduring influence of Descartes' dualistic system. When Descartes traveled to Sweden at the insistence of the queen, he brought with him a wooden automaton named Francine, a replica of his daughter, whom he had lost a few years earlier.

3 While employing NPs is often viewed as a cost-saving measure, studies indicate that this substitution may lead to higher overall expenses. Research published by the American Medical Association found that care provided by NPs in EDs resulted in a 7% increase in costs per patient, approximately $66 more than physician-provided care. Additionally, increasing the number of NPs to reduce wait times raised total healthcare spending by 15%, or $238 per case, excluding additional NP salaries (Chan, D. C., Jr., & Chen, Y. [2022]. *The productivity of professions: Evidence from the emergency department* [Working Paper No. 30608]. National Bureau of Economic Research. https://doi.org/10.3386/w30608).

4 The lifeworld became a crucial concept in the 1950s and 1960s that Heidegger used to explain the being in the world as Existenz or Merleau-Ponty as *monde vivre* or hermeneutics as communicative speech. Husserl's notion of Lebenswelt goes hand in hand with his renewed phenomenological approach in a genetic sense. Probably influenced by the way in which Natorp explains time in 1912 as an event that regains a logical function in the psychic life, Husserl understood time as a ur-experience that acquires a referential implication in the way in which it constitutes meanings in our lives.

References

Carel, H. (2008). *Illness: The cry of the flesh*. London: Acumen Publishing.

Carel, H. (2011). Phenomenology and its application in medicine. *Theoretical Medicine and Bioethics*, *32*(1), 33–46.

Carel, H. (2016). *Phenomenology of illness*. Oxford: Oxford University Press.

Carr, E. H. (1948). The political science of E.H. Carr. *World Politics*, *1*(1), 127–134.

Chan, D. C. Jr., & Chen, Y. (2022). *The productivity of professions: Evidence from the emergency department* (Working Paper No. 30608). National Bureau of Economic Research. https://doi.org/10.3386/w30608

Duong, D. (2022). Why are emergency departments closing? *CMAJ: Canadian Medical Association Journal = journal de l'Association médicale canadienne*, *194*(33), E1138–E1139.

Ekpo, E. U., Alakhras, M., & Brennan, P. (2018). Errors in mammography cannot be solved through technology alone. *Asian Pacific Journal of Cancer Prevention: APJCP*, *19*(2), 291–301.

Englander, M. (2023). Bioethics, sociality, and mental illness. *The Journal of Medicine and Philosophy: A Forum for Bioethics and Philosophy of Medicine*, *48*(2), 161–169.

Englander, M., & Ferrarello, S. (Eds.). (2022). *Empathy and ethics*. London: Rowman & Littlefield Publishers.

Essex, C. (2005). Ulysses syndrome. *BMJ: British Medical Journal*, *330*(7502), 1268.

Ferrarello, S. (2021). Ulysses syndrome: The problem of collective intentionality for newcomers. *Intersezioni – InCircolo*, (11), 375–396.

Frankl, V. (1959). *Man's search for a meaning*. Boston: Beacon Press.
Frith, C. D. (1992). *Cognitive neuropsychology of schizophrenia*. Sussex: Psychology Press.
Fuchs, T. (2012). The phenomenology and development of social perspectives. *Phenomenology and the Cognitive Sciences*, *11*(4), 541–564.
Fuchs, T. (2013). The phenomenology of affectivity. In K. W. M. Fulford, M. Davies, R. G. T. Gipps, G. Graham, J. Z. Sadler, G. Stanghellini, & T. Thornton (Eds.), *The Oxford handbook of philosophy and psychiatry* (pp. 612–631). Oxford: Oxford University Press.
Galilei, G. (1957). *The assayer.* S. Drake (Trans.). In S. Drake (Ed.), *Discoveries and opinions of Galileo* (pp. 231–280). Garden City, NY: Doubleday. (Original work published 1623).
Husserl, E. (1956). *Erste Philosophie (1923/4). Erste Teil: Kritische Ideengeschichte* [First philosophy (1923–24). First part: The critical history of ideas]. The Hague: Martinus Nijhoff.
Husserl, E. (1965). Philosophy and the crisis of European man. In Q. Lauer (Ed. & Trans.), *Phenomenology and the crisis of philosophy: Philosophy as rigorous science, and Philosophy and the crisis of European man* (pp. 149–192). New York: Harper & Row.
Husserl, E. (1970a). *Logical investigations*. New York: Humanities Press.
Husserl, E. (1970b). *The crisis of European sciences and transcendental phenomenology: An introduction to phenomenology*. Evanston, IL: Northwestern University Press.
Husserl, E. (1994). *Briefwechsel* [Correspondence]. The Hague: Kluwer Academic Publishers (Vol. III).
Husserl, E. (2003). *Philosophy of arithmetic: Psychological and logical investigations with supplementary texts from 1887–1901*. D. Willard (Trans.). Dordrecht: Kluwer Academic Publishers. (Original work published 1891).
Husserl, E. (2014). *Ideas: General introduction to pure phenomenology*, W. R. Boyce Gibson (Trans.). London: Routledge.
Husserl, E. (n.d.). *B II manuscripts* [Unpublished manuscript]. Husserl Archives, KU Leuven. Retrieved from https://hiw.kuleuven.be/digitalhusserl/manuscripts
Jaspers, K. (1959). *General psychopathology*. J. Hoenig & M. W. Hamilton (Trans.). Manchester: Manchester University Press. (Original work published 1913).
Kidd, I. J., & Carel, H. (2017). Epistemic injustice and illness. *Journal of Applied Philosophy*, *34*, 172–190. https://doi.org/10.1111/japp.12172
Merleau-Ponty, M. (1942). La structure du comportement. Paris: Presses Universitaires de France.
Oben, P. (2020). Understanding the patient experience: A conceptual framework. *Journal of Patient Experience*, *7*(6), 906–910.
Paci, E. (1972). *The function of the sciences and the meaning of man*. Evanston, IL: Northwestern University Press.
Parnas, J., Møller, P., Kircher, T, Thalbitzer, J., Jansson, L., Handest, P., & Zahavi, D. (2005). EASE. Examination of anomalous self-experience. *Psychopathology*, *38*, 236–258.
Ratcliffe, M. (2008). *Feelings of being: Phenomenology, psychiatry and the sense of reality*. Oxford: Oxford University Press.
Razavi, M., Perloff, J., & Buerhaus, P. I. (2020). Nurse practitioner-provided care costs up to 34% less than doctor-provided care. *Medical Care*. Retrieved from https://heller.brandeis.edu/news/items/releases/2020/razavi-perloff-medical-care.html

Scheler, M. (1980). *Der Formalismus in der Ethik und die materiale Wertethik*. Bern: Francke Verlag.

Schneider, K. (1950). *Klinische Psychopathologie*. Stuttgart: Thieme.

Schuhmann, K. (1977). *Husserl-Chronik: Denk- und Lebensweg Edmund Husserls*. Den Haag: Martinus Nijhoff.

Sidek, M. A. J., Amajid, K., Loh, Y. S., Rosli, M. A., Hashim, I. S., Mohd Suffian, N. A., Abdullah, N., & Midin, M. (2023). The prevalent factors of anxiety in women undergoing mammography. *Frontiers in Psychiatry, 14*, 1085115.

Stanghellini, G. (2006). *Psicopatologia del senso comune*. Milano: Raffaello Cortina.

Stanghellini, G., & Rosfort, R. (2013). *Emotions and Personhood: Exploring Fragility – Making Sense of Vulnerability*. Oxford University Press.

Straus, E. W. (1969). *Psychiatry and philosophy*. Berlin: Springer Verlag.

Toombs, S. K. (1990). The temporality of illness: four levels of experience. *Theoretical Medicine, 11*(3), 227–241. https://doi.org/10.1007/BF00489832

Toombs, K. (2001). Handbook of phenomenology and medicine. In *Handbook of phenomenology and medicine* (pp. 673–694). Dordrecht: Kluwer Academic Publisher.

Uljée, R. (2023). The unconscious and the transcendental: Husserlian phenomenology in intersubjective systems theory. *Frontiers in Psychology, 14*, 1162372.

Weber, M. (1922). *Economy and society*. Berkeley: University of California Press.

Weyl, H. (1948). Wissenschaft als symbolische Konstruktion des Menschen. *Eranos-Jahrbuch, 375–431*, GA IV, 289–345.

Yegdich, T. (1999). On the phenomenology of empathy in nursing: Empathy or sympathy? *Journal of Advanced Nursing, 30*(1), 83–93.

Zahavi, D. (Ed.). (2000). *Exploring the self: Philosophical and psychopathological perspectiveson self-experience*. Amsterdam: John Benjamins.

7

AFFECTS DISORDERS

Introduction

Husserl's insights on the *Lebenswelt*, intersubjective meaning, and the crisis of the sciences—as discussed in Chapter 6—find clinical application in the understanding of affective disorders and disruptions of selfhood. From a phenomenological perspective, affectivity is not a secondary psychological function but the very foundation of personality and meaningful experience. We are constantly called to engage with the world, and with each moment, we awaken to life within it,[1] gradually shaping different aspects of our character. For instance, as we absentmindedly prepare lunch, a memory of a recipe our grandmother once made may come to mind. Or, while dressing our child, we might notice ourselves choosing a color our parents would have rejected because it defies inherited gender norms. These subtle moments show that we inhabit the *lifeworld* not through abstract reflection, but through affective awakenings that pull us into relationship with the world.

As described in Husserl's manuscripts (Ms D 14), the world impresses itself upon us through a "battle of affections," each vying for the attention of the "I." A string of lights flickering on the horizon, for example, may not call for direct attention, but it nonetheless imprints itself affectively, structuring our perceptual field and shaping what we care about. Over time, this stream of affective impressions forms the sediment of character. What we find meaningful is often guided by what has already awakened us. Husserl refers to this tendency as *drive-related preference* (Husserl, 1966, 198)—our inclination to return to what has previously been lived as affectively significant.

As discussed in Chapter 6, this affective structure is increasingly overlooked in modern scientific and medical paradigms. In line with Husserl's critique of

DOI: 10.4324/9781003665557-7

science's detachment from the *Lebenswelt*, contemporary clinical practice often treats patients as objects of management rather than as subjects embedded in meaningful contexts. When human beings are approached through standardized checklists and guidelines—detached from their lived experience—the deeper sense of healing is lost. Professionalism risks becoming, as noted earlier, the blind application of technical knowledge, severed from reflective and empathic engagement (Englander & Ferrarello, 2023).

Further, modern society tends to equate value with utility and utility with profit. This mindset, as seen in Chapter 6, reduces truth to what is most audible, marketable, or efficient, rather than what is existentially significant. In such a framework, talents and desires are valued only if they are seen as productive. Otherwise, they are dismissed as useless. But if, as we explored previously, the telos of science was originally to serve human flourishing—not to dominate it—then this shift reflects a profound disorientation. Husserl's claim that "opiate treatments suppress symptoms but do not cure the disease" applies not only to medicine but to the broader epistemic crisis of our time.

Against this backdrop, this chapter explores affectivity as the foundation of personal meaning, agency, and psychopathology. Affects and their nuanced variations—such as affection, allure, and affective force—are our primary modes of being alive in the world. As Husserl writes, "The world that is there for me… is there for me as a world of interests [Interessenwelt], and the way the world appears to me is the way in which I am interested in this world" (Husserl, 2008, 597). This means that our world is not first given through cognition but through what matters to us—what touches us, calls us, moves us. As argued in Chapter 6, it is not the ego that constitutes meaning, but affective intentionality—the dynamic process through which we become subjects of our own life, capable of empathy, ethical responsiveness, and self-formation.

But there are moments when this process fails. Our feelings may no longer resonate with what affects us. In these cases, affectivity remains present but is no longer felt or integrated. The disjunction between affection and feeling lies at the heart of several psychopathological profiles.

In this chapter, I will first explore the concept of affect and its role in constituting meaning over time. I will then examine how affects connect with feelings in relation to their interest, value, and representational abilities. Finally, I will analyze what occurs when we are unable to feel or engage with our affects, as in cases of alexithymia; when we strongly feel and value our affects, as seen in borderline personality disorder (BPD); or when we reject certain affects and create empty representations of our feelings, as seen in individuals with narcissistic traits.

In this exploration, I will draw on Husserl's interpretation, as discussed in my previous works (Ferrarello, 2015, 2018, 2021). As shown in Table 7.1, this chapter proceeds in triads and in the rest of the book, I will dedicate a chapter to

TABLE 7.1 Chapter Structure

Level of Affective Intentionality	*Interpersonal Process*	*Clinical Disruption*
Interest	Empathy	Alexithymia
Value activity	Intersubjectivity	Borderline personality
Representation	Ethics	Narcissistic traits

each of these triads. The first triad addresses the noetic aspect of affective intentionality, expressed in three layers: embodied interest, valuing, and representation (1.1–1.6). Each layer corresponds to a way of connecting with the world, forming the second triad: empathy, intersubjective formation through shared values, and ethical duties toward others (2.1–2.3). The third triad addresses personality disorders, which arise from malfunctions in one of the layers of affective intentionality (3.1–3.3): alexithymia when defects occur in embodied interest, BPD when the valuing process is impaired, and narcissistic traits when there are issues with representation. Although this chapter's primary aim is a speculative study of the relationship between affectivity and these disorders, I will also propose active approaches for improving the quality of life for those affected.

Affects and Awakening

Affectivity is the most primordial level of activity with which we can describe life in the world before it becomes our own. Through affectivity, our body becomes aware of its potentialities as it strives toward kinaesthetic realizations (cf. Husserl, 1973, 84)—in other words, the body discovers its ability to function in the world as it develops interest in these potentialities. For example, a newborn baby might accidentally hit her own face with her hand, and through this, she discovers her hand, its possible movements, and the sensations that arise from it. From there, the world is filled with surprises. What can she do with that hand? That hand becomes a sensitive tool for distinguishing herself from the Other in the world. Through her hand, she is in the world, able to touch and perceive everything around her.

Typically, affection—such as the hand that accidentally hits our own face—awakens the subject to possibilities that manifest as interest, bodily attitudes, the desire for knowledge, and the formation of personal habits. This newborn baby can move, cry, and laugh, even in the mother's womb; however, it is when these "innate dispositions" (Husserl, 1966, 24) encounter the Other in the world that their meaning develops into long-term dispositions, such as habits that shape her character. A newborn may smile in the womb, but it is when that smile meets the Other that this innate disposition becomes a long-term habit conveying an interpersonal meaning. In this encounter, a sense emerges that connects the baby to the people around her. The repetition of their responses is an affection that animates their interest in the world, guiding them according to a preferred drive. This primal interaction creates life in the world—our life in our lifeworld. The transition from the ego's passivity to its active interest is marked by a series of indistinct moments, a "gray area," that outlines the shift from simply being affected to the explicit act of turning one's attention toward the source of the affection. This transition takes us from "I do not even know I am a body" to "Let's see what this hand can do for me here."

For this transition to occur, feelings play a crucial role. This hand may hit my face, but it can also grab my mother's finger—the latter kinaesthetic act may be preferable because it generates greater sensory pleasure. The feelings I derive from these experiences shape my tendency to repeat one kinaesthetic act more often than the other. As Husserl notes, what is sensually given to us arrives not only through interested perceptions but also through evaluation and bodily sensations such as pleasure, pain, and desire, which we use to represent what has been given to us:

> there is an original passivity not only of sensuous givens, of 'sense data,' but also of feeling and, in contrast to this passivity, there is an active, objectivating orientation, not only in perception but also in evaluation and in pleasure.
> *(Husserl, 1973, 71)*

As Husserl explains, affective data are given to us passively as sense data, but it is through feelings that they are transformed into active meaning for us. This transformation occurs through three main feeling activities: perceptive interest, evaluation, and the objectivating representation of sensuous content.

From Affections to Feelings: The Intentionality of Feelings

In the A-Manuscripts, Husserl elaborates on how feelings help us transition from passive matter to active subjects who make sense of our affects. He defines feelings and feeling-acts as second-order phenomena (non-objectifying acts) that conceptually rely on a primary act of objectification, such as perception (Melle, 1990). This suggests that before something can evoke a sensual or more complex feeling, it must first be perceived and apprehended.

Feelings have intentionality, though the structure of this intentionality remains unclear. Do feelings arise because a representation of what we have apprehended captures our attention? Or is it our bodily perception and interest that initially provoke our feelings? These questions have fueled a longstanding debate, which unfortunately cannot be fully explored here. Some scholars argue that feelings transform what they represent into an object (Smith, 1976). Others propose that an affect-like form of interest drives feelings to perceive affects and transform them into a unified sense (Goldie, 2002; Ratcliffe, 2019; Slaby, 2008). Still, others emphasize the value-based motivation behind feeling intentions (Hatzimoysis, 2003; Vendrell-Ferran, 2022).

While I have addressed the determinants of feeling intentionality in other works (Ferrarello, 2015), here I will focus on these three components—interest, value, and representation—as interrelated mechanisms by which feelings perceive the affects that awaken us from a passive, object-like state of being in the world.

Being in the Feeling: Interest

Feelings bring to predication, either affective (as in Forlè, 2019; Slaby 2008; Wehrle, 2015) or cognitive (as in Smith, 1976), matter that draws our attention to recognize an object. This process can be understood as an intentionality of feelings (whether direct or indirect), where feelings act upon affects to give them, in a sense, a voice that expresses meaning to us. It remains uncertain whether this intentionality is driven directly by the affects themselves—making it egoless—or triggered by the ego's intentional interpretation of the relationship between act and matter in feelings.

In both cases, the intensity with which these feelings emerge from background experience to prominence varies based on the primal intensity with which the ego "lives 'in' the experience" through interest (Husserl, 1973, 81):

> In the state of being awake (as a correlate of sleep) there can be no absolute lack of interest, and even what we call 'operating without interest' is still a phenomenon of relevance, one of the lowest levels of relevance.
>
> *(Husserl, 2008, 596)*

While awake, I experience something prominent that stimulates my interest, leading to the formation of new meaning in that lived experience. This awakening alters the way I represent data and find relevance in it:

> It [the great affective power] wakes me as someone who is not only a professional, but also, for example, a father. But before the moment of awakening, my fatherly interest was not active. Therefore, the child did not have the affective power to catch my attention when I saw her entering the room, and it did not have the power to motivate fatherly actions at that time. My fatherly interest now becomes activated.
>
> *(Husserl, 2008, 594)*

This quote illustrates how affective data capture my attention based on my current interest at a particular moment. Interest acts as a fundamental driver of feeling intentionality, recognizing the value of what draws our interest and motivating the ego to represent the data and derive meaning from it. Although I have described this process as happening in stages, from a genetic standpoint, it unfolds simultaneously within the continuous flow of the ego's life.

In his 1898 manuscript addressing the problem of attention as interest, Husserl demonstrates that "interest" is fundamental to an act of explicit or "focused" intentionality, which we recognize as attention. The key condition for attention is our ability to be present (*inter* and *sum*) in the matter of the intended object that prompts our awareness. This interest, according to Husserl, is not merely theoretical, as Carl Stumpf suggests, but is instead a perceptual act (Husserl, 2008, 103). For any act to sustain the motivation to perceive the object-like formation in its entirety, it requires a habitual horizon of interest (Rang, 1973, 127). Interest is a gradual and fluctuating process that significantly impacts the ego's ability to maintain attention to affects.[2]

Feeling the Sense: Valuing

The ongoing debate between Bégout (2000) and Steinbock (1995) seeks to address the issue of the primacy of sense in relation to affects and the intentionality of feelings that grasp them. Bégout argues that sense is generated by affections, whereas Steinbock contends that it is sense that directs affective forces toward meanings that become prominent for us. For Steinbock,[3] sense drives affective forces, even at the most basic constitutive level. The selectivity with which the "I" perceives certain things over others is shaped by pre-given object-like formations of sense, which are influenced by specific egoic factors and differentiations, such as the rational, emotional, and axiological constitution of the embodied subject. What we perceive and bring into the constitution of sense is grounded in affective forces as they manifest through the habits of the embodied person. According to Bégout, "the original interpretation of affection as a simple putting into relation of hyletic unities and the receptive ego is thus confirmed: affection does not always make the relationships that are grounding in the particularity of the contents" (Bégout, 2000, 192).

It is possible that both interpreters are correct, given the nonlinear nature of phenomenological time. At a very primal level, sense may not be pre-given (as Bégout suggests), but over time it becomes so, as habitual patterns of sense are repeatedly constituted through specific choices of the embodied ego (as Steinbock argues). Affective acts seem to offer a sensuousness that, over time, becomes a habitualized reference, which prompts presentative acts to bring these habitual patterns of affects to predication. The choice is rooted in an embodied valuing activity. In fact, the predication of one sense over another is influenced by repeated interest and valuing activities. We develop interest in what we find more valuable, and as a result, tend to prioritize the representation of certain matters over others.

Feeling the Content: Representation

Valuing activities guide the I's focus from one object-like formation to another in the process of generating sense. What affects me in one moment can quickly lose its impact in the next. For example, the movie I was watching became less significant when I shifted my attention to answering a friend's text message. In order to be interested—literally "to be there" (inter-esse)—the ego must perceive some form of value[4] in what it is experiencing, even if that value is assigned pre-cognitively.

"Every awakening proceeds from an impression of or from an already non-intuitively reproduced present toward another reproduced present, whose movement requires a 'bridge element' that synthesizes what is given and leads to the next coincidence (Deckung)" (Husserl, 2000, 123).

The synthesis initiated by the retentional power of what is present to me becomes a protentional synthetic activity in which all sensuous data are gathered and presented to the subject as a form of external rhythm. The impression leaves its mark in the past and projects toward the future, creating a rhythmic chain of associations. This rhythm continually affects and reveals to the ego the contents of the "now" in the ego's flowing life. "In the conscious life of the concrete ego, there is an abiding hyletic core of non-ego that yet belongs essentially to the ego. Without a realm of pregivenness, a realm of unities constituted as non-ego, no ego is possible" (Husserl, 1973, 379).

Although not entirely devoid of subjectivity, the affective data remain foreign to the ego in that their field organizes itself without the ego's direct involvement (*Ichbeteiligung*) (Husserl, 2000, 478). Every "now" that is more than a mere "now point" (*Jetzpoint*) is a living presence, structured through this rhythmic encounter between past and future. These rhythms generate coherent patterns of affective data, where future impressions affectively resonate with present impressions, sparking associative syntheses through which the I discovers itself as an affected I.

Husserl calls that which affects the ego a "prominence" (Abgehobenheit). Prominences are sensible units (Husserl, 2000, 527) that depend directly on hyletic contrast and conflict (Husserl, 2000, 196–197). By contrast and conflict, Husserl refers to the forces driving matter toward synthesis. As retentions, affects can cluster around the *Schwelle des Bewusstseins* (threshold of consciousness) and return through associations.

When we sense and perceive something, there is already an inherent valuing process that shapes our experience and influences how we organize our perception of things. Feeling acts as a preference, influencing what we choose to see and interpret as prominent, which we perceive as a motivational necessity rooted in valuing activity. However, we sometimes question why we focus our attention on certain things over others. To address this, intentional feelings require presentations in order to clearly identify the object of their act and bring it into a predicative sense for us. From the perspective of static phenomenology, this occurs in a sequence, whereas from a genetic perspective, the presentative quality is fused into the given "now," along with the valuing and sensing activities triggered or influenced by the affects (depending on whether we follow Bégout's or Steinbock's interpretation). Feelings motivate or even enable us to select what we want to sense and react to, which in turn affects us and prompts further engagement with these stimuli. The intentionality of feelings allows us to objectify the content of the affect in our actions, helping us, at times, to understand why we develop certain dispositions over others.

Feeling the Affects: Empathy, Intersubjectivity, and Ethics

As previously noted, experiencing affects is the primary way in which we engage with the world, make sense of it, and establish connections with others. Interest, valuing activity, and representation are the key mechanisms through which these feelings are activated, allowing us to connect with ourselves and others in a harmonious community. The "I" becomes aware of the affects and is present within them (interest), valuing the prominence of the affective data that demand attention and making choices based on the recognition of the sense of what affects it. Although this process does not necessarily follow a path that is linear in time, from a dispositional perspective, it leads to the development of empathy, intersubjective interconnection (or interaffectivity), and an ethical conscience, provided these feeling tools are in operation. In the following sections, I will explore how the experience of affects shapes our empathy, intersubjective connection, and ethical valuing activity, moving into the second triad.

Empathy and Interest

As it concerns the constitution of our empathetic connection with the world, we can notice how this connection occurs before we are present to ourselves as this or that person. The empathetic connection with the world is a pre-reflective and pre-predicative moment of interest in our active life. In a moment of time, undifferentiated matter becomes something specific because its parts come together and form a whole based on various criteria. This flow is not present all at once but is synthesized and diffused through egoic activities such as memory, imagination, and empathy. Empathy, in fact, is the first presenting egoic activity through which the "I" emerges and recognizes itself as distinct from the matter it perceives. Through analogizing and differentiating processes, the "I" synthesizes the affective matter that awakened it, organizing it into a meaningful sense. These embodied acts of presentification allow the subject to transform undifferentiated matter into a sedimentation that creates "the unity of world-certainty" and reveals the potential for reproductive activity (Husserl, 1966, 152).

Empathy allows us to become involved in (*inter-esse*) the matter of the other; our bodily perception becomes engaged in bringing to presence the affective awakenings of others, which rouse us from a state of rest. The primordial ego radiates affective awakenings, and the awakened ego responds by opening its horizon to a chain of possible fusions or primordial associations of matter. We become part of the world through our connection with an "other" that appears similar to us. According to Husserl (Husserl, 1966, 123), although primordial association operates independently of the ego, it awakens the ego through affective associations based on similarities and differences. Empathy is one way that our perceptive interest identifies these similarities and differences between the newly awakened embodied ego and the other.

Initially, the essential structure of the given data is recognized by an ego-less affection. This ego-less affection then integrates the given data into a system of interrelated elements, while simultaneously revealing something distinct but related. As Husserl notes, "We can secure decisive insights into the essence of association when we comprehend the (…) structure pertaining to the function of affection, its peculiarity, and its dependence on essential conditions" (Husserl, 1966, 211). Husserl describes synthetic force as a form of affection exerted by matter (Husserl, 1966, 477–478), which allows the subject—who has not yet questioned its own "thing-hood"—to discover itself as an agent.

Intersubjectivity-Value Activity to a Shared Lifeworld

In this primal flow of living presence, the ego as an agent discovers itself as the original Other, observing itself from the origin of being and time. I appear to this foundational function of existence as the primary Other. To coexist in the same world, we must share values, with the value of existence being fundamental. Although I am distinct from the affective matter that awakened me, I remain connected to it in a way that imparts meaning and value to my being. I discover myself as I-we, that is, as a primordial origin of intersubjectivity. Intersubjectivity can be understood as the relationship between myself and other entities. What is unique about this relationship is that the Other is not foreign to me but exists "within me," *Leibhaftig* (in person).[5]

When I perceive another person, the Other is genetically constituted within the flow of my own experience; my perception of the Other emerges naturally alongside my self-awareness, not before or after it, but as part of my living experience in a world imbued with values. In my simple act of living and perceiving, the Other appears as an integral part of my being-in-the-world, almost like a companion. In the formation of the intersubjective connection, the value activity through which the newly awakened "I" acknowledges the affective matter linked to its activity becomes the means by which the Other is given a distinct form and identity, allowing them to become part of the subject's lifeworld.

This path of self/other discovery is described as "the progressive development of a phenomenological community," which involves "wakeful communalization as co-searching and living life as a whole accordingly" (Fink, 1995, 191). The creation of values within this intersubjective field is essential for gaining access to a shared world. Fink's vision of communalization is inherently social, not merely academic, as he asks, "How long can I phenomenologize as solus ipse, as the 'only man'? How long can I remain at it … how long can I want to remain at it?" (Fink, 1995, 191). In his later reflections, Husserl envisions phenomenology's ultimate goal as being directed toward the social realm, stating that human life is "we-life," a pursuit of individual realization that "each has to understand in a sense appropriate to himself" while simultaneously being "a striving of the we toward unity in a we-satisfaction," culminating in "the creation of a new environing human world" (Fink, 1995, 192).

Ethics and Representational Activity

The agent subject is not only present to itself and others through empathy but also actively participates in the lifeworld through valuing activities, becoming a subject of responsibility. This subject takes charge of its own decisions through representational activity. A human subject becomes an ethical agent capable of engaging with the intersubjective community based on shared understandings of right and wrong because it can reflect on and represent the content of its feelings. According to Husserl, a human being is human precisely due to its capacity to feel, reflect on, and make those feelings present to itself. This ability allows individuals to make decisions and act wisely.

> The practical behavior of human beings is obviously determined by feeling (Fühlen). If we were to try to extinguish all feeling (Gefühl) from the human breast, then we would lose all ethical concepts, concepts like end and means, good and bad and all the affiliated special concepts and their sense.
>
> *(Stanghellini, 2004, 40)*

For Husserl, feelings are essential to being human and to behaving ethically in society with others. To make informed decisions, we must process our feelings and the affects connected to them. In this sense, we need to bring these feelings to the forefront of our position-taking, making choices based on our capacity to evaluate what matters for ourselves and others. Thus, feelings and their intentional activity at a presentational level are crucial for the existence of an ethical community.

Affects' Disorders

In what follows, I will address the final triad and provide a brief overview of the disorders that, in my view, are closely tied to an inability to process affects. This inability arises from dysfunction in one of the levels of feeling intentionality: interest, valuing, or representing. While a more detailed discussion of the three affective disorders I refer to—alexithymia, BPD, and narcissistic traits[6]—will be deferred to the following three chapters, I will provide a brief overview focused on where feeling intentionality fails in processing affects.

To summarize, I believe that alexithymia is marked by issues with empathy due to problems with the intentionality of feelings related to developing interest—the alexithymic individual has difficulty feeling their own affects. On the other hand, individuals with BPD feel very intensely. They struggle to properly value the affects that relate to them within their intersubjective community. Those who exhibit narcissistic traits, however, resist feeling altogether. In these cases, feeling intentionality is blocked at the representational level, and the individual has difficulty recognizing the impact of their actions and decisions on themselves and others. In Table 7.2, I summarize the sequence of triads examined in this chapter and include the clinical approach I will propose in the final, forthcoming triad.

Alexithymia, Interest, and Empathy

The personality trait of alexithymia is characterized by difficulties in identifying and describing personal feelings, as well as a limited capacity to consider others' emotions. As a result, individuals with these traits often struggle to develop empathy for both themselves and others. The term "alexithymia" comes from the Greek words "a-lexos" (no words) and "thumia" (mood), literally meaning "no words for mood." Originally, this condition was linked to patients with

TABLE 7.2 Affect Disorders and Approaches

Affects through Feeling Intentionality	*Lifeworld*	*Disorder/Traits*	*Approach*
Interest	Empathy	Alexithymia	Bodily activity
Value	Intersubjectivity/ interaffectivity	BPD	Value activity
Representation	Ethics	Narcissistic traits	Representational activity

psychosomatic issues. Following a study conducted by Nemiah and Sifneos (1970) on patients with psychosomatic diseases, Sifneos (1972) coined the term "alexithymia" to describe the cognitive and affective problems observed in these patients.

Alexithymia is typically described by the following features: significant difficulties in identifying and describing emotions, challenges in distinguishing between emotions and bodily sensations related to emotional arousal, a marked lack of imagination (evidenced by a scarcity of fantasies), a cognitive style that is concrete and focused on reality (also referred to as externally oriented thinking or "pensée opératoire"), and a high degree of social conformity with limited awareness of their own inner world (von Rad, 1983). Furthermore, Bach et al. (1996) demonstrated that alexithymia and somatization are distinct constructs that can coexist.

Given the link between feelings and physical movement, I believe alexithymia is associated with the first degree of feeling intentionality. The inability to find words for the affective content of feelings is primarily related to a physical disconnection from the affect, with representational issues being secondary. As we noted earlier, interest is a bodily form of attention, where the body is primordially engaged with what has drawn the I's attention. This trait has been mostly observed in individuals with psychosomatic disorders, suggesting they have difficulty being bodily present with the affects that arise in their subjectivity. This results in an impairment in bodily engagement with their feelings and prevents them from processing these emotions through physical activity.

Consequently, individuals with alexithymia struggle to develop empathy, strengthen intersubjective connections within their immediate community, and make affectively informed ethical decisions involving others. Over time, this may lead to depressive moods, detachment, panic disorders, and other psychological issues stemming from an inability to process the affects impacting their lives, leaving them overwhelmed by these emotions without fully perceiving them (Haviland et al., 1988; Sifneos, 1988).

Although treatment for alexithymia generally involves talk therapy and medications to manage related issues like anxiety, depression, and substance abuse (Da Silva et al., 2018; Ogrodniczuk, 2007), I believe more focus should be placed on its bodily roots in the intentionality of feelings. In line with Vanheule et al. (2011), who argue for a new framework focused on interpersonally embedded affect regulation for alexithymia-related disorders, I believe an approach that emphasizes the bodily nature of this condition is essential. Therefore, incorporating physical activities such as dancing, playing, or mindful movement, followed by active efforts to name the emotions associated with these movements, can, over time, help individuals develop a vocabulary to express at least a basic pattern of feelings.

BPD, Value Activity, and Intersubjectivity

In the case of BPD, the intentionality of feelings encounters difficulties in properly valuing affects, particularly those that arise from interactions with others. Individuals with BPD tend to assign excessive value to passive affects or experience an overwhelming number of affects, leading them to feel the emotional impact more intensely than others.

According to Biosocial Theory (Trull et al., 2018), during emotional development, the intersubjective and interaffective needs of individuals with BPD are not adequately met. Their emotional vulnerability, which is biologically based, is often handled in ways that are perceived as invalidating, minimizing, or trivializing. As a result, these individuals develop traits such as impulsivity, poor social functioning, emotional sensitivity, heightened reactivity, and a slow return to emotional baseline (Trull et al., 2018). These challenges often lead to feelings of sadness, hostility, and fear (Fertuck et al., 2006). Some researchers attribute these issues to large-scale cognitive deficits (LeGris & van Reekum, 2006; Lenzenweger & Desantis Castro, 2005), which sometimes extend to affective decision-making processes. For example, individuals with BPD tend to make impulsive decisions in delay-discounting tasks, favoring immediate rewards over long-term gains (Sánchez-Navarro et al., 2014; Van Reekum et al., 1994), and struggle with decisions involving potential losses (Gratz et al., 2013).

Laboratory studies also reveal high emotional reactivity in individuals with BPD, often marked by shame (Kuo & Linehan, 2009), anger (Minzenberg et al., 2007), fear, and anxiety (Dixon-Gordon et al., 2015), as well as heightened amygdala reactivity (Shenk & Fruzzetti, 2011). These individuals are more likely to perceive negative evaluations or criticism from others as harsher than intended (Shenk & Fruzzetti, 2011) and to misinterpret positive cues in a negative light, leading to feelings of rejection (Peters et al., 2017; Staebler et al., 2011).

The most common response to perceived rejection is rumination, defined as repetitive, unproductive thoughts (Berenson et al., 2011). Rumination often leads to "emotional cascades," where distress is amplified and discharged through impulsive actions aimed at escaping emotions. This process is linked to heightened experiences of anger (Peters, 2015), shame (Selby et al., 2015), lower engagement in present-focused awareness (Gottman, 1993), and difficulty managing intense emotional arousal (Dixon-Gordon et al., 2015).

Individuals with BPD tend to feel overwhelmed by the emotional world around them, struggling to properly assess and value what their affective experiences are conveying. What others might perceive as overreactions are, for those with BPD, responses to an intense array of affects that they feel directly involved with. Mancini and Stanghellini (2020) identified three forms of logic underlying the constitution of the lifeworld in individuals with BPD: (1) the logic of intimacy, which is centered around belongingness and mutual recognition; (2) the logic of spontaneity, which values authenticity; and (3) the logic of instantaneity, which prioritizes intensity. The "*ordo amoris*" that structures the reality for individuals with BPD is deeply invested in this "visceral need for belonging, acceptance, and love." Their actions are driven by the intensity of emotional values, which are constantly frustrated by ethical norms and social conventions that shape their shared interpersonal world (Mancini & Stanghellini, 2020). Any effort to soothe emotions or delay decisions diminishes the immediacy with which this normative intensity must be expressed.

These logics are central to the way individuals with BPD construct their lifeworld, contributing to the disturbance in the interaffective resonance of their reality. Affective resonance refers to the pre-reflective, embodied sharing of emotional states between individuals, where one person's affective expression evokes a corresponding affective reaction in another, without conscious imitation or interpretation. For instance, when a patient with BPD enters the room appearing agitated, the therapist may suddenly feel a surge of anxiety or urgency. Even before any words are exchanged, the patient's dysregulated emotional state has reverberated through the relational field. This is affective resonance—an unmediated transmission of mood that demands awareness and regulation, especially in emotionally intense therapeutic dyads. This concept helps distinguish empathy from emotional contagion: the clinician *feels with* the patient but does not become overwhelmed by the affect.

The lifeworld of someone with BPD often feels frightening and exhausting, as the continuity of its affective structure fluctuates as rapidly as their emotions. In this context, even a small event like an expected smile or an unanswered phone call can disrupt their sense of belonging in the affective world. The value placed on such seemingly minor interactions can threaten their connection to their social environment, resulting in a deep sense of axiological instability.

This instability in the constitution of values and logic mirrors the instability of the lifeworld for individuals with BPD. They may feel detached from their social surroundings and pressured to be different, leaving them in a dilemma where they are unable to engage in fulfilling interaffective resonance. By shedding light on the axiological steps involved in the constitution of meaning, we can better understand where intervention is needed to address this blockage. I believe that the disturbance in affective resonance can be greatly reduced if clinicians focus on the axiological processes that shape the content of lived experience for individuals with BPD. Focusing on the continuity of reality, independent of the emotional and axiological disruptions caused by the value assigned to specific lived experiences, can contribute to stabilizing their interaffective and intersubjective world, thus enhancing their sense of belonging.

In conclusion, the instability in the behavior of individuals with BPD reflects the instability of their lifeworld. Attention to the existential consequences of the axiological processes in their meaning-making experience is crucial to preventing disruptions in the affective resonance that connects them to their intersubjective and interaffective world.

Narcissistic Personality Disorder, Presentational Acts, and Ethics

In individuals with narcissistic traits, the intentionality of feelings seems to encounter difficulties at the representational level. Although affects are properly felt through interest and valuing activities, certain affects—likely because they are too overwhelming—become blocked, disrupting the natural flow of affective representation. As a result, what is represented is often devoid of emotional depth. Their decisions and actions are not rooted in immediate, embodied affects, which leads to a lack of ethical consideration for both others and themselves. Narcissistic individuals often avoid feeling their emotions because doing so would be too painful.

People with narcissistic traits or personality disorder seem to lack the emotional tools necessary to reconnect with their feelings in a healthy way. It is difficult for them to engage in deep self-reflection because they lack the empathetic drive to show compassion toward themselves. Consequently, their self-reflection only touches the surface of their being. Their sense of self is based on fleeting images, shaped by how others perceive them, or is reified in material objects. This makes them highly vulnerable to criticism, even though they often project an air of superiority over others (e.g., Campbell et al., 2002; Gabriel et al., 1994) and believe themselves to be unique (Emmons, 1987), which can be linked to a heightened sense of entitlement (Campbell et al., 2004). Any negative remark feels like a personal attack on their entire being, as if the other person is trying to erase them. They feel empty because they cannot connect with their emotions, and they compensate for this emptiness with grandiose fantasies and an inflated ego, believing this to be the best strategy for reaffirming their existence.

If narcissistic individuals are able to fully reflect on themselves and reach the deepest part of their being, they may undergo a healing transformation, as in Ovid's interpretation of the Narcissus myth. In the mid-1980s, Young developed schema therapy to help narcissists recognize the behavioral patterns underlying their condition. Similarly, Johnson (1987) argued that effective treatment requires narcissists to accept their vulnerability and develop a mature awareness of their behavior. These approaches are still in use today.

The acceptance gained through such therapies may initially bring a strong sense of depression and sadness as individuals become more aware of their responsibility for their actions. However, this acceptance is often followed by a sense of completeness, as the fragmented parts of their personality become fully integrated. A key element of this process is establishing a trusting relationship with the therapist, which allows the client to feel their emotions without fear of judgment. Murray-Jobsis (1990a, 1990b, 1990c) demonstrated how such a relationship can help clients redefine the boundaries between internal and external realities, fostering acceptance of an imperfect world (see also my *Human Emotions and the Origins of Bioethics*, chapter 5). Baker (1981), drawing on Mahler's (1968) work, also developed hypnotic techniques and self-psychology methods to help narcissistic clients revisit a pre-verbal stage and create new corrective experiences in the present. His fifth, sixth, and seventh exercises focus on reinforcing the therapist as a "good object," providing the client with the emotional stability they lacked during their upbringing. In particular, the seventh exercise helps integrate positive and negative experiences, while the therapist aids the client in eliminating harmful mental objects. In this sense, fantasy and imagination—more than meditation—can help reinforce emotional constancy for narcissistic individuals.

Baker also highlighted the importance of empathy in helping narcissists develop an observing ego. Hypnotic techniques such as the affect bridge (Watkins, 1978), future projections (Phillips & Frederick, 1995), ego-strengthening exercises (Frederick & McNeal, 1999), and Ego State Therapy (Watkins & Watkins, 1997) may reduce treatment duration from the typical two to three years to just over a year.

I believe that whenever life events threaten our intimate sense of self (or the image with which we identify), a "narcissistic wound" is exposed, creating the potential for narcissistic tendencies to emerge. I propose combining the positive aspects of the aforementioned treatments into an intentionality-oriented approach to maintain emotional health throughout life. By promoting self-acceptance, ego-strengthening, and the exploration of feelings related to traumatic experiences, individuals can reconnect with the intentionality behind their actions. Grounding narcissistic individuals in their own bodies, as part of a larger system, can help overcome painful emotional blockages and foster a sense of intimacy.

In particular, those with narcissistic traits would benefit from developing the representational aspect of feeling intentionality to recognize and confront the painful affects that prevent them from connecting with their true selves and others. The ultimate goal is to restore the natural flow of affective syntheses, reigniting empathy and intersubjective connections. This would allow narcissists to become more present with their emotions and act ethically and mindfully toward others.

Narcissists struggle to access the organic presence of their bodies, finding it difficult to accept their physical imperfections or even the reality of aging. Their bodies feel almost shameful to them, disconnected from their sense of self. This inability to accept their physicality leads to grandiosity, a fixation on image, and a disconnection from the bodies of others. Therefore, practical exercises that stimulate awareness of the body's passive syntheses (its basic functions) rather than the empty projections formed from traumatic experiences are essential. Once this reconnection is achieved, it becomes possible to revisit the traumatic events in a healthier way. Often, the unethical behavior of narcissists stems from this blocked intentionality, which prevents them from accessing the affects tied to their wounds and from connecting with the meaningful aspects of themselves and others. Addressing this blockage may help alleviate the loneliness and emptiness they experience.

Conclusion

In the following three chapters, I will dive into each of these problems: alexithymia, BPD, and Narcissistic Personality Disorder (NPD). In this chapter, I explored the importance of affectivity in enabling human beings to be part of a shared world. I demonstrated how the intentionality of feelings is key to engaging with affects and understanding their significance in shaping who we are as human beings. I outlined three levels of this intentionality—interest, value activity, and representation—which, while not necessarily sequential, are interconnected in the process of meaning-making. Each of these stages corresponds to an aspect of our being-in-the-world, manifesting through empathy, intersubjectivity, and ethics.

In the latter part of the paper, I discussed how certain personality traits or disorders can be linked to affective disorders that disrupt the functioning of feeling intentionality and limit access to the lifeworld. For example, in the case of alexithymia, a lack of bodily interest impedes the development of empathy, making it difficult for individuals to form emotional connections with themselves and others. People with alexithymic traits struggle to feel and engage with their own emotions. On the other hand, individuals with BPD tend to assign excessive value to many of the affects they experience. This heightened intensity often disrupts the balance of their interaffective world. In contrast, individuals with narcissistic traits often avoid feeling certain affects, likely because some emotions are too painful to confront. This avoidance obstructs the representational flow through which they make sense of their existence in the world, leading to ethically questionable behavior that may lack consideration for others.

For each of these challenges, I proposed practical solutions aimed at enhancing contact with affects in areas where blockages are most evident. By addressing these blockages, individuals can improve their connection to their emotional experiences, fostering a healthier engagement with their affective world and interpersonal relationships.

Notes

1 See, for example, Husserl: "While taking an evening stroll on the Loretto Heights, a string of lights in the Rhine Valley suddenly flashes into our horizon; it immediately becomes affectively and unitarily prominent, without necessarily leading to an attentive turning toward it" (Husserl, 1966, 202).

2 As Husserl explains, after a while, the I loses its interest in a certain thing and gets caught up with something else. This loss of interest is also a gradual process, in which

something affects me less and less until the point that I become completely indifferent. The affective force of the object slowly fades away in a process of retentional change (...). And finally, everything runs together as one; all retentional ebbs and flows form one unity in which a multifaceted sense is implicitly lodged, for it has flowed into it through multifarious particular lines of unity, but in such a way that no affective pull proceeds from this unity" (Husserl, 1966, 220).

3 As Steinbock remarks, "if sense constitution did presuppose affection, would not the very constitution of sense somehow presuppose, paradoxically, that sense was already constituted so that it could exert an affective force on me in order to be constituted?" (Steinbock, 1995, 154)

4 "The same holds true for the axiological role of feelings, as value-apprehension and value-judgments. Value-perception also presupposes a neutral perception, the presentation of an object as object. In a parallel or even simultaneous manner, this perception is accompanied by a sensual feeling caused by the object. Sensual feelings then give rise to value-apprehensions and value-judgments, which lead to proper feelings like joy, disgust, or happiness as their effects. Proper feelings, like joy or disgust, are thus founded in value-apprehensive consciousness ('im werterfassenden Bewusstsein'; Husserl, Ms. A VI 12 II/132a).

5 The sources Husserl borrowed to develop his theory of intersubjectivity are especially indebted to Brentano (1973), Stein (1989), and Fink (1995). From Brentano he took the theory of intentionality to explain the subject-object relationship and from Stein the notion of empathy to clarify the manner in which we perceive otherness.

6 I will refer to individuals with narcissistic traits as "narcissists" or "individuals with NPD," while fully acknowledging that narcissism, in and of itself, is not a formal diagnosis according to the DSM. Rather, it refers to a constellation of traits that may, in some cases, meet the criteria for NPD, but often exist along a spectrum of personality features.

References

Bach, M., de Bach, D., & Zwaan, M. (1996). Independency of alexithymia and somatization: A factor analytic study. *Psychosomatics*, *37*(5), 451–458.

Baker, E. L. (1981). A hypnotherapeutic approach to enhance object relatedness in psychotic patients. *International Journal of Clinical and Experimental Hypnosis*, *29*(2), 136–147.

Bégout, B. (2000). *La généalogie de la logique: Husserl, l'antéprédicatif et le catégorial.* Vrin.

Berenson, K. R., Downey, G., Rafaeli, E., Coifman, K. G., & Paquin, N. L. (2011). The rejection-rage contingency in borderline personality disorder. *Journal of Abnormal Psychology, 120*(3), 681–690.

Campbell, W. K., Bonacci, A. M., Shelton, J., Exline, J. J., & Bushman, B. J. (2004). Psychological entitlement: Interpersonal consequences and validation of a self-report measure. *Journal of Personality Assessment, 83*(1), 29–45.

Campbell, W. K., Rudich, E., & Sedikides, C. (2002). Narcissism, self-esteem, and the positivity of self-views: Two portraits of self-love. *Personality and Social Psychology Bulletin, 28*(3), 358–368.

da Silva, A. C. N., Vasco, A. B., & Watson, J. C. (2018). Alexithymia and therapeutic alliance: A multiple case study comparing good and poor outcome cases. *Research in Psychotherapy (Milano), 21*(2), 313. https://doi.org/10.4081/ripppo.2018.292

Dixon-Gordon, K. L., Weiss, N. H., Tull, M. T., DiLillo, D., Messman-Moore, T., & Gratz, K. L. (2015). Characterizing emotional dysfunction in borderline personality, major depression, and their co-occurrence. *Comprehensive Psychiatry, 62*, 187–203.

Emmons, R. A. (1987). Narcissism: Theory and measurement. *Journal of Personality and Social Psychology, 52*(1), 11–17.

Englander, M., & Ferrarello, S. (Eds.). (2023). *Empathy and ethics*. Rowman & Littlefield Publishers.

Ferrarello, S. (2015). *Husserl's ethics and practical intentionality*. Bloomsbury.

Ferrarello, S. (2018). Husserl's ethics and psychiatry. In M. Englander (Ed.), *Phenomenology and the social context of psychiatry: Social relations, psychopathology, and Husserl's philosophy* (pp. 161–181). Bloomsbury Academic.

Ferrarello, S. (2021). Meaning-making activity in the emotional experience of borderline personalities. *Psychopathology, 54*, 221–231.

Fertuck, E. A., Lenzenweger, M. F., Clarkin, J. F., Hoermann, S., & Stanley, B. (2006). Executive neurocognition, memory systems, and borderline personality disorder. *Clinical Psychology Review, 26*(3), 346–375.

Fink, E. (1995). *Sixth Cartesian Meditation: The idea of a transcendental theory of method*. R. Bruzina (Trans.). Indiana University Press.

Forlè, F. (2019). Bodily expressions, feelings, and the direct perception account of social cognition. *Phenomenology and the Cognitive Sciences, 19*(5), 1019–1034.

Frederick, C., & McNeal, S. (1999). *Inner strengths*. Routledge.

Gabriel, M. T., Critelli, J. W., & Ee, J. S. (1994). Narcissistic illusions in self-evaluations of intelligence and attractiveness. *Journal of Personality, 62*(1), 143–155.

Goldie, P. (2002). Emotions, feelings, and intentionality. *Phenomenology and the Cognitive Sciences, 1*, 235–254.

Gottman, J. M. (1993). A theory of marital dissolution and stability. *Journal of Family Psychology, 7*(1), 57–75.

Gratz, K. L., Tull, M. T., Matusiewicz, A. M., Breetz, A. A., & Lejuez, C. W. (2013). Multimodal examination of emotion regulation difficulties as a function of co-occurring avoidant personality disorder among women with borderline personality disorder. *Personality Disorders, 4*(4), 304–314.

Hatzimoysis, A. (2003). *Philosophy and the emotions* (pp. 105–112). Cambridge University Press.

Haviland, M. G., Shaw, D. G., MacMurray, J. P., & Cummings, M. A. (1988). Validation of the Toronto Alexithymia Scale with substance abusers psychotherapy. *Psychosomatics, 50*, 81–87.

Husserl, E. (1966). *Analysen zur passiven Synthesis. Aus Vorlesungs und Forschungsmanuskripten 1918–1926*. M. Fleischer (Ed.). Nijhoff.

Husserl, E. (1973). *Zur Phänomenologie der Intersubjektivität. Dritter Teil (1929–1935)*. I. Kern (Ed.). Nijhof.

Husserl, E. (2000). *Aktive Synthesen: Aus der Vorlesung 'Transzendentale Logik' 1920/21. Ergänzungsband zu 'Analysen zur passiven Synthesis'* [Active syntheses: From the lecture 'transcendental logic' 1920/21'. Complementary text to 'Analysis of passive synthesis']. R. Breeur (Ed.). The Hague: Kluwer Academic Publishers.

Husserl, E. (2008). *Die Lebenswelt. Auslegungen der vorgegebenen Welt und ihrer Konstitution. Texte aus dem Nachlass (1916–1937)*. R. Sowa (Ed.). Springer.

Husserl, E. (n.d.a). *Manuscript D 14, 6a*. Husserl Archives, KU Leuven.

Husserl, E. (n.d.b) *Manuscript A VII. Mundane Phenomenology.* Husserl Archives, KU Leuven.

Johnson, S. M. (1987). *Humanizing the narcissistic style*. W.W. Norton.

Kuo, J. R., & Linehan, M. M. (2009). Disentangling emotion processes in borderline personality disorder: Physiological and self-reported assessment of biological vulnerability, baseline intensity, and reactivity to emotionally evocative stimuli. *Journal of Abnormal Psychology, 118*(3), 531–544.

LeGris, J., & van Reekum, R. (2006). The neuropsychological correlates of borderline personality disorder and suicidal behaviour. *Canadian Journal of Psychiatry. Revue Canadienne de Psychiatrie, 51*(3), 131–142. https://doi.org/10.1177/070674370605100303

Lenzenweger, M. F., & Desantis Castro, D. (2005). Predicting change in borderline personality: Using neurobehavioral systems indicators within an individual growth curve framework. *Development and Psychopathology, 17*(4), 1207–1237. https://doi.org/10.1017/s0954579405050571

Mahler, M. S. (1968). *On human symbiosis and the vicissitudes of individuation: Infantile psychosis* (Vol. 1). International Universities Press.

Mancini, M., & Stanghellini, G. (2020). Values in persons with borderline personality disorder: Their relevance for the therapeutic interview. *Research in Psychotherapy: Psychopathology, Process and Outcome, 23*(1), 449.

Melle, U. (1990). Objektivierende und nicht-objektivierende Akte. In S. IJsseling (Ed.), *Husserl Ausgabe und Forschung* (pp. 35–49). Kluwer.

Minzenberg, M. J., Fan, J., New, A. S., Tang, C. Y., & Siever, L. J. (2007). Frontolimbic dysfunction in response to facial emotion in borderline personality disorder: An event-related fMRI study. *Psychiatry Research, 155*(3), 231–243.

Murray-Jobsis, J. (1990a). Renurturing: Forming positive sense of identity and bonding. In D. C. Hammond (Ed.), *Handbook of hypnotic suggestions and metaphors* (pp. 326–328). W. W. Norton & Company.

Murray-Jobsis, J. (1990b). Suggestions for creative self-mothering. In D. C. Hammond (Ed.), *Handbook of hypnotic suggestions and metaphors* (p. 328). W. W. Norton & Company.

Murray-Jobsis, J. (1990c). Ego building. In D. C. Hammond (Ed.), *Handbook of hypnotic suggestions and metaphors* (pp. 136–139). W. W. Norton & Company.

Nemiah, J. C., & Sifneos, P. E. (1970). Affect and fantasy in patients with psychosomatic disorders. In O. W. Hill (Ed.), *Modern trends in psychosomatic medicine* (Vol. 2, pp. 26–34). Butterworths.

Ogrodniczuk, J. S. (2007). Alexithymia: Considerations for the psychotherapist. *Psychotherapy Bulletin, 42*, 4–7.

Peters, J. R. (2015). *The rewarding nature of anger rumination in borderline personality disorder: An fMRI investigation* [Doctoral dissertation, University of Kentucky]. UKnowledge. https://uknowledge.uky.edu/psychology_etds/57

Peters, J. R., Eisenlohr-Moul, T. A., Upton, B. T., Talavera, N. A., Folsom, J. J., & Baer, R. A. (2017). Characteristics of repetitive thought associated with borderline personality features: A multimodal investigation of ruminative content and style. *Journal of Psychopathology and Behavioral Assessment, 39*(3), 456–466. https://doi.org/10.1007/s10862-017-9594-x

Phillips, M., & Frederick, C. (1995). *Healing the divided self.* Norton.

Rang, B. (1973). *Kausalität und Motivation. Untersuchungen zum Verhältnis von Perspektivität und Objektivität in der Phänomenologie Edmund Husserls*. Martinus Nijhof.

Ratcliffe, M. (2019). Emotional intentionality. *Royal Institute of Philosophy Supplement, 85*, 251–269.

Sánchez-Navarro, J. P., Weller, J. A., López-Navarro, J. M., Martínez-Selva, J. M., & Bechara, A. (2014). Suboptimal decision making in borderline personality disorder: Effect of potential losses. *The Spanish Journal of Psychology, 17*, E38. https://doi.org/10.1017/sjp.2014.39

Selby, E. A., Fehling, K. B., Panza, E. A., & Kranzler, A. (2015). Rumination, mindfulness, and borderline personality disorder symptoms. *Mindfulness, 7*(1), 228–235.

Shenk, C. E., & Fruzzetti, A. E. (2011). The impact of validating and invalidating responses on emotional reactivity. *Journal of Social Clinical Psychology, 30*(2), 163–183.

Sifneos, P. E. (1972). *Short-term psychotherapy and emotional crisis*. Harvard University Press.

Sifneos, P. E. (1988). Alexithymia and its relationship to hemispheric specialization, affect, and creativity. *Psychiatric Clinics of North America, 11*, 287–329.

Slaby, J. (2008). Affective intentionality and the feeling body. *Phenomenology and the Cognitive Sciences, 7*(4), 429–444.

Smith, Q. (1976). Husserl and the inner structure of feeling-acts. *Research in Phenomenology, 6*(1), 84–104.

Staebler, K., Helbing, E., Rosenbach, C., & Renneberg, B. (2011). Rejection sensitivity and borderline personality disorder. *Clinical Psychology & Psychotherapy, 18*(4), 275–283. https://doi.org/10.1002/cpp.705

Stanghellini, G. (2004). *Disembodied spirits and deanimated bodies: The psychopathology of common sense*. Oxford University Press.

Steinbock, A. J. (1995). Phenomenological concepts of normality and abnormality. *Man and World, 28*, 241–260.

Trull, T. J., Solhan, M. B., Tragesser, S. L., Jahng, S., Wood, P. K., & Piasecki, T. M. (2018). Affective instability: Measuring a core feature of borderline personality disorder with ecological momentary assessment. *Journal of Abnormal Psychology, 117*, 647–661.

Vanheule, S., Verhaeghe, P., & Desmet, M. (2011). In search of a framework for the treatment of alexithymia. *Journal of Psychology and Psychotherapy, 84*, 84–110.

Van Reekum, R., Links, P. S., & Fedorov, C. (1994). Impulsivity in borderline personality disorder. In K. R. Silk (Ed.), *Biological and neurobehavioral studies of borderline personality disorder* (pp. 1–22). American Psychiatric Association.

Vendrell-Ferran, I. (2022). Feeling as consciousness of value. *Ethical Theory Moral Practice, 25*, 71–88.

von Rad, M. (1983). *Alexithymie. Empirische Untersuchungen zur Diagnostik und Therapie psychosomatisch Kranken. Monographien aus dem Gesamtgebiet der Psychiatrie*. Springer-Verlag.

Watkins, J. G. (1978). *The therapeutic self.* Human Sciences.

Watkins, J. G., & Watkins, H. H. (1997). *Ego states theory and therapy*. Norton.

Wehrle, M. (2015). "Feelings as the motor of perception"? The essential role of interest for intentionality. *Husserl Studies, 31*(1), 45–64.

8

EMOTIONAL BLINDNESS

A Phenomenological Account of Alexithymia and Empathy

Introduction

Saramago redefines human nature and its moral status through the mental experiment pursued in his famous novel, *Blindness*, where he imagines the population suddenly affected by a fast-spreading epidemic of blindness that throws society into chaos and desperation. He shows how blindness can shape people's lives on different levels and focuses in particular on the moral throwbacks of the epidemic and their emotional consequences. In this chapter, I will focus on the description of a peculiar form of blindness, the emotional one and its practical influence on individuals' lives. Emotional blindness (alexithymia) is in fact a condition that, according to epidemiological studies, seems to affect 10% of the general population (Salminen et al., 1999). There are individuals who know that there are emotions they should feel but they cannot perceive them; they might understand their existence but they cannot directly come in contact with them. In the same way as blind persons who use their cane to see what is around them, alexithymic individuals use their cognitive understanding to perceive the emotions that are around them and develop empathy with themselves and others.

Struggling to put into words what we feel is an experience that all of us endured to a different degree. Yet, systematically being unable to perceive the bodily feelings that are moving from within and coupling them with the right sensations is a lived experience that radically undermines our ability of enjoying life and living fulfilling relationships with others.

DOI: 10.4324/9781003665557-8

Below in the note I cite a poem[1] on alexithymia where the author, Panday, shares with us how alexithymia feels in daily life with others:

> I wrote this <poem> to explain that sometimes a person can be filled with so much life and can be exploding with passion or they could be more gentle and passive, with calmer thoughts BUT none of this would actually matter if a person can't actually feel or show anything- emotions. You can be the best dancer in the room but if you can't feel the music, it's not the same. You're somewhat numb.

This image—dancing without music—beautifully encapsulates the paradox of alexithymia: a life lived in full motion, yet stripped of emotional resonance. Emotional disconnection is not the absence of vitality but the inability to inhabit its rhythms. The result is not apathy but a profound and often invisible sense of numbness—one that leaves individuals feeling alienated from themselves and from others.

Unfortunately, in our society, we have not been educated on how to relate to individuals experiencing this kind of blindness to the point that they become almost invisible to our eyes as well. As the author puts it, they would feel that they would "continue to be nothing" since nothing is what they can feel. There are online spaces where people suffering from this condition can gather and exchange a few words, like this user:

> For some time I have been saying "I am aware of physical changes in my body but I don't know what emotion to call them". So finding the term Alexithymia was – well I don't know how to describe how I felt![2]

This person is aware of its own physical changes but it is certainly challenging for him/her (more often him in case of alexithymia) to label them and couple them with significant meanings. This person adds,

> As a child I remember that an icecream van drove around our rural area – maybe once a week – it played a happy tune to let us know that it was close and the other children got "excited" and ran up the drive to be ready for its arrival – I did not feel excitement so I used to say that I did not like icecream. I did not dislike icecream I was just not excited by it.

Being aware of other people's reactions sheds a light on how alexithymic individuals should feel when certain events occur. Accordingly, they doubt what is the right way to feel because they cannot properly name or feel the affection that they sense. As this other user writes,

> I understand other people's emotions in a theoretical or logical kind of way. Your child dies? I understand that that is devastating for you. You will need

> time to adjust. You will not be able to function normally for some time. You will exhibit emotional behaviour. That is justifiable, understandable. I will make myself available for you to tell me how you feel. I will reassure you that there is nothing wrong with you because you feel these emotions – but empathy – I suppose not.

As shown in Chapter 7, in alexithymia, there is a basic cognitive understanding of what it should be reasonable to feel in certain circumstances and what others should feel in the same circumstances; there is also genuine care for others but all these emotional expressions are understood more than actually felt by the individual.

Hence, in this chapter, I will expand on the theoretical structure I presented in Chapter 7 and I will discuss how practically alexithymia unfolds in real life. The Husserlian phenomenological approach to affectivity will help to understand how the empathetic life of alexithymic individuals is impacted based on a basic and complex definition of phenomenological empathy. In conclusion, I will propose therapeutic exercises that might help alexithymic individuals to improve their empathetic skills. Ultimately, this chapter is to address the questions: how do you build your clinical decision-making process on your phenomenological understanding of lived experiences and how do you take into account the values of the person?

What Is Alexithymia

Alexithymia is a multifaceted psychological construct characterized by difficulties in recognizing, understanding, and expressing one's emotions. First identified and coined by psychoanalyst Peter Sifneos in the 1970s, the term "alexithymia" originates from the Greek words "a" (lack), "lexis" (word), and "thymos" (emotion), indicating a deficit in verbalizing emotions. This condition has significant implications for emotional processing, interpersonal relationships, and mental health, and it has garnered substantial attention across multiple disciplines. Alexithymia is a personality trait characterized by difficulties in identifying and describing personal feelings and a lack of consideration for others' emotions. As a result, individuals with these traits find it challenging to develop empathy toward themselves and others.

Originally associated with patients affected by psychosomatic problems, alexithymia involves an inability to adequately identify physical sensations as manifestations of emotions, leading to difficulties in discriminating between feelings and bodily sensations. Alexithymia refers to "the inability to adequately identify physical sensations as somatic manifestations of emotions" (Di Tella & Costelli, 2016, 41) or a failure to realize that "a number of bodily feelings… are/indicate sensations" (Dellantonio & Pastore, 2017, 268). Beyond somatic dissociation, alexithymia is marked by a constricted imaginative life and externally oriented cognitive style. Alexithymic individuals tend to focus on factual, observable aspects of experience while avoiding introspection or reflection on their internal emotional world (Bach et al., 1996). This operational thinking style—what Marty and de M'Uzan (1963) called *pensée opératoire*—is pragmatic, devoid of fantasy, and often yields narratives that are emotionally flat, self-centered, and devoid of empathy (Nemiah, 1977). Alexithymic persons may recount events in a detached, third-person manner, offering exhaustive detail while omitting inner perspectives or social context, making therapeutic encounters particularly challenging. This emotional disconnection has profound implications for interpersonal relationships. As Parker et al. (1993) observe, individuals with alexithymia often fail to perceive the emotional cues in others' facial expressions and may show diminished empathic capacities. They are also prone to difficulties in distinguishing their own perspectives from those of others (Taylor, 1984), which compounds social isolation and complicates therapeutic engagement.

The cognitive style characterizing alexithymia leads to constricted imaginative processes and a concrete, reality-based approach, with a strong inclination toward social conformity and a lack of connection with their own emotional reality (Bach et al., 1996). Accordingly, individuals tend to focus on external events and factual details rather than their internal emotional states. Such individuals may prioritize practical matters over emotional introspection. This condition is commonly associated with certain psychiatric and medical conditions, such as depression, anxiety disorders, post-traumatic stress disorder, eating disorders, and psychosomatic illnesses.

Assessment of alexithymia typically involves the use of self-report questionnaires, with the most widely employed instrument being the Toronto Alexithymia Scale (TAS-20). The TAS-20 comprises 20 items designed to measure difficulty of identifying feelings, difficulty of describing feelings, and externally oriented thinking (Bagby et al., 1994).

Neuroscientific research has provided insights into the neurobiological basis of alexithymia. Functional magnetic resonance imaging studies have revealed alterations in brain regions involved in emotional processing, such as the anterior cingulate cortex, insula, and prefrontal cortex (Van der Velde et al., 2013). These brain regions play crucial roles in emotional awareness, regulation, and empathy, suggesting that alexithymia may be linked to disturbances in these neural circuits.

Alexithymia can emerge early in life, and certain developmental factors may contribute to its development—even the loss of an arena where to express feelings through movement (Taylor et al., 1997). Childhood trauma, adverse experiences, and insecure attachment patterns have been associated with the development of alexithymia. Moreover, cultural factors can influence emotional expression norms, potentially impacting the manifestation and recognition of alexithymic traits across different cultural contexts.

The Lived Experience of Alexithymia

This phenomenon heightens vulnerability to mental disorders, diminishes the efficacy of psychotherapy, and has adverse impacts on the emergence and intensity of psychopathological symptoms (Semerari, 2011). Despite the variety of areas touched by this problem, this chapter will focus on how this phenomenon connects with empathy, especially in daily bodily activities.

In daily life, alexithymic people seem to strongly rely on outlets to express their bodily feelings; engaging in sports, especially high-risk ones, is a way to adapt their emotional regulation (Cazenave et al., 2008; Woodman et al., 2009). A person experiencing alexithymia might discover it simpler to recognize emotions in situations with elevated risks, where emotions like fear are more readily noticeable compared to other contexts. Consequently, they initially undergo the emotion of fear and subsequently perceive the corresponding decrease in emotion after completing the activity (Castanier et al., 2011; Woodman et al., 2009).

In my philosophical practice, I encountered alexithymia indirectly. Originally, my client was the wife of the person suffering from alexithymia. She came to my office dressed in black, concerned about her life and at the same time very warm and considerate in the way she related to me. She had two children. They had to face a relocation from another European city and she was in big distress. Having to handle two children was hard but what made everything more challenging was her husband. She did not feel supported by him; rather, she felt constantly judged by him and his family. In his life, everything seemed to have to look perfect, she and their children included. He never seemed to have had important ups and downs in his emotional life as she admittedly did. To her eye, he seemed to always have everything under control. She decided at some point after her second child to start wearing only black because she wanted that to be her signature; she wanted to look as "cool" as he was. At night before sleeping, she would consistently dream of another life. She fantasized in minutious detail habits, routines, and joys of another life. When she would fall asleep, the narration would end and then restart from where it ended the next night.

I investigated with her if the husband was lacking respect toward her, emotionally or physically; if there was any trace of abuse or gaslighting. None of this. He was cold. Emotionally remote. Distant. He could understand her. He was very empathetic with the struggles she was going through and he was willing to change because he did not want to lose her and this important relationship with her. Yet, the ways in which he could empathize with her were not sufficiently warm for her.

After a few sessions, it became more and more evident to me that her problem was to be found in the way in which she related to her husband. He might have suffered from alexithymia. I suggested to her strategies to recover the ownership over her body, her time, and, so to speak, her colors. Slowly, she started wearing colored clothes again and living more in the present rather than in her dreams. The husband met with a psychotherapist and it was confirmed that he was suffering from alexithymia. For the two of them, it was challenging to find an emotional place where to meet and build their emotional life. She had to learn what kind of advantages his emotional stability was bringing to the couple, his love language, and his way of caring; he had to learn how to see emotionally despite his blindness and to be there for her in the ways he could.

It is not easy for an alexithymic person to recover the emotional nuances of their own feelings and even access them—even if this kind of blindness generates deep sorrow and sadness. As we can read in this forum dedicated to people suffering from alexithymia:

> I feel like I can't access my own feelings. I feel something is going on but I can't find words to describe it. Like I've never learnt how to do it. When I am with my boyfriend – he kept asking me how I feel in this situation, how does the situation makes me feel… but my answer is always "okay", "good", "don't know"… it is really frustrating for him and I can relate that he isn't satisfied with my responses.

In similar words, this other user describes his willingness for a more emotional life and a more harmonious relationship with the partner. People suffering from this condition experience feelings and can see what other people are going through but they have extreme difficulty in perceiving and labeling their own feelings with words. It is as if they cannot be there with them. Hence, a deep sense of frustration follows.

> So I can't express and name my own feeling but I can deal with the feelings of others. I can sympathize with them and I can read and name their feelings.

A similar sentiment is expressed by another user, who likewise reflects on the difficulty of accessing personal emotions despite being attuned to the emotional states of others.

> I just discovered today what alexithymia was after I got into a huge falling out with my fiancee, who I've been with for about 5 years and currently live with. Most of our fights revolve around my inability to read my own emotions and hers and they've been happening more frequently in the past couple of months.

For some, even discovering the name of this condition can be liberating, as it can indicate a rational path one can follow to overcome blindness or to learn how to emotionally see in a different way. Being able to see one's own emotions and read them becomes a challenging effort that often fails them to the point that they seem to not value the persons they are close to in their lives.

> I love my fiancee very much but I really feel that my alexithymia is sabotaging our relationship. I tried everything to resolve it. I went to therapy, I started meditating, etc. I also tried communicating with her in her love language more (something I've had trouble with for a long time) to let her know that I'm on her side. Even though I have trouble reading my own emotions, I genuinely feel that this relationship is right for me but there's a voice in the back of my mind telling me that I don't deserve her because I have tremendous difficulty responding to her emotions and I feel defective when I have these thoughts so it becomes a never-ending thought loop that has been destroying us. Even if she does tell me what she feels, either it doesn't register or I think she's overreacting.

It becomes difficult for them to express their value system and to show that they are "on the side" of the people they love. It may be liberating for them to find ways to express their value system to loved ones, even if the full emotional and ethical picture still eludes them.

In fact, although empathy is not completely impaired as it might be in the case of sociopaths, cognitive empathy is there to acknowledge the lack of it and its need for improvement. Cognitive empathy is often used as the cane to navigate the emotional blindness in their interaffective world. According to a study, cognitive empathy is not always impaired in alexithymic individuals as

> alexithymia does not only involve a diminished ability to identify and describe one's own emotions. Furthermore, it is related to a deeper disability of emotion regulation, which becomes visible through impaired emotional concern for others and higher levels of personal distress.
>
> *(Alkan Härtwig et al., 2013)*

For Husserl, cognitive empathy is the main form of empathy we use toward foreign humanity (such as babies or animals, to use his examples); the *Einfühlung* is no longer confronted to the "extraordinarily distant analogy *(ausserordentlichf erne Analogie*)" (Husserl, 1973, 117). As one can read in Husserl's famous 1935 letter to Lévy-Bruhl:

> it is a possible and highly important and great task to 'empathize' (einzufühlen) with a humanity living self-contained in living generative sociality and to understand this humanity as having, in and through its socially unified life, the world, which for it is not a 'world-representation' but rather the world that actually exists for it.
>
> *(Husserl, 2008b, 3)*

Empathizing with a humanity that lives within its own "generative sociality" points to a central task of phenomenology: the effort to understand the world not only as it is constituted for oneself, but as it is experienced and lived by others within their own communal context. Husserl emphasizes that other communities do not merely hold different "representations" of the world; rather, their world is experientially and meaningfully real to them, shaped through the structures of their intersubjective life. This form of empathy requires a higher imaginative effort from the empathizer. Similar to how abnormal empathy works, in alexithymia we need to imagine what it would be like to be that body. In Husserl's Arbeitsmanuskripte from 1921, we can read,

> I see a human being, but he has no arms. I recognize him, I empathize with him, but I see that he is blind. […] But what if, as a human being, I see an animal? First of all, a superior animal. It still looks like a human being: in a way, it is a human being disfigured (verzerrter) in his embodied aspect […].
> *(Husserl, 1973, 126)*

Empathy compels us to imagine what it would be like to inhabit that body and live as that individual. It demands a rigorous, imaginative, and affectively attuned effort to understand how the world *shows itself* for others from within their own lifeworld. In this sense, empathy is not sentimental identification but a methodologically grounded, ethically motivated task that requires humility, openness, and an acknowledgment of our own limits. This process bears similarities to how individuals with alexithymia are often required to navigate their experiences. As one of the users on this forum asks,

> Would it be possible to learn my way through 20/20 difficulties describing feelings also? If there was a textbook on this just told me everything I'd be much better off.

and another replies,

> i have no idea, but id just pay attention to people and words they use. i mean hey, they get emotions, so why not use words they use to describe feelings that logically fit into place of any scenario or conversation?

This proves how even though access to their feelings seems cognitively and emotionally limited, it is yet possible for them to understand how to emotionally see and find an imitative access to overcome the impairment. Henceforth, in what follows, I will provide a medical and phenomenological description of what alexithymia is, why I consider it an affect disorder, how alexithymic individuals relate to empathy, and what solutions phenomenology can offer to improve this affect disorder.

Phenomenological Approaches to Alexithymia

Phenomenological approaches to alexithymia generally focus on understanding the subjective experiences of individuals with this condition. Phenomenology seeks to explore the lived experiences and the first-person perspective of those who have difficulty identifying, describing, and expressing emotions.

In an article on the topic, Svenaeus applies Heidegger's existential-phenomenological framework to the interpretation of alexithymia (1999). Drawing on Heidegger, he emphasizes that feeling, language, and bodily being are integral to how humans generate and receive meaning as being-in-the-world. Understanding, in Heidegger's sense, is not merely cognitive but must be attuned, embodied, and articulated to be meaningful. This attunement (*Befindlichkeit*) should not be reduced to discrete psychological emotions but refers to the situatedness of the self within a cultural and historical context into which one is thrown. Heidegger's concept of *Stimmungen* (moods) shapes how individuals perceive and relate to the world, themselves, and others. Moods are not incidental; they structure what matters to us by grounding our orientation within a meaningful totality of relevance. Svenaeus draws parallels between the alexithymic individual and Heidegger's concept of *das Man*—the inauthentic form of being-in-the-world characterized by social conformity, externalization, and a flight from existential self-awareness. Using McDougall's term "normopath" (1980, 1982), he aptly describes the alexithymic individual as one living solely in the external world, lacking access to subjective values and emotional depth—echoing Heidegger's *Verfallensein*, the existential fallenness into impersonal, collective life.

For Heidegger, authentic existence (*Eigentlichkeit*) is made possible through the attunement of anxiety, a fundamental mood (*Grundstimmung*) that reveals the world's meaning as contingent on one's own being. In contrast, *das Man* avoids this anxiety, instead immersing itself in superficial activity and collective norms, thereby losing the potential for authentic meaning-making (Heidegger, 1927/1962, 184–191). Svenaeus argues that alexithymic individuals similarly flee from existential anxiety, resulting in a flattened emotional world where others are perceived not as fellow *Dasein* but as instrumental objects.

Language, in this context, also loses its existential richness. The speech of alexithymic persons resembles Heidegger's concept of *Gerede* (idle talk): a form of communication devoid of emotional resonance and reflective depth (167–170). Although Heidegger maintains that total emotional detachment is existentially impossible—since all being-in-the-world is attuned in some way—*das Man*'s default attunement is curiosity (*Neugier*), which reflects goal-directed and externalized engagement (170–173). Similarly, alexithymic individuals exhibit a rigid, operational approach to language and relationships, lacking empathy and narrative depth (Nemiah, 1977).

Svenaeus also engages with psychoanalytic and cultural interpretations, noting a shift in recent scholarship from viewing alexithymia as an intrapsychic deficit to understanding it as a failure in the communicative field between analyst and analysand (Langs, 1978; von Rad & Lolas, 1982). Kirmayer (1987) highlights the cultural construction of emotional expressivity, suggesting that norms for articulating feelings are not universal. From a Heideggerian view, these cultural contexts shape *Mitsein* (being-with), where attunement and language are embedded in shared worlds.

While Heidegger gives less direct attention to the body, Svenaeus supplements this with Merleau-Ponty's *Phénoménologie de la Perception* (1945), which conceptualizes the body as a "lived" or phenomenological body rather than a mere object. In alexithymia, the body is no longer experienced as subjectively lived but appears as a foreign, external object—an "it" rather than "mine" (Krystal, 1982). This estrangement contributes to somatization, where unprocessed affect accumulates as psychosomatic pain.

Svenaeus contends that while emotional attunements such as joy, sorrow, and dread open the world to meaningful engagement, their absence in alexithymia results in existential closure. In such cases, attunement withdraws from the interpersonal and linguistic realms, concentrating instead on the body as undifferentiated pain. This somatic pain, though not devoid of meaning, marks the remnant of emotional life trapped in bodily sensation. The alexithymic body thus becomes the site of a mute and unmediated attunement—no longer participating in the shared world but suffering in isolated corporeality.

Svenaeus' reading situates alexithymia not merely as a cognitive-emotional deficit, but as an existential condition of disrupted being-in-the-world. It is a disorder of attunement, language, and embodied subjectivity, rendering true intersubjectivity and authenticity elusive.

While still phenomenological and partially aligned with Svenaeus' findings, my approach is grounded in Husserlian phenomenology of affect. Unlike Svenaeus, my phenomenological account of alexithymia focuses more on the dynamics of affection and personal habit in order to explore how alexithymia hinders individuals from accessing their own emotions.

An Husserlian Approach

As mentioned in the previous chapter, Husserl describes the common phenomenon of accessing one's own content of experience as a "battle of affections," that is, the affections struggle to get the attention from the I (Husserl, 1931, Ms. D, 14). Affects trigger both lower and higher feelings, allowing us to engage with the world. These feelings help us to understand ourselves as both subjects and objects of our experiences, creating empathetic connections with others and guiding ethical choices. However, when feelings fail to process affects properly, it can lead to affective disorders. As Husserl explains (*Phenomenology of Intersubjectivity*, 1973), affective data are initially received passively, but feelings transform them into active sense and meaning. This transformation happens through intentionality, which operates on the affects to determine their meaning for us. As mentioned in Chapter 7, this process unfolds through three main activities: perceptive interest, evaluation, and objectivating representation (Forlè, 2019; Slaby, 2008; Wehrle, 2015).

In alexithymia, the issue lies predominantly in the first step: interest. Interest, as Husserl describes, is essential for attention, a perceptive act that helps the ego focus on affective data. In alexithymia, this process seems to function in a peculiar way, impacting the individual's ability to determine the meaning belonging to their feelings. As in the case of my client, her husband genuinely loved her but was unable to be interested in the sense of being present with the feelings that connected him to her. As a result, he could not fully participate in or experience a true sense of belonging to his own emotional life. This impairment can hinder empathy, limiting affective engagement with others, and leading to emotional disorders like depression or panic (Husserl, 2008a; Rang, 1973).

Husserl's phenomenology of affect helps explain how we become aware of emotions through a layered process that begins with being affected by something and culminates in the formation of meaningful emotional experience. This process relies on what Husserl calls perceptive interest—the ability to be bodily and attentively present with what affects us. In alexithymia, this basic level of engagement is often disrupted. Individuals may register that something is emotionally significant but fail to access or articulate the corresponding feeling. They remain cognitively aware that an emotional response is expected, yet the emotion itself remains unavailable or unformed. As one individual described in a support forum: "*It's like I have the manual for human emotions, but the wiring just isn't there.*" Hence, they can extend cognitive knowledge on this perceptive process but lack the automatic movement necessary to enact the connection between themselves and the other. The problem lies not only in the verbal expression of feelings but also in the earlier, more embodied stage of emotional life where affective data should be transformed into felt meaning.

Clinically, this can manifest in various ways. A person may experience physiological symptoms of panic without being able to name the anxiety behind them. As it was for my client's husband, others may struggle in relationships, knowing intellectually that their partner is upset but feeling emotionally flat or disconnected. In some cases, alexithymic individuals may thrive in high-performance environments—such as competitive sports—where emotional detachment can be an advantage. However, over time, the inability to be fully present with one's own emotions can hinder empathy, lead to ethical disorientation, and contribute to depressive states or chronic detachment. To address alexithymia, it is crucial to explore the nature of empathy and how interest influences our capacity to engage with the world through feelings.

The Problem of Empathy in Alexithymia

The problem of empathy in alexithymia is a significant and multifaceted issue. One of the primary challenges is that individuals with alexithymia find it difficult to recognize and comprehend the emotional states of others. One user expressed, "*I can see someone is in pain, but there's a delay in me. I don't know what I'm feeling, and by the time I figure it out, the moment to act has passed.*" A therapist working with an alexithymic adolescent observed, "*He would often say, 'I know she's upset, but I don't know what to do unless someone tells me step-by-step.*'" These remarks illustrate how empathy, in the alexithymic structure, often fails to arise in synchrony with the emotional needs of others. Their limited emotional awareness and expression make it challenging to pick up on subtle emotional cues, facial expressions, and vocal intonations, leading to misinterpretations or a lack of appropriate emotional responses.

According to Husserl's intentionality of feeling, our ability to develop empathy is strongly connected to our ability to feel bodily interest in the affects that awaken us from our object-like state. What has not been felt yet becomes "something" when its parts associate into a whole, according to the criteria dictated by affections and feelings by means of presenting egoic activities such as memory, phantasy, and empathy. In fact, empathy is one of the very first egoic activities which presents itself to our subjectivity by awakening the I to recognize itself as different from the matter it perceives; here we mean perceive as that in which the subject is bodily present. Through an analogizing and differentiating approach, the I synthetizes the affect matter it was awakened by in order to organize it into a sense—that is what a perceiving I does. Such embodied presentifications allow the undifferentiated matter to become a sedimentation that establishes "the unity of world-certainty" and discloses the possibility of reproductive activity (Husserl, 1966, 152). Through empathy, we are in (*inter sumus*) the matter of the other; our bodily perception is interested in making present what others' affects awakened us from our state of rest. The primordial ego irradiates affective awakenings; the awake ego reacts and opens its horizon to a chain of other possible fusions or primordial homogeneous associations of matter. We become part of the world in connection with a "first other" that looks similar to us. In the case of my client, she could perceive the connection with her husband; their bond was present but the feelings that usually surround that bond were not, so to speak, alive.

For Husserl (1966, 123), while primordial association is independent of the ego, it awakens the ego through affective associations based on similarities and differences. Empathy is one of the ways through which our perceptive interest recognizes differences and similarities between the just-awoken embodied ego and the other. At first, it is the ego-less affection that seizes the undifferentiated matter and transforms it into a unit of given data; then the matter self-organizes in data within a system of interrelated units. While doing so, the structure of something different from, and yet related to, the data awakens the subject. Husserl writes, "We can secure decisive insights into the essence of association when we comprehend the (…) structure pertaining to the function of affection, its peculiarity, and its dependence on essential conditions" (Husserl, 1966, 211). The synthetic force through which the affects become data felt by the subject (1966, 477–478) transforms the subject, which does not yet question its thinghood, into a living agent. This living agent experiences itself as bodily bound to the world through which it awakens to itself. This connection is a first empathetic layer that establishes the continuity of the subject with the other living agents. It seems that in alexithymia this first living embodied connection is difficult to recover and perceptively experience. Everything becomes colored in black, like my client's clothing. She is deeply affected by her husband's way of being and unconsciously begins to mimic him—without realizing that she is, in fact, mirroring his emotional blindness.

Movement, Enaction, and Empathy

As we saw thus far, alexithymic individuals have the ability to cognitively acknowledge the lack of their empathetic connection and recognize where an openness to the other would be needed. Yet, they lack the automatic movement necessary to enact the connection between themselves and the other. They do not seem to feel the affects that trigger the bodily interest and move their attention toward a spontaneous pairing direction. In fact, the coupling of self and the other is not based on a deliberative reflection, that is a cognitive form of empathy that acknowledges the similarities between oneself and the other, but it is rooted in a habitual body schema where the self awakens as operating in an ongoing automatic coupling procedure. By bodily schema (Merleau-Ponty, 1945; Spence & Holmes, 2004), here it is meant the tridimensional pattern of habituations and automatic responses that the body gives to the input of the world which allows it to be passively and actively engaged with it (de Vignemont et al., 2021). Very simple examples of bodily schema could be reaching for a cup or moving in a crowded space—the body schema is constantly updated based on sensory information and experiences. It should be through the automatic procedure embodied by the bodily schema that the self awakens to the affects that are shaping its bodily presence and comprehend its own emotions and the emotions of the other. As Thompson remarks (2007, 393), this is a fundamental level of empathy that allows one to live within the experience of another as a living bodily subject. This does not seem to occur in people suffering from alexithymia. Their interest, is in a certain way, impaired because the perceptive movement that should set in motion the coupling process is malfunctioning and does not allow bodily schemas to develop in that direction. Affects remain so to speak uncoupled and not felt.

Hence, how can we help people suffering from alexithymia to solve this problem? According to some scholars, perception is action and cannot be isolated from it (Gibson, 2014; Noë, 2004; Varela et al., 2017). A person with high alexithymic traits shared, "*I walk too close or too far from people, and I don't notice until they step away or say something. I don't pick up the vibe.*" This lack of pre-reflective adjustment reflects a breakdown in the sensory-motor tuning required for bodily copresence. Perception is an active, ongoing process that involves and allows constant interaction between the subject and the outside world. According to these scholars, this interaction is possible because through the ongoing interactive process the subject recognizes the lawful connection between sensory and motor systems. That is, in this process an ongoing bodily engagement with the world is in action which cannot be reduced to passive reception of sensory data; that is so because the ongoing engagement with the lawful connection is a selfless process that makes the world as it is according to its lawful linkages between sensory and motor systems (Varela et al., 2017, 173).

At its most sensuous level the empathetic coupling involves the ability to connect the sensory stimuli we receive with our movement and engage with the lawful connection that couples the two together. This requires our *phronesis* (from Greek, practical reason), that is, a high-functioning activity of our practical knowledge which knows how to activate the appropriate norm according to the sensory data and stimuli we were subjected to. This activation is not performed by the subject alone but it involves the collaboration between subject and object.

For example, I am walking with a friend and we both regulate each other's walking speed and distance. We both adhere to the data that the sensory and motor systems give us in relation to the implied law of walking together as friends rather than as lovers. Hence, coupling refers to the ability to effectively link the sensory stimuli we receive with our movements, thereby mastering the lawful relationship between the two. In other words, perceptual experience is based on our practical knowledge.

> ...to feel a shape or texture of a surface is ... to allow one's movement to be moulded by that which one touches. For something to feel this way or that (round, large, flat, rough, soft) is for it to condition the possibilities of movement of the palpating hand or body part in corresponding ways.
>
> *(Noë, 2004, 108)*

The way in which we perceive other minds and we encounter the other in the world according to their structural similarities is strongly connected to perceptive movement and the enactive qualities of the subject capable of engaging with the norm that allows the coupling process of sensory data and stimuli to be. This basic empathy—which Hollan (2012) distinguishes from complex empathy as this latter entails conscious cognitive engagement and enactive acknowledgment of common basic norms—is more difficult to improve as it depends on our affective visceral life. While basic empathy implies a perceptual way to understand the emotional state of the other and the goals they are set to, complex empathy involves a complex understanding of how things should be in order to be empathetic. Alexithymic individuals may have difficulties attuning to the former rather than the latter. If by being empathetic we understand the more complex phenomenon of affective understanding and being nice to others in order to avoid upsetting or shaming someone, then this is something that alexithymic individuals might excel at. Yet, they might not be able to attune to the implied perceptive norm that can make them ready to give someone a tissue when they are about to cry or stop talking when someone is getting upset (although they would be happy to).

To use one last example, on a first date dinner, the two people will know how to adjust to each other, how to sit at the appropriate distance, how long they should talk, and how they should use certain words to avoid hurting each other's sensitivity. This might be lacking in the alexithymic person, unless they have experienced several first dates and have a cognitive understanding of how things should go. The alexithymic individual, unless equipped with a learned script or prior experience, may find these norms opaque. One individual admitted, "*I Google how to behave on dates. I need rules because I don't feel what's appropriate.*"

The basic norms regulating these encounters cannot be reversed; there is no perspective to see the common norm from different sides for them because at that basic empathetic level there is still no differentiation as the two subjects have not yet thematized the content of their lived experience. So they are as a whole coupling together in the flow of data of life. It is a moment-by-moment automatic reference to the norm that allows the harmonious interaction in which the bodily schemas of their subjectivity unfolds and this is the area that should be reinforced through therapy for the alexithymic individuals. As Cook and colleagues remark, training to better associate emotional expressions and faces (see Cook et al., 2013) might improve the recollection of emotional memories (see Luminet et al., 2006). Or, fostering linguistic intervention to help labeling affect with appropriate words, thus facilitating the lexicalization of emotional aspects as connected to specific emotional stimuli and events. Research shows that affect labeling enhances emotion regulation (Lieberman et al., 2011) and may draw on cognitive empathy to support the development of basic, embodied empathy in individuals with alexithymia. The impoverished linguistic style of alexithymic individuals may be enriched by training them to use metaphors (Kousta et al., 2011) and mental imagery (Holmes & Mathews, 2010). A recent series of innovative experiments by Kidd and Castano (2013) suggests that reading literary fiction (as opposed to nonliterary texts) can improve people's ability to identify and understand others' subjective states—although often dyslexia seems to accompany alexithymia (Mellor & Dagnan, 2005; Nesaimoghadam et al., 2020)—hence, the aid of audiobooks might be key in that sense.

Possible Paths

Having brought to light the important distinction between basic bodily empathy and complex cognitive empathy, and having shown the peculiar functioning of perceptive movement that impedes the body with alexithymia from being present in the feeling of the other, we can now propose some therapeutic suggestions.

These approaches, grounded in Husserl's phenomenology, may offer support to individuals with alexithymia. These paths aim not at reinforcing representational understanding of emotion, but at restoring the bodily intentionality through which affective life becomes experientially available.

Alexithymic individuals may benefit from cultivating perceptual experiences that enable them to move within the emotional field, rather than simply reflect upon it. According to Husserl, it is through *affective awakening*—the bodily response to the world's solicitations—that the ego emerges into its own self-awareness. In this light, we might understand empathy as not beginning in thought, but in bodily attunement. Practices that encourage rhythmic bodily synchronization—such as group walking, slow choreography, or collective vocal exercises—can help revive the *pre-reflective bodily schema* through which the world becomes affectively accessible. These responses operate both passively and actively, structuring the way one is attuned to the world (Vignemont et al., 2021). For individuals with alexithymia, this schema does not appear to support the automatic perceptual coupling that underlies basic empathy. Thus, therapies should focus not on emotion as content to be interpreted but as movement to be reinhabited.

As Thompson (2007, 393) remarks, this bodily resonance is a fundamental level of empathy, one that allows us to *live within* the experience of the other. Yet in alexithymia, this resonance is either absent or fragmented. To remedy this, therapeutic settings could involve structured intersubjective spaces—such as paired somatic mirroring, simple group rituals, or even shared attention tasks—where perceptive movement is gently facilitated and bodily interest in the presence of the other is reawakened.

As mentioned before, perception is not the reception of internal representations but the enactment of a sensorimotor loop that discloses the world through lawful coupling between movement and sensation (Gibson, 2014; Noë, 2004; Varela et al., 2017). From this view, empathy can be reframed as a bodily skill—one that arises when the subject is capable of letting their own movement be shaped by the emotional textures of the other. Such therapeutic work would not aim to teach emotion cognitively but to cultivate the felt sense of *letting the other's mood guide one's perceptual rhythm*. To feel another's sadness, for example, is not first to label it but to *slow down* with them, to match the silence or hesitancy in their speech, and to withdraw one's own claims to space. These are not learned scripts but embodied adjustments that emerge from the flow of shared temporality.

To work with this, therapy might focus on situations where bodily norms are shared and felt without needing to be named—such as those mentioned above, dancing in synchrony, or playing in musical ensembles. In these contexts, emotional attunement is practiced not through introspection but through coordinated action, where each body adjusts to the affective timing of others. Crucially, in these activities the underlying norm is not hidden: it can be supported by external structures like rhythm, breath, or score, offering the alexithymic person both perceptual immersion and conceptual scaffolding.

Finally, therapeutic space must remain respectful of the alexithymic person's value system. Their discomfort with emotional labeling should not be bypassed but gently explored through phenomenological description: "How did that moment feel in your body?" or "Was there a shift in your pace, your breath, your posture?" By cultivating the intentionality of feeling in its embodied roots—and not merely its cognitive or linguistic elaboration—we invite alexithymic individuals to encounter the possibility of affective meaning once again.

Conclusion

In this chapter, I have traced the phenomenological contours of alexithymia by focusing on the bodily and affective dynamics that make empathy possible. Rather than treating alexithymia as a merely cognitive or linguistic deficit, I have argued—drawing on Husserl's theory of intentionality—that it involves a deeper disturbance in the structure of embodied affectivity. The capacity to feel, resonate with, and respond to others does not arise first through mental representations but through a bodily schema that enables perceptual coupling with the world and with others.

Ultimately, caring for alexithymic individuals through a phenomenological lens means honoring their mode of being-in-the-world and working within its structures—patiently, bodily, and with shared rhythm—until emotional meaning becomes once again perceivable. It is not a matter of teaching empathy but of rekindling the bodily conditions through which empathy can arise.

Notes

1 You can retrieve this poem online at https://hellopoetry.com/solar-hugs-and-lunar-kisses/: Krithi Panday, Alexithymia:
2 Unless indicated otherwise, this and all the following first-hand quotes are retrieved from alexithymia forum at https://www.alexithymie.com/en/post/1278/questions_about_progress_with_symptoms.

References

Alkan Härtwig, E., Aust, S., & Heuser, I. (2013). HPA system activity in alexithymia: A cortisol awakening response study. *Psychoneuroendocrinology, 38*(9), 2121–2126. https://doi.org/10.1016/j.psyneuen.2013.03.023

Bach, M., Bach, D., & de Zwaan, M. (1996). Independency of alexithymia and somatization: A factor analytic study. *Psychosomatics, 37*(5), 451–458.

Bagby, R. M., Parker, J. D. A., & Taylor, G. J. (1994). The twenty-item Toronto Alexithymia Scale—I. Item selection and cross-validation of the factor structure. *Journal of Psychosomatic Research, 38*(1), 23–32. https://doi.org/10.1016/0022-3999(94)90005-1

Castanier, C., Le Scanff, C., & Woodman, T. (2011). Mountaineering as affect regulation: The moderating role of self-regulation strategies. *Anxiety, Stress & Coping, 24*(1), 75–89.

Cazenave, N., Le Scanff, C., & Tim, W. (2008). Skydiving as emotion regulation: The rise and fall of anxiety is moderated by alexithymia. *Journal of Sport and Exercise Psychology, 30*(4), 424–433.

Cook, R., Brewer, R., Shah, P., & Bird, G. (2013). Alexithymia, not autism, predicts poor recognition of emotional facial expressions. *Psychological Science, 24*(5), 723–732.

de Vignemont, F., Pitron, V., & Alsmith, A. J. T. (2021). What is the body schema? In Y. Ataria, S. Tanaka, & S. Gallagher (Eds.), *Body schema and body image: New directions*. Oxford: Oxford University Press.

Dellantonio, S., & Pastore, L. (2017). *Internal perception: The role of bodily information in concepts and word mastery*. Springer.

Di Tella, M., & Castelli, L. (2016). Alexithymia in chronic pain disorders. *Current Rheumatology Reports, 18*(7), Article 41. https://doi.org/10.1007/s11926-016-0592-x

Forlè, F. (2019). Bodily expressions, feelings, and the direct perception account of social cognition. *Phenomenology and the Cognitive Sciences, 19*(5), 1019–1034.

Gibson, J. J. (2014). *The ecological approach to visual perception.* London: Routledge.

Heidegger, M. (1962). *Being and time* (J. Macquarrie & E. Robinson, Trans.). Harper & Row. (Original work published 1927).

Heidegger, M. (1927/1986). *Sein und Zeit*. Tübingen: Max Niemeyer Verlag. 1996. *Being and time.* J. Stambaugh (Trans.). Albany: State University of New York.

Hollan, D. (2012). Emerging issues in the cross-cultural study of empathy. *Emotion Review, 4*(1), 70–78.

Holmes, E. A., & Mathews, A. (2010). Mental imagery in emotion and emotional disorders. *Clinical Psychology Review, 30*(3), 349–362.

Husserl, E. (1931). *Affektivität im Allgemeinen und in Bezug auf Wachheit und Schlaf* (manuscript), Ms. D 14.

Husserl, E. (1966). *Analysen zur passiven Synthesis. Aus Vorlesungs- und Forschungsmanuskripten 1918–1926.* M. Fleischer (Ed.). Den Haag: Nijhoff.

Husserl, E. (1973). *Zur Phänomenologie der Intersubjektivität. Dritter Teil (1929–1935)*. I. Kern (Ed.). Den Haag: Nijhoff.

Husserl, E. (2008a). *Die Lebenswelt. Auslegungen der vorgegebenen Welt und ihrer Konstitution. Texte aus dem Nachlass (1916–1937)*. R. Sowa (Ed.). Dordrecht: Springer.

Husserl, E. (2008b). Edmund Husserl's letter to Lucien Lévy-Bruhl. *The New Yearbook for Phenomenology and Phenomenological Philosophy, VIII*, 1–6.

Kidd, D. C., & Castano, E. (2013). Reading literary fiction improves theory of mind. *Science, 342*(6156), 377–380.

Kirmayer, L. J. 1987. Languages of suffering and healing: Alexithymia as a social and cultural process. *Transcultural Psychiatric Research Review* 24:119–36.

Kousta, S. T., Vigliocco, G., Vinson, D. P., Andrews, M., & Del Campo, E. (2011). The representation of abstract words: Why emotion matters. *Journal of Experimental Psychology: General, 140*(1), 14–22.

Krystal, H. (1982). Alexithymia and the effectiveness of psychoanalytic treatment. *International Journal of Psychoanalytic Psychotherapy, 9*, 353–378.

Lieberman, M. D., Inagaki, T. K., Tabibnia, G., & Crockett, M. J. (2011). Subjective responses to emotional stimuli during labeling, reappraisal, and distraction. *Emotion, 11*(3), 468–480.

Luminet, O., Vermeulen, N., Demaret, C., Taylor, G. J., & Bagby, R. M. (2006). Alexithymia and levels of processing: Evidence for an overall deficit in remembering emotion words. *Journal of Research in Personality, 40*(5), 713–733.

Marty, P., & de M'Uzan, M. (1963). La Pensee Operatoire. *Revue Francaise de Psychanalyse*, *27*, 1345–1356.

McDougall, J. (1980). *Plea for a measure of abnormality*. New York: International Universities Press.

McDougall, J. (1982). Alexithymia, psychosomatosis, and psychosis. *International Journal of Psychoanalytic Psychotherapy, 9*, 379–388.

Mellor, K., & Dagnan, D. (2005). Exploring the concept of alexithymia in the lives of people with learning disabilities. *Journal of Intellectual Disabilities, 9*(3), 229–239.

Merleau-Ponty, M. (1945). *Phenomenology of perception*. London: Routledge.

Nemiah, J. C. (1977). Alexithymia. Theoretical considerations. *Psychotherapy and Psychosomatics*, *28*(1-4), 199–206. https://doi.org/10.1159/000287064

Nesaimoghadam, B., Yaghoobi, A., Rashid, K., & Kordnoghabi, R. (2020). The effect of sand play therapy on reducing alexithymia in dyslexic students. *Journal of Educational Psychology Studies, 17*(38), 85–104.

Noë, A. (2004). *Action in perception*. Cambridge, MA: MIT Press.

Parker, J. D., Taylor, G. J., & Bagby, R. M. (1993). Alexithymia and the recognition of facial expressions of emotion. Psychotherapy and psychosomatics, 59(3-4), 197–202.

Rang, B. (1973). *Kausalität und Motivation. Untersuchungen zum Verhältnis von Perspektivität und Objektivität in der Phänomenologie Edmund Husserls*. Den Haag: Nijhoff.

Salminen, J. K., Saarijärvi, S., Äärelä, E., Toikka, T., & Kauhanen, J. (1999). Prevalence of alexithymia and its association with sociodemographic variables in the general population of Finland. *Journal of Psychosomatic Research, 1*(1), 75–82. https://doi.org/10.1016/S0022-3999(98)00053-1

Semerari, A., Carcione, A., Dimaggio, G., Nicolò, G., & Procacci, M. (2007). *Psychotherapy of personality disorders: Metacognition, states of mind and interpersonal cycles*. London: Routledge.

Sifneos, P. E. (1972). *Short-term psychotherapy and emotional crisis.* Harvard: Harvard University Press.

Sifneos, P. E. (1988). Alexithymia and its relationship to hemispheric specialization, affect, and creativity. *Psychiatric Clinics of North America, 11*(2), 287–292.

Slaby, J. (2008). Affective intentionality and the feeling body. *Phenomenology and the Cognitive Sciences, 7*(4), 429–444.

Spence, C., & Holmes, N. P. (2004). The bodily self: Sensory–motor integration and the sense of self. In G. Knoblich, I. M. Thornton, M. Grosjean, & M. Shiffrar (Eds.), *Human body perception from the inside out* (pp. 147–169). Oxford: Oxford University Press.

Svenaeus, F. (1999). Alexithymia: A phenomenological approach. *Philosophy, Psychiatry, & Psychology, 6*(2), 71–82.

Taylor, G. J. (1984). Alexithymia: concept, measurement, and implications for treatment. *The American Journal of Psychiatry, 141*(6), 725–732. https://doi.org/10.1176/ajp.141.6.725

Taylor, G. J., Bagby, R. M., & Parker, J. D. A. (1997). *Disorders of affect regulation: Alexithymia in medical and psychiatric illness.* Cambridge: Cambridge University Press.

Thompson, E. (2007). *Mind in life: Biology, phenomenology, and the sciences of mind.* Harvard: Harvard University Press.

van der Velde, J., Servaas, M. N., Goerlich, K. S., Bruggeman, R., Horton, P., Costafreda, S. G., & Aleman, A. (2013). Neural correlates of alexithymia: A meta-analysis of emotion processing studies. *Neuroscience & Biobehavioral Reviews, 37*(8), 1774–1785. https://doi.org/10.1016/j.neubiorev.2013.07.008

Varela, F. J., Rosch, E., & Thompson, E. (2017). *The embodied mind: Cognitive science and human experience.* Cambridge, MA: MIT Press.

von Rad, M. (1983). Alexithymie. Empirische Untersuchungen zur Diagnostik und Therapie psychosomatisch Kranken. In *Monographien aus dem Gesamtgebiet der Psychiatrie* (Vol. 30). Berlin: Springer-Verlag.

von Rad, M., & Lolas, F. (1982). Empirical evidence of alexithymia. *Psychotherapy and Psychosomatics, 38*(1), 91–102. https://doi.org/10.1159/000287618

Wehrle, M. (2015). "Feelings as the motor of perception"? The essential role of interest for intentionality. *Husserl Studies, 31*(1), 45–64.

Woodman, T., Huggins, M., Le Scanff, C., & Cazenave, N. (2009). Alexithymia determines the anxiety experienced in skydiving. *Journal of Affective Disorders, 116*, 134–138. https://doi.org/10.1016/j.jad.2008.11.022

9

BORDERLINE PERSONALITY DISORDERS, AFFECTS, AND VALUE DISRUPTIONS

Introduction

In Chapter 8, I explored the relationship between affect, empathy, and alexithymia, demonstrating how a lack of spontaneous bodily presence in the affects (*interest*) can lead to diminished empathetic connections with others. In this chapter, I will focus on the second triad described in Chapter 7. I will examine how a highly engaging valuing activity applied on affects can lead to a disruptive representational pattern of the affects; what one might call this, an excess of empathy, which disrupts the balance between the individual and others. Therefore, this chapter addresses the issue of the relationship between emotions and reality, focusing on how the evaluative components of our emotions can complicate the process of making-meaning from our affective experiences. I will draw on Husserl's concept of intentionality and affect to propose an alternative approach that harmonizes meaning and emotion.

This chapter will address these points through a phenomenological description of the mereological constitution of contents in the intentional acts of people affected by Borderline Personalities (BPD) or emotionally unstable personality disorder (EUPD). The goal is to see how this mereological constitution leads to a disturbance in the affective resonance[1] of our interaffective[2] and intersubjective[3] lifeworld.[4] To my understanding, this disturbance occurs because the existential quality implied in the axiological property of meanings has the power to overrule its logical[5] components, thus affecting the intersubjective interactions of everyday life.

This chapter will first examine the emotional patterns of individuals affected by the disorder. Next, it will analyze the role of mereology in shaping the

DOI: 10.4324/9781003665557-9

meaning-making process within intentional acts. Finally, it will demonstrate how this process typically functions in those impacted by the disorder. The aim is to highlight a key factor contributing to the disruption of intersubjective relationships in these individuals, providing clinicians and caregivers with alternative strategies to address the issue, alleviate the disruption, and promote emotional integration.

What Is BPD/EUPD?

Individuals with BPD/EUPD[6] disorders often face ongoing challenges in managing their emotions, leading them to impulsive and self-harmful behaviors, which frequently result in tumultuous and unstable relationships (American Psychiatric Association, 2013). Despite the significant impact of BPD on healthcare systems (Bagge et al., 2005; Comtois et al., 2003) and the economic burden on individuals and society (van Asselt et al., 2007), many clinicians are hesitant to work with these patients due to the potential risks they pose to themselves and others (Dixon-Gordon et al., 2017). This hesitancy, coupled with reduced social support networks, often further diminishes the individual's ability to manage emotional distress (Hughes et al., 2012). Gaining a deeper understanding of the emotional dysregulation underlying BPD could benefit both patients and healthcare professionals working with them.

In individuals with BPD/EUPD, early emotional and social development is often marked by unmet intersubjective and interaffective needs. According to biosocial theory (Linehan, 1993), the social environment inadequately responds to the emotional vulnerability of the child, often in ways perceived as invalidating, dismissive, or trivializing. This interaction exacerbates the child's innate emotional sensitivity, resulting in impulsivity, poor social functioning, heightened emotional reactivity, and difficulty returning to emotional baseline (Linehan, 1993). Such patterns can lead to emotions like sadness, hostility, and fear (Trull et al., 2008).

Some researchers suggest that these difficulties may stem from larger cognitive deficits (Fertuck et al., 2006; Lenzenweger et al., 2004), which extend to affective decision-making. For instance, individuals with BPD/EUPD tend to make poor decisions, prioritizing immediate rewards over long-term gains (LeGris et al., 2014; van Reekum et al., 1994), particularly when dealing with uncertain outcomes or potential losses (Sánchez-Navarro et al., 2014). Laboratory studies have also highlighted the presence of intense emotional reactivity, such as shame (Gratz et al., 2013), anger (Kuo et al., 2013), fear, and anxiety (Dixon-Gordon et al., 2015), often accompanied by heightened amygdala responses (Minzenberg et al., 2007).

Moreover, individuals with BPD/EUPD are prone to interpreting negative feedback more harshly than intended (Shenk & Fruzzetti, 2011, 2014) or misreading positive cues as negative, often leading to feelings of rejection (Gardner et al., 2010; Staebler et al., 2011). The most common reaction to perceived rejection is rumination, defined as repetitive, unproductive thoughts (Peters et al., 2015; Selby et al., 2009). This rumination can escalate into "emotional cascades," where distress intensifies and leads to impulsive actions to escape overwhelming emotions. Such rumination is strongly associated with anger (Berenson et al., 2011), shame (Peters et al., 2014), reduced present-focused awareness (Selby et al., 2015), and difficulty managing intense emotional arousal (Gottman, 1993).

Phenomenological Psychopathology of BPD/EUPD

Phenomenological psychopathology provides a rich framework for understanding BPD by delving into the lived experiences of emotional instability and fragmented identity. One of the core contributions comes from the works of Karl Jaspers, who emphasized the need for *Verstehen*, or empathetic understanding, in psychopathology. Jaspers argued that the subjective experiences of individuals with BPD reveal a deep struggle with emotional dysregulation, where feelings of emptiness and impulsive behaviors stem from an inability to maintain a stable self-concept (Jaspers, 1963). This fragmented sense of self is not simply a symptom but a fundamental disruption in how individuals perceive and relate to themselves and their world. Jaspers' insights into how existential anxiety and crises of identity manifest in BPD patients have laid the foundation for a phenomenological approach to the disorder.

Following his intuitions, the works of Hans Köhler (2015) and Thomas Fuchs (2005) have further deepened our understanding of the emotional and interpersonal dimensions of BPD. Köhler explored how emotional dysregulation in BPD disrupts the temporal structure of lived experience, leading to a sense of fragmentation not only in identity but also in the perception of time (Köhler, 2015). This contributes to the erratic and impulsive behaviors commonly seen in BPD, where patients live in a continuous present, disconnected from past and future. Fuchs expanded on this by examining the role of embodiment and affectivity, arguing that the emotional instability of BPD patients leads to a disconnection from their own bodies and the world around them (Fuchs, 2005). Fuchs' notion of "affective attunement" highlights how the emotional experiences of BPD patients become disjointed, causing a breakdown in the intersubjective connections that are essential for a coherent sense of self and stable relationships (Fuchs, 2013).

Anderson and Stanghellini have also contributed significantly to the phenomenological study of BPD, focusing on the intersubjective dimension of the disorder. Anderson, building on the work of phenomenologists like Merleau-Ponty, emphasized how BPD individuals experience an existential alienation, where their emotional turmoil makes it difficult to establish meaningful connections with others (Anderson, 2012). Stanghellini's exploration of *pathic intersubjectivity* in BPD reveals how the intense emotional fluctuations seen in the disorder can lead to an unstable perception of others, often oscillating between idealization and devaluation (Stanghellini, 2004). This makes it difficult for individuals with BPD to form stable, enduring relationships, which further compounds their emotional dysregulation. Through these phenomenological perspectives, BPD is understood not merely as a clinical diagnosis but as a peculiar form of lived experience in which individuals relate and engage with their emotional and social worlds.

First-Person Lived Experience

Narratives from BPD/EUPDs' first-person lived experience seem to confirm the traits discussed above. Here, for example, Jill writes:

> I know I keep having these ups and downs, but if I don't get off this roller coaster, I'm worried he's just going to get sick of it and leave me.
>
> *(cited in Dixon-Gordon et al., 2017, 429)*

Emotional reactivity and instability severely affect the romantic relationships of individuals with BPD/EUPD. The instability of their interaffective world undermines their sense of belonging, which is crucial for both personal and social well-being. It is as though their emotional life is constantly under threat, leaving them vulnerable to being disconnected from their own lifeworld at any time. Unfortunately, these threats are not merely perceived; despite having significant people in their lives, the emotional volatility in BPD/EUPD creates significant strain on their relationships, making it difficult to predict the longevity of any meaningful connection. This, in turn, fuels a vicious cycle, further escalating their emotional reactivity.

> I had always felt 'different' growing up. I didn't have a stop button when it came to regulating my emotions. Even the 'good' emotions, exhausted me.[7]

Emotional reactivity can often leave individuals feeling powerless. The intensity of their emotional responses may create a sense of losing control over their emotional choices. The overwhelming nature of their reactions can strip them of their ability to make decisions calmly, leaving them drained by the constant emotional turbulence. As a result, these individuals frequently experience emotional exhaustion, even though, from an outside perspective, their lives may appear calm and stable. On this point, Natasha continues:

> Over the years I've heard people say the following statements to me, repeatedly; "You're getting obsessed again!", "You're so sensitive!", "Stop

> overthinking and analysing everything!" "You're so weird." "You were really inappropriate last night." "You are too intense." "You are too much." "You are so over the top."

Feeling a distinct separation between oneself and others creates a sense of stigma that hinders the healthy development of an intersubjective community. Emotional reactivity disrupts the harmony between oneself and others, and with that disconnection there's a risk of losing the sense of belonging to one's own life-world. This, in turn, fuels feelings of isolation and shame, which further intensify self-destructive emotions and repetitive negative thinking. There is often a perceived pressure to be different and happier in order to fit into the social and intersubjective context. While conforming to this expectation might alleviate the sense of loneliness, doing so would be nearly impossible without compromising their authentic self. So, Jesse writes:

> I was told to 'stop wasting people's time' and I was 'being a burden and impacting my friends too much.' They even said that I shouldn't be so unhappy because my family always went on nice holidays (...). I was regarded as being 'too difficult to deal with' which didn't correlate with how I had been seen previously. When it wasn't an easy fix, they thought I wasn't trying to help myself and were frustrated.

The most logical feeling that follows from this implied obligation is the sense of self-exclusion:

> My feelings were completely dismissed, and I was told that 'I hadn't experienced any trauma so I shouldn't be struggling'. (...) I had no explanation for how I was feeling so it became internalised.

Jesse did not experience any trauma, and she came from a stable, affluent family. This created an unspoken expectation for her to feel happy in order to belong to her emotional and social world. Although this expectation may have arisen from Jesse's own ruminative thoughts or distorted emotional perceptions, as mentioned earlier, the existing social and clinical systems still fall short in providing adequate support for this emotional disorder. As a result, it is likely that what Jesse (and many others with BPD/EUPD) felt was, to some degree, a reflection of a genuine social expectation. Jesse probably sensed something that was, in fact, reinforced by the attitudes and behaviors of those around her. In another testimony, a participant writes:

> Before my diagnosis I was so confused as to why I felt the things I did, and so I breathed a sigh of relief when my psychiatrist spoke about EUPD to me

> as it all just made so much sense. EUPD is exhausting and I feel like my mind is on overdrive 24/7. When struggling to explain myself to others, I was told that this was all a made up thing in my head and that I shouldn't be trusted, because if I could make something like this up then what else would I be making up?

Receiving a diagnosis is often one of the initial and crucial steps for individuals with BPD/EUPD to feel acknowledged and validated within their emotional and social worlds. The constant emotional exhaustion and operating on a different emotional wavelength from others make it extremely challenging to clearly express themselves and feel connected to their community. However, when the language of scientific diagnosis is shared more broadly in society, it can help foster intersubjective dialogue, easing the process of regaining a more stable sense of belonging.

Thinking of Our World

To phenomenologically reflect on this lived experience, let's consider these questions: How do we mentally integrate our experience of the world? How does something external become part of our subjective experience? And how do we use that experience to inform our everyday actions? Mereology, the study of parts and wholes, can offer insight into these questions and help clarify the issues that arise from emotional dysregulation in individuals with BPD/EUPD. The term mereology was coined in 1927 by Leśniewski[8] from Greek μερος, ("part") and λόγος (study); it indicates the study of parthood relations with the goal of describing the relations of parts to whole and the relations of part to part within a whole—in this case, the whole is represented by the content of the acts that animate one's lived experience. Even though the term is fairly new, its roots date back to antiquity.[9]

Through our lived experiences, what initially exists outside our personal perception as neutral beings gains emotional significance and cognitive detail, transforming into something uniquely personal. As Husserl puts it, the diverse elements of things, spaces, and geometries come together in a unified structure, allowing us to recognize a single, cohesive object in consciousness. He uses the term "foundation" to describe the relationship between dependent and independent objects, as well as between concrete and abstract contents. For instance, independent objects, like the leg of a table, can exist on their own once separated, whereas non-independent objects, like the color green of grass, exist only in relation to the whole.

Husserl explains that a founded act inherently depends on the acts that underlie it, which helps form our understanding of particular objects as part of a greater whole. "When I say 'this', I do not merely perceive, but rather on the basis of the perception a new act of intending-this is established that is directed to it and is dependent upon it, despite its difference" (Hua XIX/1, 683). He identifies two forms of foundation[10]: categorial and ontological. In categorial foundation, an abstract concept, such as "school," grounds the particular qualities of individuals, like children being identified as students. The abstract concept of the school is fundamental for identifying the children as students. In ontological foundation, however, the relationship is reversed. Here, the concrete objects—such as students—are essential for recognizing abstract entities, like a school. Without the students, the concept of the school would not exist in the same way. Thus, the interplay between abstract and concrete objects is foundational to understanding how we experience and interpret the world.

Axiology of Affects in BPD/EUPDs

The categorial foundation of meaning (Sinn) for individuals with BPD/EUPD appears to be destabilized due to existential interference from axiological acts that influence the affects operating in the foundational process. As described in Chapter 7, according to Husserl, axiological acts are responsible for bringing pre-predicative material into existence, with *Daseinswert* signifying the primordial value of "being there" (*wertvoller Leistungen*) (Hua-Mat IX, 137–143). This value is recognized as a *Gutwert* (good-value or "goodness"), signifying a fundamental recognition of existence that we primitively recognize as a value, and which originally comes into being as a temporal unit, manifesting its "there-ness" for us. This primitive being-a-value-for represents a necessity that converts the concreta of my affects to prominence, that is, into units acknowledged as wholes. For most, this recognition enables the concrete aspects of experience to stand out and be valued as distinct entities. However, for BPD/EUPD individuals, this process can falter. The concrete elements of their lifeworld are not always perceived as *Gutwert* or *Daseinswert*, leading to a suppression or negation of their existence. Normally, as we showed in Chapter 7, converting the concreta to prominence produces a *Wertsein* (being-value), meaning a unit valued exactly because it comes into being and is perceivable as prominent among other beings. Hence, the *Daseinswert* is an axiological core that, in its there-ness or *wertvoller Leistung* (full-valued functioning), calls for the constitution of other prominent units that transform the concreteness of experience into personal meanings. What is there for me or any personal user has always a core existential value. This axiological core expressed through the *Daseinswert* represents that affective necessity which moves life forward through an infinite system of life goals (*Lebensziele*, Hua-Mat IX, 140).

Typically, this process results in *Wertsein* (being-value), wherein the concreteness of an experience becomes meaningful and is perceived as significant. However, in the context of BPD/EUPD, this core can be tinged with negativity, resulting in a distorted perception of their lifeworld. For instance, if I say Mario is a good person, I am saying that this person I call Mario is good. He exists in the world in this given moment as a good person. If he is neither good nor bad, he will still be Mario and being Mario is acknowledged as a positive value because of its being-there-for me in my lifeworld. In BPD/EUPDs' lifeworld, it happens that Mario will not be, in the sense of being-there-for-one's-lifeworld, if the axiological instantiation of its meaning is perceived as a negative one. Mario can literally disappear as an affective presence in my lifeworld. The ontological foundation is weakened by the categorial one and the resulting sense that fills their lifeworld with meaning is severely impoverished by this dynamic interaction.

The Axiological Acts and the Concreteness of Life

Let's continue with the example of Mario. I came to know Mario through an intentional act in which I reflected on my lived experience and transformed the scattered elements of this experience into a unity that means, for me, "he is Mario." Per se, Mario appears to me as a person through a manifold of appearances that bring together chaotic matter into an intelligible form (Hua XVI, 49–50). "The proper appearance and the improper appearance are not separate things; they are united in the appearance in the broader sense" (Hua XVI, 49). Real and ideal, the affects we perceive and the conceptual are given simultaneously. "This <the real> appearance is not presentational, although it does indeed make its object known in a certain way" (Hua XVI, 50); the real is not presentational because it is given to us first in a perceptually instinctive manner.

In the first section of the fifth Logical Investigation, Husserl defined this structure using the notion of intentional essence. From sections 20 to 22, he described the essence of intentional acts not as acts in which "we live" (Hua XIX, 411; En. tr. 119), but as phenomena that appear to us when we reflect on them. An intentional essence is what makes an act objectifying—that is, an act in which the object is presented to us.

The primary structure of an intentional essence consists of a correlation between matter and quality—the concretum and abstractum I mentioned earlier. They are inseparable (Hua XIX, 122) because quality is the way in which matter presents itself, while matter is what the quality presents. The former stands for the representational component of the intention, the latter for its sensory component.

> The quality can be combined with every objective reference (...) and only determines whether what is already presented in definite fashion is intentionally present as wished, asked, posited in judgment, etc. The Matter must be

> that element in an act which first gives it reference to an object (…) but also the precise way in which it is meant.
>
> *(Hua XIX, 121)*

The matter is that aspect of the intentional essence that determines "that it grasps the object but also as what it grasps it." Husserl continued, "the intentional essence does not exhaust the act phenomenologically" (Hua XIX, 416; En. tr. 123). We could not speak about intentional essences if "the fullness or vividness of the sensuous contents" (Hua XIX, 415; En. tr. 121) did not help to "build" the act.

Besides quality and matter, the intentional essence needs the concreteness of life in order to operate. Fullness is what exceeds and animates the intentional essence; it is fullness that causes the act of apprehension (*Auffassung*) and thus enables the intentional act to grasp the content of the lifeworld. When we examine the intentional essence, it becomes apparent that there is an emotional sensuousness and material concreteness toward which the quality of our intentional act reacts, determining it according to a specific quality. "We can only direct ourselves feelingly to objects that are presented to us by interwoven presentations (…) only its union with a representation gives it a certain relation to an object" (Hua XIX, 388; En. tr. 107). "The special essence of pleasure demands a relation to something pleasing (…). They all owe their intentional relation to certain underlying presentations" (Hua XIX, 390; En. tr. 109).

It seems that in the intentional acts which animate the lived experience of BPD/EUPDs, the quality/abstract/categorial part of the act, which coexists with its matter/concretum/ontological part, begins to undermine the concreteness or fullness of the matter. Once again, Mario is a fullness whose life interacts with mine, but the quality with which I determine his matter—in particular, the axiological one (good, bad, neutral)—does not interfere with the concreteness of this fullness. Yet, this axiological quality has the power to bring his matter into existence for me: "I see Mario. He's a good person."

For BPD/EUPDs, however, this axiological quality might cloud its matter because of its negative value. Mario's being and the fullness of life in general might become obscured to the point to experience an existential sense of loneliness and isolation. It is as if the axiological quality overpowers any ontological one, given the existential significance of axiological acts. This dynamic negatively influences the continuity that BPD/EUPDs perceive in the contents of their interaffective and intersubjective lifeworld. Fullness is what animates our lived experience and compels us to engage with the world around us. Instinctively, we know that this fullness exists and persists whether we can engage with it or not. In the case of BPD/EUPDs, the ontological quality of this reality and the sense (Sinn) it can produce is severely weakened.

Consequences of the Mereology in Meaning-Making Experience in BPD

As Staiti remarks, "in phenomenology, intuition represents the apex of an experiential process, that is, the congruence between the sense as it is thought and the sense as it has been actually experienced" (2019, 63). How this congruence comes together in the intentional content is explained through the notion of mereological foundation. As explained above in phenomenology, foundation (*Fundierung*) describes a mereological relationship of parts and whole in which a complex experience and its object can be analyzed according to their mutual inferences.

As seen above, in BPD/EUPDs, the concreteness of the intentional content is mostly shaped by axiological acts that glue together the representational content of the lived experience in a biased way. To build on Mario's example, Mario loves Giulio. Giulio comes into existence in Mario's emotional life as a positive value. Similarly to any other intentional act, emotional acts are also constituted of a form (Mario loves Giulio, i.e. subject + verb + object) and a matter (the emotional what that is in the act of Mario loving Giulio). Any matter is generally qualified by a position-taking with which we can tell whether the subject refers to reality (Mario loves Giulio, his partner) or fantasy (Mario loves Giulio, his imaginary friend). The position taken in emotional acts—such as "I love," "I respect," "I value"—needs to be completed by the emotion that qualifies that position-taking and the objectivating acts that make sense of their content matter. Mario loves, respects, and admires Giulio because he knows Giulio (epistemological, doxic, logical position); the logical position is what allows him to bring Giulio's matter to the predicative form—Giulio. The position-taking proper to the emotional acts needs a logical layer for the emotional content matter to be brought to the fore. If this layer is missing, what remains is a blind motivational necessity that moves Mario's romantic feelings toward his object of love but without being able to express its being in words or being aware of their existential concreteness. When the concreteness of the ontological foundation is undermined by a lacking categorial foundation, the inevitable result is to feel left with a sense of necessity whose axiological interpretation often assumes negative tones.

Axiological properties in general, like those that characterize emotional acts, need objectivating predicative acts to bring that motivating/-ed matter to the fore (I feel something I cannot explain to someone). The intentional essence of the emotional content needs to be meant in order to be epistemologically understood, yet their axiological quality can already be perceived in intuition (the essence of the beloved person as a positive value, for example). Axiological properties do not necessarily refer to the "real" object; as said above, Giulio can be just Mario's fantasy, or he might no longer be living, or he could be the character of his favorite play. Axiological properties relate to the content-object in the same way as logical properties do. Yet, in general, while logical properties are necessary for the content to preserve its objectual unity, sameness, and ontological identity, axiological properties can color the existential core of that sameness.

I think that the magnitude of the disruption occurring in BPD/EUPDs' meaning-making process is very impairing for the constitution of their interaffective and intersubjective lifeworld. While axiological properties usually combine with epistemological ones in such a way that their foundation adds something to the epistemological whole, in BPD/EUPD's acts, the axiological contents are the main supervenience that guarantees the continuity of the object as a content of their intentional act. At any moment, the emotional content of their life can disintegrate. From this perspective, impulsivity is the most logical answer to a reality that could escape them in one moment or another. Rumination is another coping strategy to hold on to a reality that could be completely different just a few minutes later. By going over and over the same thought, one can have the illusion to belong to and to be part of the world for as long as the thought is there (although the value attributed to that portion of the world is saying otherwise). Living in this way, of course, involves visible distress, disorienting feelings, and frustration.

Potential Treatment

The treatments that today are provided to heal the emotional dysregulation proper to this disorder are often based on CBT, mindfulness- and acceptance-based exercises (McMain et al., 2013). These activities are often very tiring and do not win over the forms of self-medication with which BDP/EUPDs engage to ease the pain. Yet, when well-practiced, they may *reduce* distress tolerance due to fatigue and self-regulatory deficits (Evans et al., 2014). Maladaptive strategies, such as avoidance, suppression, and substance abuse, are more appealing at the beginning when cognitive and mindful exercises result still too challenging. If the practices of this former are prolonged, it can easily lead to greater psychopathology overall (Aldao et al., 2010). Refining the skills with which BPD/EUPDs can be beneficial to regain a space of belongingness to the intersubjective society and to readjust the affective resonance before lacking.

Phenomenological psychopathology proposes approaches that focus on the subjective and relational dimensions of the disorder. Similar to my proposal, central to these treatments is the restoration of intersubjectivity and emotional integration, rather than solely addressing behavioral symptoms. One key aspect is the focus on *affective attunement*, as highlighted by Fuchs (2007). Fuchs argues that BPD patients often struggle with emotional regulation because they experience a disruption in their embodied, affective resonance with others. By creating a therapeutic space that allows for shared emotional experiences and their axiological acts to be observed as they unfold, therapists can help patients reconnect with their own emotions and develop a more coherent sense of self. This approach aims to stabilize the patient's experience of affect and reduce the emotional instability that characterizes BPD (Fuchs, 2007).

Another important aspect of treatment in phenomenological psychopathology is the emphasis on *existential dialogue*. Rooted in the work of Jaspers and expanded by contemporary scholars such as Stanghellini (2016), existential dialogue encourages patients to explore the deeper meaning of their emotional experiences and identity crises. For individuals with BPD, feelings of emptiness, abandonment, and a fragmented sense of self are common. Existential dialogue helps patients articulate these experiences, often by examining how they relate to time, space, and social interactions. Stanghellini suggests that this type of reflective process can lead to a better understanding of one's emotional life, improving emotional regulation, and fostering a greater sense of belonging in the world (Stanghellini, 2016).

Phenomenologically informed therapies also incorporate methods like *mindfulness* and *body awareness*, which emphasize a present-focused attention to one's emotions and bodily sensations. By helping BPD patients become more aware of their embodied states and how these are linked to their emotional experiences, these techniques aim to bridge the gap between emotion and action. In line with the work of scholars such as Ratcliffe and Gallagher, these treatments focus on how patients can reintegrate disrupted bodily and emotional experiences, thereby creating a more stable sense of self and improving interpersonal relationships (Gallagher, 2005; Ratcliffe, 2008).

Integrating these approaches with my view of the axiological components of the interaffective dissonance, I think it can be very productive to apply the results of the mereological investigation conducted above on the understanding of BPD/EUPD's specific meaning-making process. I believe that the disturbance in the affective resonance characterizing this disorder can be greatly attenuated if due attention would be paid to the axiological instantiation in the meaning content of the lived experience. I believe that it would be helpful if the clinicians would focus on healing the existential blindness with which the content of experience is brought to existence in BPD/EUPDs' case. Insisting on the continuity of the reality independently of the emotional and axiological disruption caused by the value assigned to the concreteness of a certain lived experience can contribute to the stability of their interaffective and intersubjective world, hence increasing their sense of belongingness. What becomes frightening and exhausting from the perspective of BPD/EUPDs is that the continuity of their experience would come and go as easily as their emotions come and go. Not only the love of their parents but even their very existence can disappear at the same speed as their emotions. Here, of course, I do not mean to say that they actually think that their parents would no longer exist if negative emotions occur in relation to them; what I am saying is that their parents would stop resonating with them and accordingly BPD/EUPDs would exclude them from their sphere of belongingness. The rollercoaster they live on is not about emotions but is about existence and nonexistence. The value attributed to a smile when it was expected or to a phone call that was not answered has the power to disrupt their sense of belongingness to their affective lifeworld.

The instability that characterizes BPD/EUPDs' behavior simply mirrors the instability of the lifeworld. I think that paying attention to the existential outcome of the axiological instantiation in the meaning-making experience of BPD/EUPD is crucial to prevent that the affective resonance that connects these individuals to their intersubjective and interaffective world is not disrupted. To my knowledge, this co-foundational component of meaning has not been sufficiently emphasized in the current literature and certainly deserves more attention.

Conclusion

In conclusion, the mereological foundation of the affects that inform the way in which BPD/EUPDs mean their lived experience often suffers from an existential and interaffective disruption. Axiological qualities—the values assigned to specific experiences—can cloud the perception of reality within their interaffective lifeworld, leading to significant emotional disturbances. Therapeutically, it may be beneficial to transform moments of invalidation into reflective pauses, reducing the intensity of existential intersubjective conflicts (e.g., feelings of abandonment). The goal is to enhance the clarity and emotional stability of their experiences, akin to tuning a disturbed radio frequency into something more coherent and, ideally, even enjoyable.

The application of mereological analysis to this meaning-making process highlights how clinicians can focus on healing the occasional existential blindness in these patients. By emphasizing the continuity of reality—despite emotional and axiological disruptions—therapists can help stabilize the patients' intersubjective and interaffective world, thus enhancing their sense of belonging. Addressing the existential impact of the disorder is crucial to ensuring that the emotional resonance connecting BPD/EUPDs to their social world is not further disrupted, thereby fostering emotional and relational stability.

Notes

1 I will define affective resonance as "the capacity to share or become affectively aroused by others' emotions" (Decety, 2011; Decety and Cowell, 2014).

2 I will use interaffectivity henceforth in this sense "*interaffectivity* is regarded as an intertwinement of two cycles of embodied affectivity, thus continuously modifying each partner's affective affordances and bodily resonance" (Fuchs & Koch, 2014). "Interaffectivity includes body feedback (i.e., the impression function within self and other) which is necessary for interbodily resonance. Components of interbodily resonance are: mirroring or complementing movements, body awareness (via proprioceptive body feedback), and kinaesthetic empathy; they are psychotherapeutically important in phenomena such as somatic countertransference (Pallaro, 2002)."

3 Intersubjectivity can be described as a relationship between me and another. The peculiarity of this relationship lies in the fact that the other is not alien to me, but is "within me" in a way that his or her "otherness" can be investigated beginning with the way in which that "otherness" is imminent in my ego. The other's otherness is present to me "in person," in Husserl's terms (Husserliana, XIV–XVII). At the end of the fourth text in *Husserliana XV*, Husserl writes "starting from intersubjectivity, it is possible to establish the intersubjective reduction by placing between brackets the world in itself and thus achieving the reduction to the universe of the intersubjective that includes in itself all that is individually subjective" (1973c, 69).

4 For this concept, I will draw completely on Husserl's writings. In his *Crisis* (1936/1970), he writes: "In whatever way we may be conscious of the world as universal horizon, as coherent universe of existing objects, we, each 'I-the-man' and all of us together, belong to the world as living with one another in the world; and the world is our world, valid for our consciousness as existing precisely through this 'living together.' We, as living in wakeful world-consciousness, are constantly active on the basis of our passive having of the world… Obviously this is true not only for me, the individual ego; rather we, in living together, have the world pre-given in this together, belong, the world as world for all, pre-given with this ontic meaning… The we-subjectivity… [is] constantly functioning" (1936/1970, 108–109).

5 Here, I will use the term logical in the same way as Husserl used it in his Logical Investigations as a term closer to epistemology than symbolic logic.

6 From now on, I will refer to Borderline Personality Disorder or Emotional Unstable Personality Disorders with these acronyms.

7 This and the following excerpts are retrieved from https://www.time-to-change.org.uk/blog/unhelpful-attitudes-made-me-feel-isolated.

8 In literature, "mereology" is also devoted to the study of system decomposition as in General Systems Theory (Mesarović et al., 1970; Winther, 2011). It is not until Leśniewski's *Foundations of the General Theory of Sets* (1916) and his *Foundations of Mathematics* (1927–1931) that we arrive at a general formulation of the theory of part-relations; yet, since Leśniewski's work was largely inaccessible to nonspeakers of Polish, we have to wait the publication of Leonard and Goodman's *The Calculus of Individuals* (1940), partly under the influence of Whitehead, to read about mereology as matter of interest for modern ontologists and metaphysicians.

9 The roots of mereology in antiquity can be traced back to the Presocratics and continuing throughout the writings of Plato (especially the *Parmenides* and the *Theaetetus*), Aristotle (especially the *Metaphysics*, but also the *Physics*, the *Topics*, and *De partibus animalium*), and Boethius (especially *De Divisione* and *In Ciceronis Topica*). Mereology occupies a prominent role also in the writings of medieval ontologists and scholastic philosophers such as Garland the Computist, Peter Abelard, Thomas Aquinas, Raymond Lull, John Duns Scotus, Walter Burley, William of Ockham, and Jean Buridan, as well as in Jungius's *Logica Hamburgensis* (1638), Leibniz's *Dissertatio de arte combinatoria* (1666) and *Monadology* (1714), and Kant's early writings (the *Gedanken* of 1747 and the *Monadologia physica* of 1756).

10 See: "The apprehension of a sensuous feature as a feature, or of a sensuous form as a form, points to acts which are all founded, and in this case as relational kinds of acts" (Hua XIX, 792; En. tr. 110).

References

Aldao, A., Nolen-Hoeksema, S., & Schweizer, S. (2010). Emotion-regulation strategies across psychopathology: A meta-analytic review. *Clinical Psychology Review*, *30*, 217–237.

American Psychiatric Association. (2013). *Diagnostic and statistical manual of mental disorders* (5th ed.). Arlington, VA: American Psychiatric Publishing.

Anderson, J. (2012). Affective alienation and intersubjectivity in borderline personality disorder. *Phenomenological Studies in Psychopathology*, *67*, 89–102.

Aristotle. (1984). *The complete works of Aristotle: The revised Oxford translation*. J. Barnes (Ed.). Princeton University Press. *(Includes: Metaphysics, Physics, Topics, De partibus animalium)*.

Bagge, C. L., Stepp, S. D., & Trull, T. J. (2005). Borderline personality disorder features and utilization of treatment over two years. *Journal of Personality Disorders*, *19*, 420–439.

Berenson, K. R., Downey, G., Rafaeli, E., Coifman, K. G., & Paquin, N. L. (2011). The rejection-rage contingency in borderline personality disorder. *Journal of Abnormal Psychology*, *120*, 681–690.

Comtois, K. A., Russo, J., Snowden, M., Srebnik, D., Ries, R., & Roy-Byrne, P. (2003). Factors associated with high use of public mental health services by persons with borderline personality disorder. *Psychiatric Services*, *54*, 1149–1154.

Decety, J. (2011). Dissecting the neural mechanisms mediating empathy. *Emotion Review*, *3*(1), 92–108.

Decety, J., & Cowell, J. M. (2014). The complex relation between morality and empathy. *Trends in Cognitive Sciences*, *18*(7), 337–339.

Dixon-Gordon, K. L., Weiss, N. H., Tull, M. T., DiLillo, D., Messman-Moore, T., & Gratz, K. L. (2015). Characterizing emotional dysfunction in borderline personality, major depression, and their co-occurrence. *Comprehensive Psychiatry*, *62*, 187–203.

Dixon-Gordon, K. L., Peters, J. R., Fertuck, E. A., & Yen, S. (2017). Emotional processes in borderline personality disorder: An update for clinical practice. *Journal of Psychotherapy Integration*, *27*(4), 425–438. https://doi.org/10.1037/int0000044

Evans, D. R., Eisenlohr-Moul, T. A., Button, D. F., Baer, R. A., & Segerstrom, S. C. (2014). Self-regulatory deficits associated with unpracticed mindfulness strategies for coping with acute pain. *Journal of Applied Social Psychology*, *44*, 23–30.

Fertuck, E. A., Lenzenweger, M. F., Clarkin, J. F., Hoermann, S., & Stanley, B. (2006). Executive neurocognition, memory systems, and borderline personality disorder. *Clinical Psychology Review*, *26*, 346–375.

Fuchs, T. (2005). The phenomenology of body, space, and time in borderline personality disorder. *Psychopathology*, *38*(5), 251–259.

Fuchs, T. (2007). The temporal structure of intentionality and its disturbance in schizophrenia. *Psychopathology*, *40*, 229–235.

Fuchs, T. (2013). Affective attunement in borderline personality disorder: Disconnection and resonance. *Journal of Phenomenological Psychology*, *44*(2), 144–160.

Fuchs, T., & Koch, S. C. (2014). Embodied affectivity: On moving and being moved. *Frontiers in Psychology*, *5*, 508.

Gallagher, S. (2005). *How the body shapes the mind*. Oxford: Oxford University Press.

Gardner, K. J., Qualter, P., & Tremblay, R. (2010). Emotional functioning of individuals with borderline personality traits in a nonclinical population. *Psychiatry Research*, *176*, 208–212.

Gottman, J. M. (1993). A theory of marital dissolution and stability. *Journal of Family Psychology*, *7*, 57–75.

Gratz, K. L., Tull, M. T., Matusiewicz, A. M., Breetz, A. A., & Lejuez, C. W. (2013). Multimodal examination of emotion regulation difficulties as a function of co-occurring avoidant personality disorder among women with borderline personality disorder. *Personality Disorders: Theory, Research, and Treatment*, *4*, 304–314.

Hughes, A. E., Crowell, S. E., Uyeji, L., & Coan, J. A. (2012). A developmental neuroscience of borderline pathology: Emotion dysregulation and social baseline theory. *Journal of Abnormal Child Psychology, 40*, 21–33.

Husserl, E. (1970). *The crisis of european sciences and transcendental phenomenology: An introduction to phenomenology*. Evanston, IL: Northwestern University Press.

Husserl, E. (1973c). *Zur Phänomenologie der Intersubjektivität: Texte aus dem Nachlass. Dritter Teil 1929–1935* [On the phenomenology of intersubjectivity. Texts from the estate. Part 3]. I. Kern (Ed.). The Hague: Martinus Nijhoff (Hua XV).

Jaspers, K. (1963). *General psychopathology*. J. Hoenig & M. W. Hamilton (Trans.). Manchester: Manchester University Press.

Jungius, J. (1638). *Logica Hamburgensis*. Hamburg. (Refer to modern studies or translations such as: Dobre, M. (2013). *Jungius and the Rise of Modern Logic*. Springer.)

Kant, I. (1747). *Gedanken von der wahren Schätzung der lebendigen Kräfte* [Thoughts on the true estimation of living forces]. Königsberg: Martin Eberhard Dorn.

Kant, I. (1756). *Monadologia Physica* [Physical monadology]. Königsberg: Martin Eberhard Dorn.

Köhler, H. (2015). The temporal disintegration of lived experience in borderline personality disorder. *Phenomenology and the Cognitive Sciences, 14*(4), 457–471.

LeGris, J., Toplak, M., & Links, P. S. (2014). Affective decision making in women with borderline personality disorder. *Journal of Personality Disorders, 28*, 1–22.

Leibniz, G. W. (1666). *Dissertatio de arte combinatoria* [Dissertation on the art of combinations]. Leipzig: Johann Grossius.

Leibniz, G. W. (1714). *Monadology* [Monadolgie]. In Nicholas Rescher (Ed.), *Gottfried Wilhelm Leibniz's Monadology: An edition for students* (1991). Pittsburgh, PA: University of Pittsburgh Press.

Lenzenweger, M. F., Clarkin, J. F., Fertuck, E. A., & Kernberg, O. F. (2004). Executive neurocognitive functioning and neurobehavioral systems indicators in borderline personality disorder: A preliminary study. *Journal of Personality Disorders, 18*, 421–438.

Leonard, H. S., & Goodman, N. (1940). The calculus of individuals and its use in ontology. *The Journal of Symbolic Logic, 5*(2), 45–55.

Leśniewski, S. (1992). *Collected works*. S. J. Surma, J. T. Srzednicki, & D. I. Barnett (Eds. & Trans.). New York: Kluwer Academic Publishers. (Original works published 1916 and 1927–1931).

Linehan, M. M. (1993). *Cognitive-behavioral treatment of borderline personality disorder*. New York: Guilford Press.

McMain, S. F., Links, P. S., Guimond, T., Wnuk, S., Eynan, R., Bergmans, Y., & Warwar, S. (2013). An exploratory study of the relationship between changes in emotion and cognitive processes and treatment outcome in borderline personality disorder. *Psychotherapy Research, 23*, 658–673.

Mesarović, M. D., Macko, D., & Takahara, Y. (1970). *Theory of hierarchical, multilevel systems*. New York: Academic Press.

Minzenberg, M. J., Fan, J., New, A. S., Tang, C. Y., & Siever, L. J. (2007). Frontolimbic dysfunction in response to facial emotion in borderline personality disorder: An event-related fMRI study. *Psychiatry Research: Neuroimaging, 155*, 231–243.

Pallaro, P. (2002). Somatic countertransference: The therapist in relationship. In P. Pallaro (Ed.), *Authentic movement: Moving the body, moving the self, being moved* (pp. 176–193). London: Jessica Kingsley.

Peters, J. R., Geiger, P. J., Smart, L. M., & Baer, R. A. (2014). Shame and borderline personality features: The potential mediating role of anger and anger rumination. *Personality Disorders: Theory, Research, and Treatment*, *5*, 1–9.

Peters, J. R., Smart, L. M., & Baer, R. A. (2015). Dysfunctional responses to emotion mediate the cross-sectional relationship between rejection sensitivity and borderline personality features. *Journal of Personality Disorders*, *29*, 231–240.

Plato. (1997). *Complete works*. J. M. Cooper & D. S. Hutchinson (Eds.). London: Hackett Publishing. (Original works include: Parmenides, Theaetetus).

Plato. (1892). Parmenides and Theaetetus. In B. Jowett (Trans.), *The dialogues of Plato*. Oxford: Oxford University Press.

Ratcliffe, M. (2008). *Feelings of being: Phenomenology, psychiatry, and the sense of reality*. Oxford: Oxford University Press.

Sánchez-Navarro, J. P., Weller, J. A., López-Navarro, J. M., Martínez-Selva, J. M., & Bechara, A. (2014). Suboptimal decision making in borderline personality disorder: Effect of potential losses. *The Spanish Journal of Psychology*, *17*, 1–9.

Selby, E. A., Anestis, M. D., Bender, T. W., & Joiner, T. E. (2009). An exploration of the emotional cascade model in borderline personality disorder. *Journal of Abnormal Psychology*, *118*, 375–387.

Selby, E. A., Fehling, K. B., Panza, E. A., & Kranzler, A. (2015). Rumination, mindfulness, and borderline personality disorder symptoms. *Mindfulness*, Advance on, 228–235.

Shenk, C. E., & Fruzzetti, A. E. (2011). The impact of validating and invalidating responses on emotional reactivity. *Journal of Social and Clinical Psychology*, *30*, 163–183.

Shenk, C. E., & Fruzzetti, A. E. (2014). Parental validating and invalidating responses and adolescent psychological functioning: An observational study. *The Family Journal*, *22*, 43–48.

Staebler, K., Helbing, E., Rosenbach, C., & Renneberg, B. (2011). Rejection sensitivity and borderline personality disorder. *Clinical Psychology & Psychotherapy*, *18*, 275–283.

Staiti, A. (2019). *The intelligibility of nature: A phenomenological essay on the natural sciences*. New York City: Springer.

Stanghellini, G. (2004). *Disorders of personhood: Schizophrenia and pathic intersubjectivity*. New York City: Springer.

Stanghellini, G. (2016). *Lost in dialogue: Anthropology, psychopathology, and care*. New York City: Oxford University Press.

Trull, T. J., Solhan, M. B., Tragesser, S. L., Jahng, S., Wood, P. K., Piasecki, T. M., & Watson, D. (2008). Affective instability: Measuring a core feature of borderline personality disorder with ecological momentary assessment. *Journal of Abnormal Psychology*, *117*, 647–661.

Van Asselt, A. D. I., Dirksen, C. D., Arntz, A., & Severens, J. L. (2007). The cost of borderline personality disorder: Societal cost of illness in BPD patients. *European Psychiatry*, *22*, 354–361.

Van Reekum, R., Links, P. S., & Fedorov, C. (1994). Impulsivity in borderline personality disorder. In K. R. Silk (Ed.), *Biological and Neurobehavioral Studies of Borderline Personality Disorder* (pp. 1–22). Washington, D.C.: American Psychiatric Association.

Winther, R. G. (2011). Part–whole science. *Synthese, 178*(3), 397–427.

10

AFFECTS AND NARCISSISM

Introduction

"It's all about them." "Run, as fast as you can!" "How to know that you're dating a narcissist." These are just a few examples of media headlines that demonize individuals with narcissistic traits. Narcissism is often painted as a toxic personality trait to be avoided at all costs. However, such one-dimensional portrayals ignore the complexity behind narcissistic behaviors. Narcissism, when viewed through the lens of phenomenology, reveals an intricate web of emotional disconnection, intentionality, and affectivity that shapes an individual's way of relating to the world.

This chapter aims to move beyond surface-level judgments to explore the emotional and intentional structures that underpin narcissistic traits. By focusing on the theory of affects described in Chapter 7, I argue that narcissistic personality disorder (NPD) individuals[1] experience a blockage in their emotional intentionality, preventing them from forming deep, meaningful connections with themselves and others. This blockage results in a pervasive sense of emptiness and isolation, which NPD individuals attempt to fill through grandiose self-images and external validation. Understanding these emotional dynamics can offer new pathways for healing narcissistic traits, providing individuals with the tools to reconnect with their emotions and lead more fulfilling lives. As discussed in Chapter 7, individuals with narcissistic traits seem to experience difficulties with the intentionality of their feelings at the representational level. Certain overwhelming emotions become blocked, interrupting the normal process of affective representation and naming of specific affections. This leads to connecting affectively to what lacks emotional depth. Consequently,

DOI: 10.4324/9781003665557-10

their decisions and actions are disconnected from immediate, embodied emotions, resulting in a diminished sense of ethical consideration for themselves and others. NPD individuals often avoid confronting their emotions because it would be too painful to face them. In what follows, I will use Ovid's myth to look at the archetype of individuals suffering from these traits; I will then show how the intentionality of feelings characterizing this problem and I will finally offer a potential approach to soothe the impacts that this problem has on their intimate lives.

The Myth of Narcissus: A Phenomenological Interpretation of Emotional Disconnection

The myth of Narcissus has long been a symbolic representation of self-absorption and vanity, but when examined through a phenomenological lens, it also provides insight into the emotional detachment that characterizes narcissism. Narcissus, the son of the river god Cephissus and the nymph Lirope, grows up with emotionally distant parents—a factor often linked to the development of narcissistic traits (Horton, 2011; Kohut, 1971). His emotional detachment from primary caregivers prevents him from forming meaningful emotional bonds, leading to a lifelong quest for external validation. Narcissus's failure to connect emotionally with himself mirrors the experience of individuals with narcissistic traits, who often feel empty and disconnected from their own emotions.

In the myth, Narcissus becomes enamored with his reflection in a pool of water, unable to look away. He is captivated by an image of himself that is not real, just as NPD individuals today are trapped by a grandiose self-image that conceals a deep sense of vulnerability and emptiness (Kohut, 1977). The myth suggests that Narcissus's only path to healing lies in a transformation or metamorphosis. In Ovid's version of the story, Narcissus transforms into a flower, a symbol of rebirth and renewal. However, other interpretations, such as those of Parthenius and Conon, envision a more tragic end for Narcissus, who ultimately takes his own life.

This mythological narrative reflects the real-life experiences of individuals with narcissistic traits who are often resistant to self-reflection because it threatens to dismantle the grandiose self-image they have built to protect themselves from the emotional void within. The existential crisis faced by Narcissus—the disintegration of his self-image—is mirrored in the narcissist's fear of confronting their emotional disconnection. This fear leads to emotional avoidance, which prevents the individual from forming authentic connections with others. The myth serves as a cautionary tale, highlighting the dangers of emotional detachment and the need for transformation in the journey toward healing.

Affectivity and the Theory of Intentionality in Narcissism

To understand narcissistic traits from a phenomenological perspective, it is essential to examine the role of affectivity. Affects, in phenomenology, refer to the emotions and feelings that shape our lived experiences and intentional actions. As we saw in Chapters 6 and 7, Husserl considers intentionality to be the structure of consciousness that directs us toward objects in the world, and affects play a central role in this process (Hua XIII). They are, in fact, the concreteness of life that awakes our embodied subjectivity to action. Emotions are not just passive experiences but active participants in shaping our intentionality—our directedness toward the world and others. In that sense, intentionality is a complex term whose roots come from Greek *enteinein* translated into Latin as *intendere* and in Arabic with *Ma qul* or *Ma na.* The etymology refers to the connecting "tension" of "aiming at" something; this tension conjuncts our inner sense of reality to the outer world. In Plato's *Cratylus*, the intentional directedness of consciousness toward its object is described through the metaphor of an archer drawing a bow to aim an arrow at a target. Hence, first intentionality refers to this tension that invisibly connects humans to an "external something." Second, for Stoics, intentionality is *ennoemata*, that is, thoughts that replace the concreteness of what is meant through representations dwelling in our soul. A third and perhaps most interesting way to explain the intentional act is the Greek expression *paron apon*, present absence. Similarly to the *ennoemata*, the *paron apon* involves that any reflection upon my own acts sets aside the object as it appears outside of me while pointing my attention to the object as held in my consciousness, an object that is now present in me as a token of the tension that connected me to the outside world, a "presence in absence." As mentioned in Chapter 7, in people suffering from narcissistic traits, this presence is detached from the object that has been represented. Even if it should appear as its token, its representation is somewhat inflated and disconnected from what it should point it to.

Brentano and later his disciple Husserl revived the studies around intentionality by emphasizing the reflective quality of intentionality. For Brentano, intentionality refers to the "objectual in-existence" (Brentano, 1874/2008) of the content of my lived experience in a renewed form, while for Husserl it indicates the way in which consciousness aims at the object. Both cases point to intentionality as a reflective experience in which the subject transforms what was present in front of themselves into a "present absence" that continuously connects them to the world while constituting meanings and values that give a regulative sense to this interconnection. To this extent, the intentional content becomes the means one uses to shape its own reality and establish bonds with the lifeworld. In NPD, this reflection does not connect them directly with what they live in the world but it connects them to a number of projections of how they think or they wish they live in the world. For example, a person with narcissistic traits may post curated photos of luxurious vacations or constant achievements on social media—not because these moments are deeply fulfilling, but because they construct an image of success and admiration they wish to inhabit. Their reality is shaped less by their lived experience of joy, connection, or satisfaction, and more by an idealized narrative they believe others should see and validate. This projection creates a dissonance between their actual emotional life and the image they maintain, distancing them from authentic connection with both themselves and others.

Three Groups of Intentionality

In Husserl's phenomenology, we find a multitude of ways of referring to intentionality, instinctive, coitus, affective, instinct, etc.; in my research (Ferrarello, 2015), I organize these forms of intentionality into three main groups: active, passive, and practical intentionality. While active intentionality entails position-taking (*Stellungnahme*) and meaning-giving (*Sinngebung*) activity (Hua III, 207), passive intentionality is a synthetic process that takes place mainly on two ego-less organic layers: those of spontaneous and non-spontaneous syntheses (Hua XXXIII). The spontaneous syntheses bring together the percepta of our experience according to a principle of homogeneity, while the non-spontaneous one assigns a meaning to these organic data. Through the layers formed by these syntheses, we constitute the material core around which the meaning- and value-giving activity of active intentionality revolves. The transition from ego-less synthetic processes to egoic meaning-giving (*Sinngebung*) activity is characterized by practical intention. In fact, the sphere of irritability (Hua XXXIII, text 1), that is, the layer of affections and reactions, represents the lowest level of affections from which the ego emerges and reacts to the irritating affecting matter by deciding what position it is going to take (Hua XXXIII, text 1, 5, 6, 9, 10). As already described in Chapter 5, this reactive emergence is rooted in the volitional body (Hua-Mat IV, 186) which bridges nature (passive syntheses) and spirit (active intention). The ego reacts to matter by deciding whether to accept and validate that matter as its own. In NPD individuals, this ego is detached from its own matter; even though the affections coming from the organic matter awaken its reaction, it does not own these affections but it looks somewhere else to create meanings. Accordingly, a great part of the material content provided to the ego will remain in the form of passive syntheses, while just a little will be organized through values and meanings. For example, imagine someone who feels a subtle wave of anxiety after being ignored in a conversation. For most people, this bodily tension (a passive synthesis) might evolve into a conscious reflection—perhaps a realization of feeling excluded, followed by a decision to address it or seek reassurance. But for someone with narcissistic traits, this irritability does not lead to ownership of the feeling. Instead, they might bypass the anxiety entirely and reinterpret the situation as evidence that others are jealous or inferior. The original affect—feeling vulnerable—is not validated or integrated; it remains unresolved. The ego reacts, but not by forming a meaningful connection to the affect—it creates an externalized narrative instead.

While the realm of passivity provides formless matter with a logical or graspable form, the realm of activity is the constitutive pole through which a given number of synthetic layers are composed in a graspable meaning. The practical intention is the phronetic act whereby the subject resolves to move toward self-constitution, recognizing the interconnection between passive syntheses and its own activity as a self-reflective subject.

In the case of narcissism, the affects that are organized in passive syntheses do not influence their intentional acts. Accordingly, their actions are poor in meanings and values (at least for them) and detached from their personal story. As a consequence, NPD individuals experience a blockage in their affective intentionality, meaning that their emotions do not guide them toward meaningful connections with others. The representational layer of their intentions that should help determine the meaning of the contents of their experience is disconnected from the affects that are actually moving through syntheses in their actions. They instead focus on external representations. Accordingly, this external representational activity makes them trapped in a cycle of seeking external validation to compensate for their inability to access their own emotions. This emotional disconnection leads to a distorted sense of self, where the person suffering from narcissistic traits relies on grandiose fantasies and external achievements to maintain a sense of worth.

The inability to connect with their own emotions also prevents them from forming deep, intimate relationships with others. They are often unable to empathize with the feelings of others because they are disconnected from their own affective experiences. This lack of empathy further isolates them from the social and emotional world, reinforcing their sense of loneliness and emptiness. Understanding the role of affectivity in narcissism can help clinicians develop therapeutic interventions that focus on reconnecting NPD individuals with their emotions, allowing them to form more meaningful connections with themselves and others.

Practical Intentionality and Emotional Choices

Husserl's concept of practical intentionality, as already described in Chapter 5, is crucial for understanding how NPD individuals make emotional choices. Simply put, practical intentionality refers to the way in which our actions are guided by our emotions and desires. Practical intentionality is the crucial form of intentionality that bridges active to passive intentionality. It is in fact through this form of intentionality that the subject develops a form of interest that leads it to validate the cluster of affections that are passively presented to it and transform them in an active sense. Through practical intention, the subject decides to feel the affections that are engaging with their body. In fact, to use an example, while doing other things, my body decides to stop and pay attention to the feeling of hunger and acknowledge its sense. Or, on a more psychological level, my friend is talking about his plans. I want to be a good friend and keep listening to his plans, but more pressing affections are arising in that present moment. My practical intention takes an interest in it and validates those affections which make me aware of the fact that I am feeling anxious.

Practical intentionality is the connecting bridge between passive and active intentions. It expresses through an act of validation in which the volitional body (Husserl, 2012, 186) of the subject decides to pay attention to the affections and to transform them in sense through active intentionality. Thanks to practical intentionality, the subject decides to be interested (Hua XXXI, 81) in the affections, prompted by passive intentionality, that are poking its attention; then active intentionality will assign them meanings and values.

One's personality is built upon many of these moments that have the power to reduce or increase the distance with the people we love. Persons whose practical intentions repeatedly decide to cut themselves off from their affections and do not take an interest in what their affections are trying to communicate, will as a result be distant and unauthentic because the sense and values that structure their actions are not rooted in their affections. Practical intention is that act through which subjects recognize the interconnection between passive syntheses and their own feelings. Ultimately, practical intentionality is what allows for bodily resonance and interaffectivity to function because it connects our passive synthesis (e.g. our organic nature) with our ability to feel it according to certain meanings and values. The bridge between active intention and passive synthesis is represented by the practical "Ich will und ich tue" (I want, I act) which operates through the means of the emotions that awaken the volitional body to a specific action. Being unaware of what is occurring during these moments results in a high level of emotional instability which significantly impacts our feelings of well-being.

The ego reacts to passive affections by deciding whether to accept and validate what awakes its interest or not. While the realm of passivity provides formless matter with a potentially graspable form, the realm of active intention is the constitutive pole through which a given number of affective layers are composed into a graspable meaning. Affective intentionality is one mode of practical intentions in which the affections call for a graspable determination of meaning (e.g. my stomach feels affected, I answer to these affections by acknowledging that I am hungry).

Authentic Emotions and Their Intentions

An emotion to be authentic, that is, to be connected to the *authos* (from Greek, the self) who is moved by it, needs to be in contact with its intentional roots. There is a wide agreement among philosophers and psychologists that emotions are characterized by intentionality—they are about persons, objects, events, and situations in the world (see e.g., De Sousa, 2010; Frijda, 1994; Solomon, 1976). If an emotion is not directed toward an actual object, event, or situation but is instead based on something external and cognitively observed, it tends to feel distant and detached.

In particular, practical intentionality is not neutral but concerns what is specifically valuable and relevant for the subject. In a sense, emotions are ways of perceiving, namely attending to salient features of a situation, giving them a significance and weight. Referring to Gibson's (1979) concept of affordances (that means, offerings in the environment that are available to animals, such as a tree being "climbable" and water "drinkable"), one could also speak of affective affordances: things appear to us as "important," "worthwhile," "attractive," "repulsive," "expressive," and so on. Without emotions, the world would be without meaning or significance; nothing would attract or repel us and motivate us to act (Fuchs & Koch, 2014).

In the case of narcissism, the emotional disconnection caused by affective blockages leads to maladaptive choices that reinforce the narcissist's sense of isolation. NPD individuals often make decisions based on external validation rather than genuine emotional needs, which further alienates them from their own feelings and from others (Virk & Kumari, 2024). For example, a narcissist may seek out relationships that provide them with admiration and praise, but these relationships are often shallow and unsatisfying. Because the narcissist is not emotionally connected to their own needs, they cannot form deep emotional bonds with their partners. Over time, the narcissist may become bored or disillusioned with the relationship, leading to a cycle of emotional withdrawal and detachment. This pattern of behavior is driven by the narcissist's inability to recognize and act upon their own emotional needs, a failure of practical intentionality to act upon the affects.

The theory of practical intentionality also helps explain why NPD individuals are so vulnerable to criticism. Because their sense of self is based on external validation, any negative feedback is experienced as a threat to their entire identity. NPD individuals often react to criticism with anger or defensiveness because they cannot separate their self-worth from the opinions of others. This emotional vulnerability is a direct result of the narcissist's inability to form a stable, internal sense of self through affective intentionality.

The Role of Primary Caregivers in Developing Narcissistic Traits

Early childhood experiences might play a significant role in the development of narcissistic traits. Children who grow up with emotionally distant or neglectful caregivers are more likely to develop narcissistic tendencies as a way of coping with their unmet emotional needs (Donaldson-Pressman & Pressman, 1994). These children learn to seek validation from external sources because they do not receive the emotional support they need from their caregivers. This pattern of behavior continues into adulthood, where NPD individuals rely on external achievements and relationships to maintain their sense of worth.

Phenomenologically, the lack of emotional attunement from caregivers can be understood as a failure of affective resonance. Affective resonance refers to the way in which emotions are shared and mirrored between individuals, creating a sense of connection and belonging. In the case of narcissistic individuals, this resonance is disrupted, leading to a sense of emotional isolation. Children who do not experience affective resonance with their caregivers may develop a distorted sense of self, where their worth is tied to external validation rather than internal emotional experiences. Overly permissive parents, who fail to establish clear boundaries, may inadvertently contribute to similar outcomes as narcissistic tendencies. Without appropriate limits, children may struggle to develop a healthy sense of self-discipline and may become accustomed to external validation, which can lead to narcissistic traits later in life. This lack of structure prevents the development of internal emotional regulation, reinforcing a reliance on external sources for validation and perpetuating feelings of isolation and emotional disconnection (Day et al., 2020; Virk & Kumari, 2024).

People affected with narcissistic traits use their active intentions to make meanings and values that are not based on their own passive intentions, that is, on what they affectively experience, but on an externalized sense of what they are expected to feel. As it happened for a client I worked with in my philosophical practice, his parents educated him not to take an interest in his affections, as if these affections were almost despicable and reprehensible. Good behavior for his parents was all based on meanings and values construed from externalized affections. This led him to develop a pervasive sense of coldness and meaninglessness, as if true meaning could not arise from what he genuinely experienced as meaningful. His own embodied life was not regarded as a valid source of personal values or significance; instead, only society's perception of him seemed to matter. What he found pleasant to experience, such as a walk hand in hand with his wife or spending time cooking a good meal, was perceived as lame and equated to a waste of time. As shown before, the first consistent step that leads to the constitution of narcissistic traits at a very young age is characterized by a disconnection from one's own feelings and the environment that elicits them (Lowen, 1983). Affections and the feelings stemming from the connection we make with those affections are the *via regia* to understanding our interaction with reality; shutting them out means living in an alternative uprooted reality. The reactiveness at small events displayed by people affected by narcissistic traits is one of the many outcomes of this affective uprootedness.

In the case of people affected with narcissistic traits, the interaffective disturbance is generated from a detachment between active and passive intentionality. The person does not exert her practical intentionality in a bridging way, that is, they do not connect with the affective awakenings that belong to their body or to the system of affectivity by which they are surrounded. They do not take an interest in their interaffective world which, accordingly, remains for them inauthentic and poor in meaning. As we saw in the previous section, passive intentionality is what defines us as an object among other objects governed by biological and social norms; it does not require an ego to function—in fact, the subjectivity of the ego comes only at a very late stage of the process. Similar to Kohut's view of NPD (1971, 1977), we need to be part of an interaffective community, that is a social, geographical, emotional, physical, and imaginative environment in order to be and to become something (parents, friends, school, a home, etc.). The more qualities this environment shows us, the richer our passive intentional life and accordingly our emotional world.

This lack of affective resonance also prevents NPD individuals from developing emotional curiosity about themselves. Children who grow up with emotionally detached caregivers do not learn to explore their own feelings or develop a sense of emotional self-awareness. As a result, NPD individuals are often disconnected from their own emotions and struggle to form meaningful emotional bonds with others. Therapy that focuses on reestablishing affective resonance can help people suffering from narcissistic traits to reconnect with their emotions and develop a healthier sense of self.

Affective Blockages and Therapeutic Approaches

As we saw above, NPD is characterized by a pervasive pattern of grandiosity, a need for admiration, and a lack of empathy (American Psychiatric Association, 2013). From a phenomenological perspective, these traits can be understood as the result of affective blockages that prevent individuals suffering from narcissistic traits from forming authentic emotional connections with themselves and others. NPD individuals experience a disconnection between their emotional affects and their lived experiences, leading to a distorted sense of self and a reliance on external validation.

Trauma often plays a significant role in the development of these affective blockages. Individuals who experience emotional neglect or abuse in childhood may develop narcissistic traits as a defense mechanism against their unresolved trauma (Lowen, 1983). The emotional pain caused by this trauma creates a barrier between the narcissist and their emotions, preventing them from accessing the full range of their affective experiences. Therapy that focuses on addressing these affective blockages can help NPD individuals reconnect with their emotions and begin the process of healing.

The role of the therapist is to help the client to reconnect with their own passive intentionality in order to heal the sense of primal exclusion from which the client is still suffering. As described in Chapter 7, the representational activity that aims to render passively lived experience into intelligible, active meaning directs its focus toward something external. They often find it challenging to connect with the natural presence of their bodies, struggling to accept physical imperfections or the reality of aging. They tend to view their bodies with a sense of shame, creating a disconnection between their physical selves and their identity. This inability to embrace their own physicality fosters grandiosity, an obsession with their image, and a sense of detachment from others' bodies. Practical exercises aimed at increasing awareness of the body's basic functions, rather than the empty projections shaped by past traumas, are crucial in addressing this issue. Once individuals can reconnect with their physical selves, it becomes possible to revisit traumatic events in a healthier, more constructive way. The unethical behavior often exhibited by NPD individuals is rooted in this blocked intentionality, which hinders them from accessing the emotions linked to their past wounds and from forming meaningful connections with both themselves and others. Overcoming this blockage can help ease the feelings of loneliness and emptiness they frequently endure. This can be done by leveraging their practical intentionality on their volitional body so that their body can finally decide to make sense of what it is affectively experiencing in the moment. The new relationship with the therapist and exercises directed at making the client feel like a part of her social, geographical, emotional, physical, and imaginative environment support this reconnection. Through hypnotic, acceptance-based, mindful approaches, the intentional reconnection has the goal of recuperating the lower feelings and sensations that are still floating in the figurative rooms of the disconnection and give them space to become emotions.

The overall goal of therapy is to readjust the representational blocked interconnection of passive syntheses, practical intentionality, and active intentionality while tuning in body resonance to their interaffective community. The goal is to reawaken interest in their own affects and to restore their willingness to remain present with them. NPD individuals are not able to access the affections from the organic presence of their bodies. They have great difficulties in accepting any physical flaws or even their own age. What bodies are for them and what they do in their primal functioning (passive syntheses) feels almost shameful. This result is an inability to accept their own bodily functioning (practical intention) and assign them a meaning (active intention) that is commensurate with their possibility. For this reason, the awakening, represented by practical intention, must be stimulated by bodily exercises until it reaches the real ground of the passive syntheses and not the empty one created from invalidating experiences. At that point, when that reconnection occurs, it is possible to revisit the old places where the invalidating experiences took place. In fact, the difficult emotions that were once experienced do not disappear in the linearity of time, but their affections persist in a timeless now. These affections must be lived in order to make space for new emotions to arise and fit the meanings to come. People affected from narcissistic traits feel emotional blockages and are often incapable of feeling pure joy or happiness because there is a long line of emotions waiting to be lived.

Hence, grounding the meanings (active intention) of their lives and their self-esteem on something unreal and untrustworthy (empty passive intentions) prevents any healing; only dealing with the still persistent and painful emotions would help a successful reconstruction of the interaffective community and positive reactivation of bodily resonance. In this step, the epoché—that is, a temporary moment of suspension of judgments and assumptions—should be used by therapist and client to suspend any temptation to make ethical judgments or assign quick meanings to the complexity of passive syntheses.

The Trap of the Ethical Judgment

What often happens during this step of suspension is that ethical judgment gets in the way of true healing. The temptation to dismiss certain emotions by assigning trivial values or meanings often arises as a way to avoid confronting the intimate connection revealed during the suspension of judgment. As it happened with my client, any self-exploration was dismissed as lazy and pointless. His life task was to inflate his self in the eyes of the others by showing his mastery of different languages, his muscular body, and his expensive clothes. He did not take time to know what felt good for him, what made sense in his life.

For people suffering from narcissistic traits, it becomes easy to blame others for their misery thus cutting off access to the constitution of new felt meanings in life. In their normal life, potentially neutral adjectives are transformed into ethically charged ones, thus creating a blockage to the constitution of new meanings: weak instead of sad, unappreciated instead of alone, failing instead of trying. Covering up real affections with ethical judgments is another way to block the interconnection between practical, passive, and active intentions. The counselor's goal is to create an ethically neutral space of acceptance around the arousal of each sensation so that primal feelings and sensations can freely affect the subject and guide the therapist-client relationship toward a transformative healing process of sensations into affections, into emotions, and then into meanings and values.

Once this acceptance is completed and habitualized, then the client can proceed to the next step which consists of the actual constitution of meanings based on their affective experiences. At that point, meanings would be formulated on a grounded, trustworthy, and solidly based experienced reality as opposed to the grandiose empty reality created (or projected) as a shield to the distressed ego. From there, the client can begin to rebuild a personal value system that serves as the foundation of their character and shapes how they wish to live and embody their values in the real world. At that point, life will cease to be pointless, lonely, empty, or without surprises. It will quite literally become more interesting, as shown in Chapter 7, since individuals can recover their interest in their own affects and express them through representational activity.

Of course, this process is extremely difficult and painful because it implies an actual dissolution of old structures on multiple levels. Yet, if it occurs, the renewal will be complete. The person affected with narcissistic traits can transform herself into a more graceful and down-to-earth creature whose roots are safely protected by the "dirt" of the world, as the narcissus in Ovid's myth. The temptation to fall back into old habits would be continuously there as it is for the risk of any seasonal flu, but a way to recover from that sense of loneliness and desperation is possible.

Therapeutic Approaches: Reconnecting NPD Individuals to Their Emotional Affects

Traditional treatments for narcissistic traits, such as cognitive-behavioral therapy and mindfulness-based interventions, have had limited success in addressing the emotional disconnection that defines narcissism. While these approaches can help NPD individuals develop coping strategies for managing their behaviors, they often fail to address the underlying affective blockages that prevent NPD individuals from forming meaningful emotional connections.

A phenomenological approach to therapy offers a more holistic solution by focusing on the intentional structures that shape NPD individuals' emotional experiences. This approach emphasizes the importance of reconnecting NPD individuals with their basic affects and helping them develop a more authentic sense of self. Hypnosis and self-psychology, for example, have been used to help NPD individuals access their passive syntheses and reestablish affective resonance with their emotions (Baker, 1981; Mahler, 1968). By guiding NPD individuals through a process of self-reflection and emotional exploration, therapists can help them reconnect with their emotions and begin to form deeper, more meaningful relationships.

One of the key goals of phenomenologically grounded therapy is to help NPD individuals develop empathy, both for themselves and others. NPD individuals often struggle with empathy because they are disconnected from their own emotions, making it difficult for them to understand the feelings of others. By helping NPD individuals reconnect with their own affective experiences, therapy can foster greater emotional attunement and empathy, which are essential for building healthy relationships.

One primary treatment method emphasizes helping individuals with NPD reconnect with their embodied experience. Maurice Merleau-Ponty's notion of embodied intentionality is central here, where NPD individuals are encouraged to rediscover their body as the primary medium through which they experience the world. Therapies involving body awareness, such as mindfulness practices, can assist in reestablishing this embodied sense of identity. This helps individuals move away from external validation and begin to engage more deeply with authentic emotional experiences (Merleau-Ponty, 1945).

In line with existential therapy, scholars such as Jean-Paul Sartre and Karl Jaspers propose that NPD individuals can benefit from exploring the void and alienation they often feel, allowing them to confront their fears of vulnerability and meaninglessness. By doing so, they can reestablish a connection to more profound, meaningful emotions. This process ties into Husserl's concept of practical intentionality, which encourages individuals to focus on their lived experiences and reflect on the values they assign to them (Jaspers, 1959; Sartre, 1943). Through this method, therapists guide individuals with NPD to explore the values driving their actions and choices, helping them build a more authentic sense of self that is grounded in emotional depth rather than grandiosity.

Therapeutic engagement also plays a significant role in phenomenological approaches to treating NPD. Kohut, merging psychoanalysis and phenomenology, emphasized the therapeutic relationship as a mirror through which narcissistic individuals can develop a healthier sense of self. By fostering a genuine, empathetic connection between therapist and patient, Kohut's approach helps patients explore blocked emotions, creating a nonjudgmental space that supports emotional healing and connection to others. This relational method directly addresses the emotional disconnection experienced by individuals with NPD, promoting emotional and ethical awareness in their interactions (Kohut, 1971).

Lastly, emotional re-education, a concept found in phenomenological-inspired approaches like Schema Therapy, is aimed at helping NPD individuals develop emotional skills they may have missed in childhood. Drawing from the works of Frankl and contemporary phenomenologists, this therapy encourages individuals to recognize and process their emotions in a way that fosters deeper connections with others, moving beyond superficial self-perceptions (Frankl, 1969; Young et al., 2003). This approach allows patients to rebuild their emotional world, facilitating a healthier engagement with their emotions and the interpersonal relationships they often struggle to maintain.

The ultimate goal of these therapeutic approaches is to help NPD individuals move beyond their reliance on external validation and develop a more stable, internal sense of self. By reconnecting with their emotions and forming deeper emotional bonds with others, NPD individuals can begin to heal the emotional wounds that have shaped their lives and develop a more authentic and fulfilling sense of self.

Concluding Thoughts: The Path to Healing Narcissism through Affectivity

Throughout this chapter, I have emphasized the central role of affectivity, as expressed in Chapter 7, in shaping narcissistic traits and behaviors. Narcissism, when viewed through a phenomenological lens, reveals a profound disconnection between emotions and lived experiences. Affective blockages prevent NPD individuals from forming meaningful emotional connections, leading to a distorted sense of self and a reliance on external validation. However, by reconnecting with their emotions through intentionality-based therapies, NPD individuals can begin the process of healing and develop a more authentic sense of self.

Husserl's theory of affectivity provides a valuable framework for understanding the emotional dynamics that shape narcissism. By focusing on the intentional structures that guide emotional experiences and reconnect with individuals' volitional bodies, phenomenologically grounded therapies can help NPD individuals reconnect with their emotions and form deeper, more meaningful relationships. This approach emphasizes the importance of practical intentionality, emotional continuity with one's embodied life, and affective resonance in the healing process, offering a more holistic solution to the challenges of NPD.

Phenomenologically grounded therapies offer a promising solution for addressing the affective blockages that define narcissism. By helping NPD individuals reconnect with their emotions and develop a more authentic sense of self, these therapies provide a pathway to healing and personal growth. Through this process, NPD individuals can move beyond their reliance on grandiose self-images and external validation, forming deeper, more meaningful connections with themselves and others.

Note

1 I will use the term "narcissism" and "NPD individuals" to describe individuals exhibiting narcissistic traits, as Narcissistic Personality Disorder (NPD) is relatively rare. According to the American Psychiatric Association (1994), NPD affects less than 1% of the general population.

References

American Psychiatric Association. (1994). *Diagnostic and statistical manual of mental disorders* (4th ed.). Washington, D.C.

American Psychiatric Association. (2013). *Diagnostic and statistical manual of mental disorders* (5th ed.). Arlington, VA: American Psychiatric Publishing.

Baker, E. L. (1981). An hypnotherapeutic approach to enhance object relatedness in psychotic patients. *International Journal of Clinical and Experimental Hypnosis*, *29*(2), 136–147.

Brentano, F. (1874/2008). *Psychologie vom empirischen Standpunkt*. Frankfurt: Ontos Verlag.

Day, N. J. S., Townsend, M. L., & Grenyer, B. F. S. (2020). Living with pathological narcissism: A qualitative study. *Bord Personal Disord Emotional Dysregulation*, *7*, 19.

De Sousa, R. (2010). *Emotions*. Stanford: Stanford Encyclopedia of Philosophy.

Donaldson-Pressman, S., & Pressman, R. M. (1994). *The narcissistic family: Diagnosis and treatment*. New York: Lexington Books.

Ferrarello, S. (2015). *Husserl's ethics and practical intentionality*. London: Bloomsbury.

Frankl, V. E. (1969). *The will to meaning: Foundations and applications of logotherapy*. New York: Plume.

Frijda, N. H. (1994). Emotions are functional, most of the time. In P. Ekman, & R. J. Davidson (Eds.), *The nature of emotion: Fundamental questions* (pp. 112–122). Oxford: Oxford University Press.

Fuchs, T., & Koch, S. C. (2014). Embodied affectivity: On moving and being moved. *Frontiers in Psychology*, *5*, 508.

Gibson, J. J. (1979). *The ecological approach to visual perception*. Boston: Houghton Mifflin.

Horton, R. S. (2011). On environmental sources of child narcissism: Are parents really to blame? In C. T. Barry, P. K. Kerig, K. K. Stellwagen, & T. D. Barry (Eds.), *Narcissism and Machiavellianism in youth: Implications for the development of adaptive and maladaptive behavior* (pp. 161–176). Washington, DC: American Psychological Association.

Husserl, E. (1905–1920). *Zur Phänomenologie der Intersubjektivität*. The Hague: Martinus Nijhoff (Hua XIII).

Husserl, E. (1983). *Ideas pertaining to a pure phenomenology and to a phenomenological philosophy: First book*. F. Kersten (Trans.). Dordrecht: Kluwer Academic Publishers. (Original work published 1913) (Hua III).

Husserl, E. (2001a). *Analyses concerning passive and active syntheses: Lectures on transcendental logic*. A. J. Steinbock (Trans.). Dordrecht: Kluwer Academic Publishers. [Hua XXXI].

Husserl, E. (2001b). *Die 'Bernauer Manuskripte' über das Zeitbewußtsein (1917/18)* [The 'Bernauer manuscripts' on time-consciousness]. R. Bernet, & D. Lohmar (Eds.). Dordrecht: Kluwer Academic Publishers (Hua XXXIII).

Husserl, E. (2002). *Natur und Geist. Vorlesungen Sommersemester 1919* [Nature and spirit. Summer semester lectures 1919]. M. Weiler (Ed.). Dordrecht: Kluwer Academic Publishers (Hua-Mat. IV).

Jaspers, K. (1959). *General psychopathology*. J. Hoenig & M. W. Hamilton (Trans.). Manchester: Manchester University Press.

Kohut, H. (1971). *The analysis of the self: A systematic approach to the psychoanalytic treatment of narcissistic personality disorders*. New York: International Universities Press.

Kohut, H. (1977). *The restoration of the self*. Madison, CT: International Universities Press.

Lowen, A. (1983). *Narcissism: Denial of the true self*. New York: Simon & Schuster.

Mahler, M. (1968). *On human symbiosis and the vicissitudes of individuation*. New York: International Universities Press.

Merleau-Ponty, M. (1945). *Phenomenology of perception*. Routledge.

Sartre, J.-P. (1943). *Being and nothingness: An essay on phenomenological ontology*. New York: Philosophical Library.

Solomon, R. C. (1976). *The passions: Emotions and the meaning of life*. New York: Anchor Press/Doubleday.

Virk, P., & Kumari, S. (2024). Adaptive and maladaptive narcissism: Different roots and different routes to empathy. *Social Behavior and Personality: An International Journal*, *52*(6), e12969

Young, J. E., Klosko, J. S., & Weishaar, M. E. (2003). *Schema therapy: A practitioner's guide*. New York: Guilford Press.

INDEX

Note: **Bold** page numbers refer to tables and page numbers followed by 'n' refer to notes.

For Product Safety Concerns and Information please contact our EU representative GPSR@taylorandfrancis.com Taylor & Francis Verlag GmbH, Kaufingerstraße 24, 80331 München, Germany